STRONG HEARTS
WOUNDED SOULS

D0222045

STRONG HEARTS WOUNDED SOULS

Native American Veterans of the Vietnam War

TOM HOLM

 **UNIVERSITY OF TEXAS PRESS, AUSTIN**

COPYRIGHT © 1996 BY THE UNIVERSITY OF TEXAS PRESS

All rights reserved

Printed in the United States of America

First edition, 1996

Material from Arthur C. Parker, *Parker on the Iroquois*, edited by William N. Fenton (1968), pp. 52–53, reprinted by permission of Syracuse University Press.

Material from Gwynne Dyer, *War* (Copyright © 1985 by Media Resources), pp. 9, 11, 14–15, 18, 47–49, and 104–105, reprinted by permission of Wadsworth Publishing Co.

Three Warrior Songs from *American Indian Prose and Poetry* by Margot Astrov. Copyright © 1946 by Margot Astrov. Copyright renewed. Reprinted by permission of HarperCollins Publishers, Inc.

Requests for permission to reproduce material from this work should be sent to Permissions, University of Texas Press, Box 7819, Austin, TX 78713-7819.

(∞) The paper used in this publication meets the minimum requirements of American National Standard for Information Sciences—Permanence of Paper for Printed Library Materials, ANSI Z39.48-1984.

LIBRARY OF CONGRESS CATALOGING-IN-PUBLICATION DATA

Holm, Tom, date
  Strong hearts, wounded souls : the Native American veterans of the Vietnam War / Tom Holm. — 1st ed.
      p.   cm.
  Includes bibliographical references (p.   )
  ISBN 0-292-73095-0. — ISBN 0-292-73098-5 (pbk.)
  1. Indians of North America — Warfare—United States.   2. Vietnamese Conflict, 1961–1975—Veterans.   3. Indian veterans—United States.   I. Title.
E98.W2H64   1996
959.704'34.—dc20   95-4380

DEDICATED TO THE MEMORY OF

RAYMOND CLARK, NAVAJO
U.S. Army, Vietnam

FELIX IKE, SHOSHONE
U.S. Marine Corps, Vietnam

LOUIS J. IKE, SHOSHONE
U.S. Marine Corps, Vietnam

BO KNIGHT, POTAWATOMI-CHOCTAW
U.S. Navy, Vietnam

JAMES MCCARTHY, TOHONO O'ODHAM
U.S. Army, World War I

JACK I. MILES, SAC AND FOX-CREEK
U.S. Army, Korea

ENOS POORBEAR, OGLALA LAKOTA
U.S. Army, World War II

WILFRED G. SAM, SHOSHONE
U.S. Marine Corps, Vietnam

DAVID SPOTTED CORN, CHEYENNE-ARAPAHO
U.S. Marine Corps, Vietnam

JODY (BLUESKY) STEVENS, CADDO-ARAPAHO-PAWNEE
U.S. Army Reserve

ROBERT K. THOMAS, CHEROKEE
U.S. Marine Corps, World War II

PETE TREJO, APACHE
U.S. Army, Vietnam

AL TRUJILLO, NAVAJO
U.S. Marine Corps, Vietnam

CONTENTS

TABLES

ACKNOWLEDGMENTS

Because this book is largely the result of simply being around Native American veterans, it is as much theirs as it is mine. There are so many contributors, in fact, that time and space do not allow me to include all of their names. Some, in genuine humility, would not even want me to put their names in print. There are a number of others, however, who contributed so much that I cannot help but acknowledge them and express my deep gratitude. If there are any mistakes in this book, they are mine alone.

First and foremost, I must thank Harold "Hodge" Barse. Hodge started me on this project, kept me in touch with what was going on in veterans' affairs, and got me appointed to two committees on Native American veterans. His contributions actually went far beyond helping me. Hodge inspired the organization of the Vietnam Era Veterans' Intertribal Association and put Indian veterans, for the first time, on the Veterans Administration's national agenda. His hard work and number of accomplishments for our veterans are truly staggering; and he certainly deserves every Indian vet's praise. I would also like to express my appreciation to Hodge's wife, Les, and their two daughters, Sunny and Allie, for their hospitality and kindness. To say the least, I am deeply grateful to the entire Barse family.

I am equally indebted to Frank Montour, Robin LaDue, and Steven Silver. Frank guided the Readjustment Counseling Service working group on Native American Vietnam vets with patience, sound judgment, and great fortitude. He deserves at least two more Purple Hearts. Robin deserves a medal for intellect, insight, and spirit in the face of difficulty. She stuck with the RCS working group and the VA's committee on Indian veterans when most of us wanted to give up. She stuck up for the RCS survey when all of the higher level officials in Washington wanted to ignore it. Without question, she rates the title of "Warrior Woman." Steve's contributions are equally great. His wit, wisdom, knowledge, and commitment really inspired me to get this book in shape.

I want to express my appreciation to the following people for their hospitality, insights, generosity, and courage: Ed Yava, Mike Toahty, Jody Stevens, Mike Standing, Preston Impson, David Begay, Dan Brudevold, Jim Webb, Marvin Stepson, Ward Churchill, Pat Franco, Joe Lawe, Butch Knight, Johnny Botone, Jack Proctor, Joe Jojola, Bob Chiago, Jerry C. Bread, Lawrence Snake, David Ortega Shaw, Perry Horse, Lee Thundercloud, and Billy Walkabout. They are a group of outstanding men and I gratefully acknowledge their friendship.

I would also like to thank David Wilkins, his wife, Evelyn, and their children for their friendship and encouragement. I value David's support and perceptive comments. My colleagues Jay Stauss, Michelle Taigue, Ophelia Zepeda, Vine Deloria, Jr., and James Clarke were equally supportive and thoughtful. Special thanks also go to Mike Davis and Don Fixico, who read and commented on the manuscript. Every would-be author should have people like them look over their work. Their comments on the content of the manuscript and my use (or abuse) of the English language were extremely helpful. Thanks also to Theresa J. May, assistant director and executive editor of the University of Texas Press, for believing in and shepherding me through the entire publishing process. I am equally grateful to Vicki Woodruff, also of the University of Texas Press, for copyediting the original manuscript and making it a much more readable product. I must also express my indebtedness to the best word processor at the University of Arizona, Trisha Morris. She can do it all.

Too often in academia, we fail to mention the help we receive from our graduate students. I do not want to make that mistake. I am very lucky to have had Elise Marubbio, Beth Leaman, James Cedric Woods, Charles England, Sam Cook, Jim Davis, Jeff Boyd, and Earnie Frost (Jeff and Earnie are themselves Native American veterans of the Vietnam War) as students and assistants. I've bounced ideas off them, had them proctor exams, and sent them to check things in the library. Their kind of enthusiasm, intelligence, and willingness to work hard makes academia worthwhile.

Finally, I want to express my everlasting gratitude to my family. I remember with love and deepest respect my mother, my grandparents, and my uncles and aunts who have passed on. They gave me life and my tribal identity. But most importantly, I want to thank my wife, Ina, and our sons, Garett and Mike, for the honor they have done me and for the support and love they never fail to give.

T. H.

STRONG HEARTS WOUNDED SOULS

1. FORGOTTEN WARRIORS

It was nearly daybreak before the gathering began to break up. The twenty or so middle-aged Native American men who had spent those early morning hours together in a tiny dormitory room had been engaged in animated conversation: reliving vivid memories, swapping stories, and striving to put into words their thoughts and feelings about the event they had shared the evening before. The shared event was the first National Vietnam Veterans' Pow-wow, held on December 11, 1982, at the Heart of Oklahoma Expo Center in Shawnee. And judging from the electric atmosphere prevailing in the room and from the excitement and genuine feelings of joy in the veterans' voices, the pow-wow had been an uplifting, powerful, and mystical experience that few of them would ever forget.

The real highlight of the pow-wow had been the Vietnam Era Veterans' Inter-tribal Association's Special. In pow-wow parlance, a Special is a song and dance done to honor a particular person, family or group. The families of those so esteemed reciprocate the honor done them by holding a Giveaway immediately following the special dance. The Vietnam veterans' Special that night seemed unique—grandly triumphant and yet sadly reflective. Hundreds of men and women crowded the floor of the large arena. Many of the veterans held M-16 rifles high in the air as they danced. The drum matched their racing heartbeats and spurred the dancing on. The veterans lifted their faces to the high ceiling as if imploring the spirits to give them the strength to dance all night. One man stopped still in the middle of the song, hung his head, and wept when a woman placed a new Pendleton blanket over his shoulders. When the song finally came to an end, no one wanted to leave the floor. "It's too bad we couldn't fire the rifles in the air," said one man. "That would've made it even better." Another man described the moment in this way:

> Everybody was on the floor. I carried an M-16. I lifted it up and danced like I've never danced before. You could see the power of the song in the faces of the people around you. It made you feel like you finally came home.[1]

The National Pow-wow was a milestone for the Vietnam Era Veterans' Inter-tribal Association, which had come into being only the year before, in 1981. VEVITA itself was product of an earlier, much smaller pow-wow organized by Harold Barse, a Sioux-Wichita-Kiowa counselor working for the Oklahoma City Vet Center. In early 1981, Barse, a long-time friend, called to invite me to a homecoming pow-wow for Vietnam veterans to be held at the Wichita tribal complex in Anadarko, Oklahoma. As a counselor for the Readjustment Counseling Service located in the Veterans Administration, Barse was interested in how Native American veterans had fared since the war. He was concerned over the fact that in his position he had seen so few Native American veterans come in for help. The pow-wow, he thought, would serve to give the area's Indian veterans a feeling of being remembered for their sacrifices in the war and, additionally, bring them together for the first time as a group at an Indian social and cultural function. Barse intuitively thought that this kind of shared experience after the war would help in their readjustment.

Barse asked me if any major studies had been done on Native American veterans, particularly those of the Vietnam era. He was especially interested, at that time, in the incidence of post-traumatic stress disorder (PTSD) in Native Americans and whether or not it could be dealt with using standard psychotherapeutic techniques. The pow-wow he was organizing provided a means by which he could get in contact with more veterans in outlying areas in order to introduce them to Vet Center services. Although I knew of no such studies, the conversation turned out to be fortuitous because it eventually led not only to my gaining a better understanding of PTSD but also to a deeper appreciation of our own Native American traditions and ceremonies.

The pow-wow Barse organized turned out to be a remarkable success in terms of bringing together Indian veterans in a familiar and friendly atmosphere. It clearly demonstrated the cohesive social power of a cultural event. I was able to participate in the "doings" and as a result became involved in the organization of VEVITA. I was to serve on the organization's board of directors for five years. A number of Indian veterans reported to me that they had emerged from this founding event with a profound sense of well-being. Several thought, as did Barse and I, that Native American veterans of the Vietnam War had been given a measure of honor and a sense of being brought back into the tribal community. I eventually wrote a short, descriptive article on the pow-wow for the now regrettably defunct magazine, *Four Winds*.[2] It was one of the first articles of any kind done on Native American veterans of the war in Southeast Asia. Significantly, members of VEVITA formed a Gourd Dance society and several color guard units that became widely respected and eagerly sought out participants at a large number of Native American cultural events throughout the nation. They also sent a contingent of members to Washington, D.C., for the dedication of the Vietnam Veterans' Memorial in November 1982.[3] Both Barse and I had a sense that a few of our veteran brothers and sisters had made very good adjustments to civilian life following their return from the war—at least in terms of having more positive views of their wartime experiences than many of their non-Indian peers. My own earlier experience tended to bear out this idea. After having served a remarkably undistinguished tour of duty in Vietnam with the United States Marine Corps, I had returned to a long and very intensive question-and-answer session conducted by several members of my family concerning the war and what I saw and did "over there." "Over there" was their term—they avoided using "Vietnam" as if it were a curse. Later, it was arranged that a Cherokee elder, who has since passed on, conduct a Going to the Water ceremony for me to wash away the evil of war and return me to the White Path of Peace.

In the Cherokee way, indeed in the ways of many tribes, the White Path of Peace is much more than the simple absence of war. It is an ordered, universal state of being in which an individual and his or her entire society attempt to live harmoniously within a given environment. This universal order—this peace—is sacred because it was divinely created.[4] Warfare is seen as a terrible, mysterious, and yet fairly common disruption in the normal functioning of everyday life. The individual who goes to war must, therefore, be returned ceremonially to a more balanced and spiritually peaceful existence. Otherwise, the community might be disrupted to the point of internal strife and ultimate social collapse. While this seems to place a great social burden on the individual who has participated in war, it actually confers a good deal of prestige on the warrior. His or her experiences outside the White Path of Peace confirm the society's belief that war is an abnormal human activity. A war-related ceremony shares the returning warrior's guilt and battle-induced stress with the community and reaffirms individual and community identity.

The idea that perhaps there is something different in American Indian life that provides for the healing of war-induced emotional scars and gives the veteran a certain degree of pride in having served even in an unpopular war seemed reasonable and worth exploring further. On the other hand, Barse and I both were aware of the fact that there was a much greater percentage of Native American veterans who had not adjusted well in any sense of the word than had. What we needed, of course, was more and better information and a commitment from the Veterans Administration to look into the special problems of Indian Vietnam veterans. As he began to press the VA to do more for Indian veterans, I began to do research on them.

WAR-RELATED STRESS AND THE INDIAN VIETNAM VET

The Vietnam War stands to become one of the most written-about and discussed American conflicts. Scholars have assessed and reassessed its military aspects, its origins in political controversies, and its impact on domestic American social and economic problems. A large number of both good and bad novels have surfaced in the attempt to impart a feeling for the horrors of combat in Vietnam. Scholars tend to take the "big picture" approach to the war to explain all of its ramifications. Consequently, scholarly studies lack the gritty reality of what it was like seeing tracer rounds streaming over one's head, or smelling the aftermath of a napalm attack, or experiencing the utter fatigue of being a combat soldier in the field. Novelists, on the other hand, describe the filth, the danger, the tedium, and the terror of the war with great skill, but too often fail to place the war in a larger context.

There is, however, a point at which scholars and novelists meet to exchange information and present the human as well as the economic, political, and social consequences of the war. Nearly everyone who has contemplated the Vietnam War in either scholarly or literary terms can say something about those who fought there. Indeed, the veteran of the war is fast becoming the most discussed, analyzed, and written about of Vietnam War topics.[5]

The wide interest in Vietnam veterans is not all that surprising. They have experienced all aspects of the conflict—the horrors, the privations, and the stress, as well as the political, social, and economic consequences of serving in this most controversial of America's wars. There are probably other reasons for the interest in Vietnam veterans, but very likely the focus on their problems stems from the extreme politicization that the war generated among Americans. Even a cursory look through the literature on the subject of Vietnam veteran adjustment following the war reveals much about the kind of war the United States asked its young men to fight. It also reveals much about who bears the brunt of battle in America's wars and much that is sad about how the United States has treated its war veterans.[6]

To say that the Vietnam War was unpopular and a political nightmare for Americans has become axiomatic. The Vietnam veteran, perhaps due to the politicization of the American public over the war, is seen as a political creature. In other words, if warfare is politics by another means, then anyone who fights in a war is automatically viewed as having condoned its political antecedents. Thus, Vietnam veterans are either vilified or seen as heroic figures, depending on which side of the Vietnam political fence the viewer sits. Because the war was lost, however, both sides can agree that the veterans were victims of misguided political beliefs, timid strategic thought, or both. The veterans are viewed as willing or duped pawns in the hands of American imperialists or as pathetic figures who lost a war as a result of political bungling, mismanagement, and lack of determination.[7]

Vietnam veteran trauma, then, has very often been seen as a problem of individual political confusion. In a sense, the belated parades and jingoistic speeches of recent years are intended to salve the wounded souls of the veterans. But more importantly, they serve as a bromide to ease a queasy American stomach—upset from collective guilt in victimizing political warriors. The Vietnam veteran is only given the chance of either admitting guilt for committing atrocities in a "bad" war or wrapping himself in the flag and declaring that the Vietnam war was a "good" cause.[8]

Since the late 1970s, clinical psychologists have attempted to look at veteran trauma in a different, and more reasonable, light. A veteran's trauma is viewed as originating in the shock of combat. The combat soldier experiences the terror and sees the horrors of the battlefield—the appalling wounds, the sudden deaths of peers and of enemy soldiers, the destruction of human-made equipment and structures, and the devastation of the natural environment. The soldier kills and destroys—that, indeed, is his job. The bottom line is that the veteran is the survivor of a human-made, primarily male-created, catastrophe. He can feel the exaltation of surviving what could be well-termed a disaster, but at the same instance feel guilty for actually having done so. As James Webb, the author of several fine novels about the Vietnam experience, said to me: "You're putting basically normal people in an extremely abnormal situation."

Militaries, of course, attempt to prepare soldiers for the horrors of the battlefield based on previous wartime experiences. A soldier's training includes how, when, and where to apply force. It teaches him the maintenance and the use of weaponry. It also includes warnings that warfare is bloody and destructive. And no one could say that the armed forces during the Vietnam War hid the truth from soldiers about the sometimes terrible consequences of battle.

What the military during the war could be accused of, perhaps, was misleading soldiers about unit pride and group cohesion. Soldiers were trained to work as teams in combat and were encouraged to think in terms of small-unit solidarity. But combat differed in Vietnam in that soldiers served tours of duty there of usually twelve months duration (Marines and sailors served what was known as "twelve and twenty," or twelve months and twenty days). The rotation of different people in and out of a unit did not serve to create long-term bonds among the soldiers within a small unit nor did it create intense unit pride. Many men were released from the military upon the completion of their tours of duty. Most veterans, seeking to forget the combat experience totally, did not actively stay in touch with those they left behind. Those left behind often treated new replacements as expendable or as somehow not worthy of filling the roles of those soldiers who had recently returned to the United States. In time, new replacements might find a niche among the older veterans; but, even then, the older veterans would eventually rotate out of combat and the whole cycle would repeat itself.

The rotation policy seemed to create the feeling among many combat soldiers that they were simply alone in the ordeal of combat. When they came home on an individual basis, there was literally no one around them with whom they could relate based on their personal experience.

In what has become typical of American behavior after a major conflict, the veteran is expected to forget the battlefield and his comrades in arms and get on with the business of life. The battlefield, however, is not a thing that one easily forgets. If a veteran's life experiences were placed on a graph and measured in terms of his emotional responses to each one of them, combat would surely create a spike equaling and surpassing the peaks of most other meaningful experiences, like weddings, births of children, graduations, and so on. Participation in combat creates in individuals what is best called "age acceleration." A soldier in combat is exposed to the deaths of other persons who are of a similar age. He is, in effect, experiencing the kinds of emotions that many other people go through during advanced age. The soldier's actual age plays against him—he is confronting his own mortality just at the stage when he is feeling the immortality of youth. In addition, upon his return home the veteran is usually placed into an economic role or a social group befitting his biological, rather than his emotional, age.[9]

Combat in Vietnam also spawned in veterans two other kinds of emotional tensions. The generation that fought the war was, on the whole, a group that grew up in the prosperous 1950s, relatively well-off in terms of health, shelter, nutrition, and leisure time. On average, they did not go through the privations suffered by their parents during the Great Depression—"privation" here being a relative term. This is not to say that most combat veterans lived lives of luxury prior to their experience in Vietnam. Many spent their childhoods in abject poverty either on the streets of the cities or in poor rural areas. On the other hand, their lot in life did not hold the dire consequences of poverty in the 1930s. In addition, they grew up in a popular culture that glorified war, and reveled in the fact that the United States won World War II and created a prosperous and secure postwar environment for all Americans. War movies and novels treated war as a heroic rather than a horrible enterprise. When they went into combat and saw the grim realities of war and felt the privations of life in the field, the soldiers could only feel that American popular culture had deceived them. The battlefield was not like the movies, and the living conditions in the field were abominable, with bad food, filth, poor sanitation, little shelter, and numerous chances of contracting diseases. For them, warfare in Vietnam literally destroyed the illusion of American prosperity and security that popular culture had manufactured.[10]

A peculiar twist on the emotional effects of battle complicated their confusion over popular mythology and the reality of life in a combat zone. While the battlefield is a grim place, full of horrors and terror, soldiers often feel an exhilaration in combat that is difficult for them to explain. The excitement of combat is not exactly that which is often depicted in motion pictures and on television screens, but contains some elements that are. In combat, a soldier experiences feelings of pride in undertaking and completing a difficult task, in valiant deeds and courageous actions, and in the spine-tingling grandeur of a vast human endeavor, regardless of the horrors it produces. But something more primal lurks in the excitement of combat. Perhaps it is the thrill of the chase and the joy of the kill passed down to us by our hunter ancestors. It might well be, as one author has pointed out, the ultimate feeling of liberation and the greatest expression of being a male.[11] In any case, the unreasoning feeling of glory in combat conflicts with the rational understanding of warfare as an abnormal and truly terrifying experience. And it differs from all other human disasters in that central aspect.

As a whole, American society was unprepared to help the veteran deal with the emotional problems created by a long and costly war. Americans, as a result of historical precedent, extreme politicization, or the inability to accept the combat experience for what it was, simply wanted the war to go away. The veteran quickly got the feeling that his guilt, fears, internal conflicts over the nature of combat, age and role confusion, doubts, and sacrifices had little or no meaning to the rest of society. The result was self-recrimination, alienation and, too often, extreme anger.[12]

Generally, clinical psychologists have been able to pin down the root causes of war-related stress and the problems society experiences in dealing with Vietnam veterans. They have also been able to reveal posttraumatic stress as a specific and treatable emotional disorder. The symptoms of PTSD are many and somewhat complex. Veterans experience frequent inexplicable headaches, states of depression, extreme nervousness, and heightened startle responses. They also complain of flashbacks and sleep intrusions. Their problems are sometimes manifested in antisocial behavior, chemical abuse, chronic unemployment, and/or the inability to maintain close personal relationships with friends or family members. Divorce and suicide rates among Vietnam veterans are above average for the same age group of nonveterans. It has been maintained that at least 60 percent of all Vietnam combat veterans display some symptoms of PTSD to a greater or lesser extent.[13]

There are strong indications that nonwhite, minority veterans display stress symptoms to a greater degree than do other veterans. According to a 1981 study commissioned by the Veterans Administration:

> Vietnam veterans as a group were three times as likely to be stressed as Vietnam era veterans [those who served in the military in the period but did not go to Vietnam] and the latter were twice as stressed as men who did not enter the military [during the war]. Blacks and Chicanos, at every point of stressful experience, evidenced somewhat higher levels than whites. Just being in Vietnam for black respondents was as stressful as being in heavy combat for white veterans.[14]

The higher levels of stress in nonwhite, minority veterans are usually seen in terms of class rather than race. Members of the lower economic strata in American society were twice as likely to be assigned to nontechnical military occupations as members of the upper classes.[15] Minority men, also because of their lower economic and educational levels and because of government programs like Project 100,000, which lowered test-performance levels to minimal standards for military service, were more apt to enter the military in the first place, to see duty in Vietnam in nontechnical military occupations, and, therefore, to directly participate in combat.[16] It has been assumed that members of minority groups enter the service to "better themselves" in the larger society. What that usually means is perhaps elevating their economic status or legitimizing themselves as full-fledged American citizens. The military has traditionally served as a point of entry into the American mainstream. New immigrants to America, for example, literally filled the ranks of the United States Army from after the Civil War through World War I.[17] Another example of group legitimization through military service would be the Japanese Americans who joined the Army in such large numbers to prove their loyalty during World War II.[18]

But during the Vietnam War many minority men began to question the idea of joining the military to fight for a country that essentially kept them on the periphery of society, despite their best efforts to integrate. In addition, some reasoned that the Vietnamese were attempting to throw off the shackles of colonialism and were, therefore, in the same kind of struggle to attain human and civil rights that nonwhites in America were striving for. Those who entered the service and fought in Vietnam were disillusioned at best. Their service in the war gained them neither social status nor economic independence. The injustices in American society were still there. Very early in the war, Malcolm X, the charismatic minister of the Nation of Islam, noted with bitter irony: "Here lies a YM, killed by a BM, fighting for the WM, who killed all the RM." Alex Haley, who was interviewing Malcolm X for his "as-told-to" biography, discovered the note on a napkin and used it in his epilogue to the book. According to Haley: "Decoding that wasn't difficult, knowing Malcolm X. 'YM' was for yellow man, 'BM' for black man, 'WM' for white man, and 'RM' was for red man." [19] The note obviously points out that Malcolm X was convinced that black people, the victims of racism in America, were being used by whites to oppress other people of color. This short, scribbled note also foreshadowed the argument made by later black leaders that African Americans should not shed their blood for a nation that has only showed them hatred and intolerance.[20] Little wonder that many minority veterans looked upon their period of service in the war as time and effort wasted. It had gained them neither greater acceptance nor financial security. In fact, it may well have exacerbated their already stressful experiences.

Given that, it is reasonable to assume that American Indians should, like blacks and Chicanos, evidence higher levels of stressful experiences. Historically, Native Americans were stripped of numerous tribal institutions, forced to abandon many of their religious ceremonies, driven from or defrauded of their traditional homelands, and left as one of the poorest economic groups in the nation.[21] The factors of low economic and educational levels (some reservations have reported unemployment rates as high as 80 percent and education averaging at the eighth-grade level) as well as a very youthful population (the average age of Native Americans in the period of the Vietnam War was between 19 and 21) virtually assured that most Indian males would be primary candidates for military service. These factors also meant that, once in the armed forces, Indians would be assigned nontechnical military occupations. Thus, they were very likely to become infantrymen and experience combat in Vietnam.

And so they did. According to one source, more than 42,000 Native Americans served in Southeast Asia either as advisors or as combat troops between 1960 and 1973.[22] More than 250 American Indians died there: 230 between 1965, when regular ground forces were committed to the conflict, and 1973, when the ground troops were finally withdrawn.[23] Still more Indians entered the service during the period but did not go to Vietnam.

The problem that still plagues many Native American veterans is that virtually no one save their own people knows of their sacrifices in the war, much less that they had fought in numbers exceeding their proportional population. American Indians, as will be shown in chapter 4, made up more than 2 percent of all troops who served in Vietnam. Since Native Americans comprise less than 1 percent of the entire U.S. population, their proportional numbers in combat more than doubled their number in the general population. While the issue of minorities bearing a disproportionate share of the war was discussed in the nation's press during the period, Indians were not specifically mentioned in a single article.[24] Malcolm X's aforementioned note states clearly, "killed *all* [emphasis added] the RM." Evidently, Malcolm thought of Indians, as did most contemporary whites, as an insignificant or vanished race. The exhaustive VA-commissioned study *Legacies of Vietnam* lacked even a mention of Native American veterans. In later years, a scholar doing research on the war stated to me that American Indians were "an insignificant population" and therefore, presumably, not worthy of scholarly attention.

The tendency in the United States to think of Indians as historical figures who essentially have been overrun by the modern world is widespread and deeply entrenched.[25] Native Americans are viewed as having disappeared or as "remnants" of a vanishing race. More than twenty years ago Vine Deloria, Jr., commented in his landmark book, *Custer Died for Your Sins*:

> The deep impression made upon American minds by the Indian struggle against the white man in the last century has made the contemporary Indian somewhat invisible compared with his ancestors.[26]

There is no reason to believe that this situation has changed. Whites still tend to think of minority "problems" in terms of the larger minority groups. And if today's Native American population of 1.9 million individuals is conspicuous by its absence in the contemporary American mind, the Indian veterans who fought in an unpopular war are even more so. To non-Indians, they are a subcategory of a subcategory—a shadow of a shadow.

What is worse, perhaps, is the fact that Native American veterans themselves have felt overlooked, shunned, and forgotten. "Everywhere I went over there [Vietnam]," said one, "I saw skins. But nobody ever put us in the papers like they did the blacks." Another noted with irony that "all the white guys that I know who were in the 'Nam said that they were buddies with an Indian. Unless they're lying, man, there were more Indians over there than anybody knows about." The frustration of going unrecognized for their sacrifices in the war was still evident in 1989. In that year, the program for the eighth National Vietnam Veterans' Pow-wow was titled "The Forgotten Warrior" and the announced theme of the entire gathering was "Native American Veterans: Have We Been Forgotten?"[27] Nearly every voice there answered this particular question in the affirmative.

THE WORKING GROUP ON
AMERICAN INDIAN VIETNAM VETERANS

It did seem as if the Veterans Administration consciously and systematically overlooked Native Americans. By 1982 its Readjustment Counseling Service, under which the nationwide network of Vet Centers operated, had already begun the process that eventually led to the formation of different groups to advise on outreach policy for women, black, and Hispanic Vietnam veterans. The women's and black groups met in that year. Interestingly, the working group on women Vietnam veterans specifically pointed out that it included women of black, Hispanic, and Asian descent.[28] In much the same conscientious manner, the working group on black veterans issued a preliminary set of recommendations which included the need to look into "Female Concerns."[29] The Hispanic working group, which issued its report in September 1983, specifically mentioned the fact that of the more than eight thousand men killed in Vietnam from the states of Arizona, California, Colorado, New Mexico, and Texas, "over 19% had distinctive Spanish surnames."[30] But while the group forcefully pointed out that people of Latino heritage belonged to different ethnic and racial groups— Mexican, Puerto Rican, Cuban, black—it failed to mention that many tribal Native Americans from those very same states also have Spanish surnames.[31] The Readjustment Counseling Service certainly tried to gain information on the diversity of Vietnam War veterans and the special needs of various groups under that heading, and each working group conscientiously acknowledged the others' special needs, but all seemed oblivious to the fact that Native American veterans of the Vietnam War were still very much alive.

To combat the invisibility of Native American veterans within the VA, Harold Barse joined with Frank Montour, a Mohawk Vet Center counselor working in the Detroit area, to prod the Readjustment Counseling Service to set up an Indian-specific working group like the ones for women, blacks, and Hispanics. Barse and Montour made the plausible argument that Indian veterans had problems specific to their population and that the VA was falling somewhat short in its mission to them. Arthur Blank, director of the RCS, saw no reason to deny the request and acquiesced to the proposal. He appointed Barse and Montour cochairs of the project and authorized them to begin work in September 1983.[32]

With determination and a remarkable amount of energy, Barse and Montour organized the first meeting of the working group in November of that same year. The working group eventually included a number of professionals within the VA system, several of whom, in addition to Barse and Montour, were Native Americans: Steven Silver of the VA Medical Center in Philadelphia, Pennsylvania; Thomas Rascon III, a Vet Center team leader from Arlington, Virginia; Gary Collins of the Vet Center in St. Louis, Missouri; Donald Johnson of the Vet Center in Seattle, Washington; Sidney Plume, a Vet Center specialist from Phoenix, Arizona; Eddie Hoklotubbe of the Vet Center in Tulsa, Oklahoma; Harlan Whipple of St. Paul, Minnesota; and the late Raymond Clark of the Vet Center in Albuquerque, New Mexico. Robin LaDue, a Cowlitz clinical psychologist from Seattle, Washington, and I came aboard as consultants.[33]

The working group immediately set several tasks for itself, all of them linked to providing information on Native American veterans for the clinicians and counselors within the Readjustment Counseling Service system. It was decided at the outset to initiate a nationwide survey of Native American veterans of the Vietnam War, since it had already been established that there were no other sources on which to develop recommendations. Drawing on lists provided by the Vet Centers and by the Vietnam Era Veterans' Inter-tribal Association, the working group began a lengthy data collection process, which culminated in its training handbook and final report, issued in May 1992. Another interrelated project was the production of a training film, *Shadow of the Warrior*. The working group enlisted the aid of the television staff of the VA Regional Medical Education Center in St. Louis to write the script and transform it to a visual medium. The film crew recorded interviews and ceremonials in several Native American communities and edited the production into a concise, informative final package. It was distributed within the VA system in 1986.[34]

Funding for a comprehensive survey of Native American Vietnam veterans, however, was always extremely limited or nonexistent. To say we operated on a shoestring budget, as consultant Robin LaDue intimated, was a considerable overstatement. Because I had access to computer time and some funds available for data processing at the University of Arizona, I inherited the survey. The American Indian Studies Program authorized the funding for the survey to be mailed to the members of VEVITA. The survey was an ongoing process. All of the returned questionnaires were hand-coded and fed into the computer. I published a few articles based on groups of 35 and 145 completed responses and my continuing field observations. Eventually, the completed questionnaires numbered 170 and represented 77 tribal groups or combinations thereof. The survey became one of the principle contributions to the working group's final report and training handbook. Presented within the context of several other articles researched and written by professionals Steven Silver, Donald Johnson, Robin LaDue, and Harold Barse, the information from the survey supports the hypothesis that Native American traditional healing and kin relationships are beneficial to the readjustment process.[35]

There can be no doubt that the working group generated more information on Native American veterans of the Vietnam War than any other source. Yet, just a year prior to the publication of the working group's final report and handbook, upper-echelon administrators within RCS began to question the "scientific validity" of the survey. Admittedly, the survey was a sample of convenience. It did not focus on one tribal group, nor did it attempt a random sampling of a complete list of Native American veterans.

Such a survey was and remains well-nigh impossible, given the problems with over- and undersampling different tribes, funding limitations, and obtaining the actual numbers of Native Americans who served in Vietnam. As will be more fully discussed in chapter 4, the problems with identifying American Indians as a racial category are staggering: Does one use membership in a federally recognized tribe to prove an Indian identity? Self-identification? Cultural identification? Blood quantum? Or some combination of all four? If federal recognition is a criteria, then a tribal people like the Lumbees of North Carolina cannot be sampled, despite the fact that they entered the service in large numbers during the Vietnam conflict. There were a number of Yaquis from southern Arizona who served in Vietnam prior to their being recognized as a tribe by the federal government. Should they be excluded? Self-identification creates even greater problems—many individuals claim Indian ancestry on the basis of family traditions but are not linked politically to any tribe. How does one test cultural identification? Blood quantum is fast becoming an unreliable test of who is and who is not an Indian. Many Indians have married other Indians and non-Indians outside of their own groups. Today there are individuals who can claim heritage from as many as eight different tribes and nationalities. There are also people with as little as 1/64 degree Indian blood who are enrolled members of federally recognized Indian nations.

Thanks to the vigorous defense of the survey by members of the working group, the results of the survey were allowed to be published in the final report and handbook with minor changes. At least the survey sampled more than one hundred individuals, making it respectable, if not complete. It also represented people with known tribal membership. In the final analysis, the survey can serve as a springboard for further testing. The hypothesis it generated—that traditional healing helps in veteran readjustment—is still valid. What motivated the charges that the survey lacked scientific validity in the first place probably can only be found in the murky depths of bureaucratic politics.

THE VETERANS' ADMINISTRATION ADVISORY COMMITTEE ON NATIVE AMERICAN VETERANS

Whatever the case, by 1986 it had become increasingly clear that Native Americans were perhaps the least understood of all veterans. Members of Native American tribes, organizations such as VEVITA, and the working group finally called Congressional attention to the fact that Indian veterans had been virtually ignored by the VA as a group having needs particularly their own. Under the Consolidated Omnibus Budget Reconciliation Act of 1986 (Public Law 99–272), Congress required the VA to establish an advisory committee on Native American concerns. The committee's main responsibility was to evaluate ongoing VA programs from a Native American perspective and determine whether or not the VA was sufficiently addressing Native American problems. A second bill was enacted two years later extending both the committee's tenure and its focus. Under this enactment (Public Law 100–322), the committee was required to enlarge its assessment of VA programs with special reference to Native Hawaiians and submit its final report by July 1989.[36]

As chance, or perhaps circumstance, would have it, I was appointed to the advisory committee, along with two other members of the RCS working group on Indian Vietnam veterans—Robin LaDue and Frank Montour. The eighteen-member panel met a total of six times and reached very similar conclusions regarding all Native American veterans (American Indians, Native Alaskans, and Native Hawaiians) to those already reached by the RCS working group on Indian Vietnam veterans. The new panel eventually found that there was indeed a grievous lack of information on Native American veterans and that it was very likely that the veterans were underutilizing both VA benefits and health services.[37]

From an insider's view of the proceedings, it looked as if the VA advisory committee was determined to follow its own path to the point of ignoring already compiled information on Indian veterans. The work of the RCS working group on Native Americans was summarily dismissed. Perhaps this dismissal was at first not without good reason. During one meeting an RCS staffer, who had been invited to report to the committee on what his particular office had been doing for Native Americans, seemed unaware that the RCS working group on Indian veterans even existed. The VA advisory committee held the RCS's ineptitude in contempt and willingly dismissed its work. When Robin LaDue and I tried to present the working group's findings on PTSD in Indian veterans, we were interrupted continually with cries of "Mr. Chairman, Mr. Chairman" and the introductions of various onlookers who had celebrity status but made no contributions to our knowledge of the Native American veteran. We also submitted copies of our articles on Indian Vietnam veterans for the committee's perusal and possible inclusion in the final report to the VA administrator. The committee as a whole was never asked whether or not it wanted the articles, all of which had been published in reputable scholarly journals, appended to its report, even though they certainly would have supported the committee's findings.[38] I was at a complete loss as to what this rejection meant, especially when I discovered that two perceptive articles on PTSD in two Asian American Vietnam veterans had been read into the *Congressional Record* in support of Senate Bill 2521, requiring the VA to conduct a study of the problems of Polynesian American and Asian American Vietnam veterans.[39] If an article on an exceedingly small number of Asian American veterans can be placed in the pages of the *Congressional Record*, it would seem appropriate that any and all articles on Native American veterans should have been appended to the report of a minor committee formed within the VA.

The rejection of relevant information notwithstanding, the committee nevertheless continued wending its tortuous journey through the bureaucratic labyrinth that was the VA during the Reagan-Bush era. Its final report was short and to the point: Indian veterans were a forgotten people. The VA had no method of counting how many Indian veterans utilized its services. Little interagency cooperation existed between the Indian Health Service and the VA hospitals, with even less between the Bureau of Indian Affairs and the VA benefits office. Indian veterans were unable, for a myriad of reasons, to take advantage of VA-guaranteed home loans. In short, Native American veterans were being shortchanged in regard to their hard-earned benefits because their numbers were small compared to the rest of the population.[40] They were, as Vine Deloria said twenty years before, invisible.

Acting on preliminary reports from the VA advisory committee, Congress attached a provision requiring the VA to launch a full-scale study of PTSD among Asian Americans, American Indians, Native Alaskans, Native Hawaiians and "other Native American Pacific Islanders." The report of the Senate Committee on Veterans' Affairs that accompanied the act asserted that this important provision derived from S.2521, the 1986 bill that required a study of PTSD in Asian American veterans. Although the report made no mention of either the VA Native American advisory committee or the RCS working group, it did allude to an earlier nationwide study of PTSD that oversampled blacks, Hispanics, and women to gain a more accurate picture of their problems relative to the rest of the veteran population. The VA had awarded the contract for this particular study to the Research Triangle Institute, Inc., in 1984.[41]

When a second contract was awarded to RTI for the study of PTSD in Native American veterans, it became clear why nearly every high-level administrator in the VA wanted to ignore the RCS working group's survey. In 1991, a researcher from RTI contacted me for input on the institute's approach to studying American Indian veterans. He proposed that the study take place at three sites: the Navajo Nation at Window Rock, Arizona, and at Oglala Lakota Reservations at Pine Ridge, South Dakota, and Seattle, Washington. I reminded him that the study might be in danger of oversampling both the Navajos and the Lakotas and that it was in danger of ignoring that half of the total Native American population living in urban areas. Not only that, but the study would also miss completely the two states with the highest total populations of American Indians—California and Oklahoma. It was immediately after I made my points about the proposed RTI study that RCS higher-ups began to question the scientific validity of the working group survey. Why the VA Advisory Committee on Native Americans rejected the study remains a mystery. Since then, the RTI study has been modified. It is now focused on three tribes: the Navajos, the Oglala Lakotas, and the Cherokees of Oklahoma.[42]

NATIVE AMERICAN VIETNAM VETERANS: PUTTING THEIR HISTORY INTO CONTEXT

After this bureaucratic baptism by fire, I resolved to continue my own study of my veteran brothers and sisters. What follows is a look at not only their lives, but also their cultures, societies, and Vietnam experiences. It also attempts to chronicle their adjustment after their experiences on the battlefields.

The ignored survey of Native American Vietnam veterans, now a matter of public record, became a primary source of information and a revelation. Many of the respondents appended notes to the questionnaires outlining their hopes for a better understanding of why they went to war and their postwar difficulties. Some wrote about their experiences in Vietnam. Many wrote of particular incidents or gave short synopses of their entire tours of duty in Southeast Asia. Others wrote about their experiences since returning to the United States—about the ignorance and the pain they endured. But most of the answers to the questions posed in the survey demanded further explanation and consideration. In many cases, the answers were predictable, while in others the responses were completely unexpected.

First and foremost, the survey confirmed that Native Americans experienced combat in a proportion greater than their relative population. The large majority of respondents had served in infantry regiments, tank battalions, airborne and air mobile units, combat engineer companies, or artillery batteries. But even given that, the number of wounds they received as well as the number of citations and medals awarded to them for valor in combat appeared exceptionally high. It seemed obvious that these men not only saw battle in all its terrible aspects but had faced it with remarkable bravery and determination.

Another fascinating revelation was that American Indian Vietnam veterans appeared to have entered military service in the first place for reasons wholly their own. Unlike other groups, they did not enter the military necessarily to better themselves in the eyes of the dominant society. The majority of them listed tribal and/or family traditions as having a significant impact on their decisions to enlist or accept conscription in the armed forces. They seemed to be taking their cues not from the larger society but from their own social and cultural environments. Granted, their societies and cultures had been manipulated and pushed to the brink of destruction by the whites in the past; by the time of the Vietnam conflict, many of the tribes to which they belonged ironically had syncretized service in the United States military with their own customs and value systems.

The ability of Native American communities to syncretize foreign institutions, customs, and forms with their own systems led to another remarkable revelation concerning Indian Vietnam veterans. It became increasingly apparent that tribal ceremonies, either conducted to honor the warrior or purge him of the taint of combat, were helping some veterans adjust to civilian life. At the same time, however, still more veterans were suffering from the wounds inflicted on their souls than were not. Many, too many, had not taken part in any kind of ritual honoring or cleansing ceremony. Moreover, the ceremonies that some Native Americans did have did not work or had not effected the kinds of changes in their lives they had hoped for.

Each bit of information gleaned from the survey seemed to pose a different question. And each question that arose seemed to demand an explanation. While it might be true to say that Native American males during the Vietnam era were very likely to become candidates for military service because of their ages and education and economic levels, the question of why they seemed always to land directly in the middle of combat still remained. Certainly many of the Native Americans who entered the military during the period were placed in nontechnical occupations because of their lack of education—34 percent of the 170 were infantrymen in the Army or Marine Corps. But many of the units and occupations they served in—such as Special Forces, Force Recon, Airborne, and Rangers—were voluntary and required extra and very specialized training. Indians seemed to serve in elite combat units in disproportionate numbers. It became obvious that many of the veterans surveyed and later interviewed actually wanted to participate in combat. Moreover, a number of them had highly technical occupations while in the military yet still managed to see warfare in all of its bloody facets. They served as combat engineers, tank crewmen, medics and corpsmen, artillery gunners and forward observers, helicopter door-gunners, and gunboat crewmen. The answer to the question of why they saw a great deal of combat, were wounded in relatively large numbers (31 percent received wounds in action), and were so decorated for courageous actions in the face of the enemy is far more complex than just a consequence of low education and economic levels.

The notion that Native Americans entered the military for reasons other than to "better themselves" socially and economically is even more perplexing than why they saw so much combat. The idea of legitimation—the effort to prove themselves "worthy" of American citizenship—has been the usual answer given to explain Indian military service since at least World War I. Nearly 80 percent of the veterans who answered the survey volunteered for military service during the Vietnam War. In addition, the majority of them entered either the Army or the Marine Corps, the two branches of the American armed forces with infantry units and, therefore, the two branches most likely to have units in direct confrontation with enemy troops. Although the Native American volunteers tended to link family and tribal traditions with U.S. military service, the linkage itself requires further explanation. At first glance, the notion seems ludicrous—their ancestors fought against the U.S. military for generations. It is as if to say that the Indian boarding schools in the late nineteenth century promoted the retention of tribal cultures among their students.

Although not usually recognized as such, the recruitment of Native Americans for U.S. military service was as much a formulated federal policy as Indian removal, the reservation system, allotment, Indian reorganization, termination, and self-determination. Despite the military victory in two wars against the British, the United States, for much of its history, was a second-rate military power. Even during the Revolutionary War and the War of 1812 the federal government actively sought Native American allies. Indians were recruited during the Civil War by both sides in relatively large numbers. The Indian Scouting Service was formed within a year after the war's end. From the last years of the nineteenth century until at least World War I, Washington policymakers made efforts to recruit Indians in order to transform them from "savages" into fully assimilated American citizens.

It appears, however, that Native American Vietnam veterans do not see their recruitment into the military as a step toward entering mainstream American society. While they sometimes talk of serving their country, they more often associate being in the armed forces with a much older tradition—that of being a warrior in the tribal sense, with all the responsibilities, relationships, and rituals that go along with that status. This association, which needs to be examined fully, might help to explain why some Native American veterans have been aided by traditional tribal medicine and rituals related to warfare.

It became clear that in order to tell the story of the Native American veteran of the Vietnam War, I would need much more than the information taken from the RCS working group's survey. For a full and proper account, I had to talk to more veterans, ask questions of tribal elders, and read extensively in several different and seemingly unrelated academic disciplines. Through old friends and members of my own family, I was able to contact and interview a larger number of men and women directly affected by the war. I observed Native American veterans and their families in a great many settings—in their homes and at numerous tribal functions—in several states. Eventually, I talked to Indian veterans from Oklahoma, Arizona, California, Washington, Wisconsin, South Dakota, Minnesota, New York, and North Carolina. I asked questions about their early lives, their problems, their communities, their reasons for entering military service, their actions in Vietnam, and their experiences since returning from the war. On occasion, discussions with the veterans turned into group "rap" sessions in which we joked, relived the terrors, and cried together. I gathered quite a bit of anecdotal material and learned many lessons about other Native American people just observing, talking, and taking notes. Most of the research for this look at the Native American veteran of the Vietnam War was conducted on the order of ethnological field work.

A great many questions remain in spite of the great cooperation and openness of the men and women I talked with. For example, one observation confirmed an idea picked up in the survey—that many veterans in fact thought of their modern combat experience in terms of much older traditions related to warfare. It became essential to the study, therefore, to make inquiries into aboriginal Native American combat. How did different tribes view war? What motivated Native American warfare? What kinds of tactics did they use in battle? What were the underlying purposes of the ceremonies performed to send a war party into and return it from a conflict? These older traditions might give us some insight into the meaning of warfare to Native American people both in the past and present.

One cannot study aboriginal Native American warfare, however, as if it occurred in a vacuum. Since 1492, European military traditions have twisted around and through American Indian lives like a corkscrew. Tribes not only fought traditional enemies but also every imperial power that came to North American shores. And every imperial power eventually sought Native American allies in their struggle to wrest the land from its indigenous owners. Native confederacies were formed to fight the European interlopers and their tribal allies. Many of these confederacies were formed primarily for military purposes. The long conflict with the Americans turned several tribes into virtual military states, always under the threat of attack and annihilation. When many of the Native nations, exhausted from being in a constant state of war with the United States, finally came into the reservations, they lived under what amounted to martial law.

There can be no doubt whatsoever that the warfare between the Indian nations of North America and the imperial European powers effected changes in the military traditions of both the New and the Old World. The Europeans learned much by suffering several defeats at the hands of Native American war leaders and tacticians. The use of sharpshooters and skirmishers by the French armies during the Napoleonic era, for example, was probably the result of the French military experience in North America. The Americans have seemingly always attributed their victory over the British in the Revolutionary War to Indian tactics learned in the numerous colonial wars with Native American tribes. Indians, on the other hand, quickly picked up the musket and, adapting tribal battle tactics to new weaponry, were able to forestall complete subjugation for four hundred years. It may also be argued that many Native American nations have never been completely subjugated by military force.

In the give-and-take of blood on the battlefield between Native Americans and Europeans, the two peoples developed a mutual military history. Yet, at the same time, they continued to take fundamentally different views of war and its purpose. Euro-Americans, then and now, tend to look upon war as a means to a practical end. It is a method by which people, as represented by government, gain territory or impose their will on another group. There is no value in war beyond its political and/or economic gains. But for many tribes and supratribal confederacies, war was equally a physical and spiritual experience. Warriors were ritually prepared for and ceremonially returned from the battlefield. Most Native Americans fought in battle to take revenge for a fallen tribal kinsman, to test their young men in war so that they understood completely the blessings of peace, to wrest from a brave enemy his spiritual power, to take objects of sacred significance, and to achieve a degree of economic gain. Indians fought to maintain and strengthen their group identity in a particular homeland but rarely to add to tribal territory or to force another people into a position of subordination. In some cases, tribal combat was ritualized to the point of not really being true warfare. Most often it lacked the predatory quality of European conflict. On the other hand, tribal battles could become extraordinarily bloody, but it was an exceedingly rare thing for tribal warriors to look upon their enemies as inanimate objects completely lacking souls or sacred powers. Indians took these traditions, syncretized them with service in the American armed forces, and essentially developed a "newer tradition."

These attitudes toward battle are still very much alive in the ceremonies utilized to bring some Native Americans home from the jungles and rice paddies of Vietnam. Although the majority of American Indians by 1968 probably were opposed to the war in all of its political ramifications, they did not seem to have viewed their sons who had been there as political pawns. In the tribal sense, they were seen as having fought for their country: to understand combat; to honor their families; to maintain their own notion of peoplehood; and because, as Cherokee anthropologist Robert K. Thomas put it, "That's what young men do."

Once the Vietnam War is understood as a visceral as well as a political experience, the story of the American Indian veteran can be placed in context. The Native American veteran possesses a long history and particular heritage of arms as part of a chain of being that extends back to a time before the coming of gunpowder, soldiers in uniform, and power politics. Indian veterans are products of a long-standing set of values that linked trade with diplomacy rather than with profits, equated peace with an ordered universe rather than the simple absence of war, and viewed those who went to war as individuals who have seen and done extraordinary things. And, because they have done extraordinary things, they not only have gained wisdom but have special problems and needs.

As to the feelings of the Native American veterans themselves, there is a dichotomy in the way they view their service in Vietnam. On the one hand, they see themselves as warriors in the tribal sense. Certainly on the battlefield they performed as courageous, knowledgeable, tenacious, and professional soldiers. They saw the horrors of war and, by contrast, knew the wisdom of peace. At the same time, they hold deep seeds of resentment toward those who they feel utilized their valorous deeds in combat to an unjust and, in many ways, cowardly end. They often resent having fought a war as United States soldiers, while the Americans have not honored American Indian treaty or human, civil, preconstitutional, or sovereign rights. They feel forgotten and treated unfairly despite the fact that they shed blood and had their blood shed in a white man's war. But many also knew not to expect concessions or even sympathy from the whites. Although they fought for the nation as a whole, they realized that in the long run there was only one given: that their own people would honor their sacrifices as warriors and treat them accordingly within the boundaries of their own tribal traditions. These boundaries also determine the context in which their history should be presented.

Vine Deloria, Jr., once explained why many Native Americans themselves, from traditional tribal elders to younger scholars, have often expressed dissatisfaction with the way in which the social sciences have approached research on American Indians. As Deloria put it:

> Indians have found even the most sophisticated academic disciplines . . . woefully inadequate because the fragmentation of knowledge that is represented by today's modern [scholarship] does not allow for a complete understanding of a problem or of a phenomenon. Every professor or professional must qualify his or her statements on reality and truth with the admonition that the observations are being made from a legal, political, sociological, anthropological or other perspective. These statements then are true if confined to the specific discipline and its methodology by which they are formed . . . Social science in the western context describes human behavior in such restrictive terminology that it describes very little except the methodology acceptable to the present generation of academics and researchers.[43]

Native Americans, according to Deloria, reject a given discipline's methodology when its "truths" fail to explain personal and communal experience. Herein lies the key to presenting information within an Indian context. To explain Indian veterans, one cannot simply jump into their personal lives, fit their stories within a single, given methodology, and then reach for a sweeping conclusion. Native American veterans identify themselves with a community (tribe) and with that community's specific traditions. Their sense of peoplehood is directly linked to place (homeland/holyland) and a shared sacred history. They tend to think of themselves as warriors of an older, sacred tradition, but placed in a changed set of circumstances. It is my intention to tell the story of these forgotten warriors, which is both personal and communal, from every angle, including the cultural, psycho-social, and historical. In other words, I will attempt to tell their story as a tribal storyteller would—explain everything that is known, even that which is taken from western knowledge, but, as Deloria continues, "admit that something mysterious remains after all is said and done."

This is, then, *a* history and not *the* history of the Native American veteran of the Vietnam War. Because they are links in a chain of being that extends back before the written word, this history bridges a time span much greater than the lengths of the veterans' individual lives. It is an attempt to understand how tribal traditions of warfare developed, why Native Americans became part of the American military, what veterans saw and did in Vietnam, and how the experience has affected their lives subsequently. These warriors' stories can be told chronologically, moving from general tribal ways of war to the specific experiences of a relatively small number of people. But their story is not strictly linear. Some Indian veterans have been able to work though the trauma of the Vietnam War by returning to ancient tribal customs and ceremonies. In the end, they have completed the circle, coming home to the traditions and spiritual experiences of their warrior ancestors. Their story substantiates what has long been apparent and what tribal societies know so well: that warfare takes a grievous emotional toll on those who survive the battlefield. It also adds dimension to the concept that understanding the role of warfare in a culture leads to a better understanding of those we ask to sacrifice their lives in battle.

2. AN OLDER TRADITION

Native American Warfare and the Warrior's Place in Tribal Societies

The warrior's cause is always just.
— STANLEY HOLDER (WICHITA), VIETNAM VETERAN, USMC

The paradox is seemingly always with us. Unless humans are completely devoid of even a touch of humanity, they automatically wince at the prospect of war and its terrible consequences. Yet at the same time, many people cannot help but feel a tingling sensation of sheer pride and even joy upon being told of gallant deeds amidst the carnage of the battlefield. There are many examples of gallantry that particularly move us: the stand at Bunker Hill; the bloody and unnecessary charge of the Light Brigade; General Robert E. Lee's final salute to his Yankee opponents at Appomattox; Chief Joseph's eloquent and courageous surrender; Audie Murphy's selfless valor against the Germans throughout World War II. Truly, we hate war but love the warrior. Stanley Holder's words can be interpreted to mean this: a warrior's gallantry translates almost any given cause into something great and meaningful and even virtuous.

Warrior traditions abound. And nearly every society, from the earliest to the most modern, has engaged in some form of violence aimed at another group. But in order to understand the older traditions that American Indian Vietnam veterans habitually refer to when explaining their own reasons for entering military service, or that helped some of them adjust after the war, an attempt must be made to explain the meaning of warfare to the societies that gave these veterans birth. What are their warrior traditions? How are they different from others? Why should they make a difference in an American Indian veteran's postcombat adjustment?

HUMAN AGGRESSION AND THE DEVELOPMENT OF WAR

It has been argued that aggression and violence in both humans and animals generally occur on two distinct levels that sometimes intertwine. The first is ritualistic aggression. Most species participate in some form of ritual combat. It is highly individualistic, marked by displays of aggressive behavior—strutting, puffing up, chest-beating, baring of teeth—and is aimed primarily at a member or members of the aggressor's own group to establish some form of dominance. Sometimes ritual aggression can be interspecific. All a lion usually needs to do to scare off a thieving jackal from its kill is to bare its teeth and roar. The second level of aggression is predation. Predatory animals are armed with stout teeth and sharp claws intended for use in killing other species as quickly as possible. Sometimes predators display ritual behavior before hunting, but this is usually connected with species that hunt in groups or pairs.

Humans seem remarkably maladapted to either form of aggression. They do not have large fangs to frighten or to kill. Humans have no horns, antlers, claws, or brightly colored or inflatable patches of skin that may be displayed to intimidate other species or even members of the same group. Bipedalism, and the increased height that comes with it, might help to intimidate others; but for the most part, physically speaking, humans should be among the most passive of all creatures.[1]

That people are actually among the most aggressive creatures in the world is largely the result of the human ability to reason and fashion implements. Weapons, even crudely chipped rocks, can both kill and intimidate. For much of human history, however, people probably reserved predation for other species. Humans armed themselves and joined together to hunt and bring down even the largest and most dangerous of prey animals. Hunting-gathering groups might well have raided or engaged in pitched battles with other groups of people, but generally historians and anthropologists agree that this form of warfare, if indeed it can be so labeled, was relatively bloodless and highly ritualized.[2] In short, human hunters apparently had the capacity to slaughter other humans in battle, but did so only occasionally and for reasons other than predation.

Gwynne Dyer, author of the popular, well-written, and informative book simply entitled *War*, argues effectively that civilization, militaries, and mass slaughter are siblings born of the notion that humans have dominion over their environments. Human control of nature led to an ever-escalating pattern of violence. According to Dyer:

> The essence of the Neolithic revolution was not the discovery between 9000 and 7000 B.C. . . . that food could be obtained more reliably and in far greater abundance by planting and harvesting crops and taming and breeding animals, nor even the huge increase in population density that these discoveries made possible. It was the insight that human will and organization could exercise control over the natural world—and over large numbers of human beings. . . . It can never be proved, but it is a safe assumption that the first time five thousand male human beings were gathered together in one place, they belonged to an army . . . it is an equally safe bet that the first truly large-scale slaughter of people in human history happened very soon afterward.[3]

From that point, according to most military historians, humans moved on to even greater massacres. Alexander the Great improved tactics and management techniques to make his army more mobile and efficient. The Roman legions improved on Alexander's techniques and invented more effective weaponry—the short sword, the pilium, and numerous siege engines. And it must be remembered that military effectiveness is normally measured in terms of an army's ability and willingness to destroy things and kill people. Technology continued to improve military efficiency through time. Humans lengthened their hunting spears into pikes, modified their hand axes into halberds, did away with cumbersome shields by producing chain-mail and steel body armor, improved the bow, invented the crossbow, and, finally, utilized gunpowder to its fullest potential. Battles became larger in terms of both time and space and thus became more lethal to greater numbers of human beings. Warfare developed, in various places at different times, to the point that entire societies could be completely and utterly obliterated.[4]

The greatest trick in this lengthy and incredibly violent evolution, however, was not necessarily to keep ahead of a given opponent's technology (although that certainly helped), but to be able to control ever-increasing numbers of people and convert individualistic hunter-warriors into anonymous soldiers in the ranks of mass armies. The tradition of Homeric heroism is often credited with keeping warriorhood alive despite the fact that, through time, leadership has become more managerial than demonstrative and that technology has made the act of killing more impersonal.[5] Wars might very well be economically based and politically justified, but human beings probably still answer a call to arms more for the sake of honor, personal glory, and a warrior tradition than for any other reason. The interesting paradox of this kind of warrior tradition is that tactical leadership in battle gains the individual soldier far more rewards than does a spontaneous act of physical bravery, which is the hallmark of Homeric heroism.

Historians generally see this chronology of violence as an evolutionary progression of improved technology and human dominance over other humans. The earliest military states were dictatorships of the tyrannical sort in which the highest military leader usually proclaimed himself to be a god or at least a representative of the gods. Soldiers in the ranks became servants of the despotic leader who became increasingly identified with the state.[6] State survival became the ultimate goal, and warfare became the means by which states pursued their political aims. States demanded that their subjects owe them first allegiance. Other states became "others," "outsiders," "enemies," "infidels," and worse.

The development of the tools with which these states fought wars was not, however, a steady process. When an army used new technology in battle it was usually quickly matched by the other side. Armies were often symmetrical in terms of arms until another great leap in technological development occurred. But with technological development, killing not only became easier but often made the technology itself the reason for war. Historically, if a state had a new weapon, it was a safe bet that the weapon would be utilized, if for no other reason than to test its destructive power. Thus, human beings "progressed" from relatively bloodless raiding, as practiced by hunting-gathering groups, to mass warfare, when armies met other armies on the battlefield, to industrialized, total war, when noncombatant factory workers became primary military targets. Warfare became more and more deadly to greater numbers of people, simply because the state and technology dehumanized potential enemies. Warfare became less a ritual and more a form of predation.[7]

This punctuated equilibrium theory of the evolution of warfare is Eurocentric to be sure. Indeed, it seems that warfare itself is a chronology of Western technological development and the evolution of a particular way of viewing human conflict in political terms. True, the Chinese may have invented gunpowder and rockets, but Europeans turned these ingenious, and originally not very deadly, Oriental inventions into instruments of mass slaughter. Western expansionism virtually assured that the European propensity for military innovation would spread worldwide.

That other non-Western societies had to adapt to European methods of warfare to stave off Western expansion for a time obscures the fact that these other cultures had originally taken different and oftentimes less horrendous paths in making war. The Chinese general Sun Tzu wrote a treatise on the subtleties of combat from long distance and the use of frightening masks to rout enemies rather than destroy them, in approximately the same period that Alexander the Great was slaughtering great numbers of Persians in headlong charges with lance and sword.[8] By the middle of the seventeenth century, the Japanese had already adopted guns, fought numerous battles with them—one of which settled into an extended stalemate of trench warfare a full four centuries before World War I—and had given them up in order to preserve their own ancient forms of ritual warfare.[9] Meanwhile, in Native North America, tribes and supratribal confederacies developed their own unique forms of combat and, in many cases, elevated ritual warfare into a kind of spiritual contest that almost defies definition in Western terms.

WARFARE IN ABORIGINAL NORTH AMERICA: AN OVERVIEW OF ITS ORIGINS AND MOTIVES

It can quickly be concluded that Native Americans did not develop warfare to its most destructive and sanguinary potential. Although a few groups, like the Aztecs and the Iroquois confederacy, were able to assemble large numbers of warriors into very real armies, mass slaughter on the scale of that habitually carried out by Assyrian, Greek, and Roman armies in ancient times did not occur in aboriginal North America. The Spanish records of Aztec atrocities in war are decidedly under a cloud of suspicion. After all, the Spanish conquistadors and Catholic priests were attempting to justify their own bloody campaign of conquest made on Aztec civilization. And the League of the Hodenosaune, or Iroquois, seemed to have been more concerned with adopting captives taken in raids than territorial expansion and the destruction of entire societies.[10] In short, American Indian battles in pre-Columbian times might have been quite bloody, as some tribal oral traditions indicate, but predatory warfare appears to have been very rare.

Scholars have debated the nature of aboriginal Native American warfare for a number of years. Some have argued that the main thrust of conflict in Native North America was territorial, but with a difference particular to North America. This argument asserts that the aboriginal tribes were seemingly always engaged in several forms of organized and semiorganized violence simply to survive as identifiable groups in particular environments. While a number of tribes developed "true" warfare, in the Western sense, for political reasons, the majority of tribes limited violence to intratribal squabbles and intertribal raiding. True warfare is, by definition, a political act, and only those groups possessing "real" or "true" political organization could conduct it. This analysis, of course, implies that the majority of tribes in North America were small, kinship-based groups with few or no political institutions. It also assumes, in the Clausewitzian sense, that war is strictly a political activity. In a larger cultural context, the argument implies that close kinship in tribes precludes the establishment of hierarchical military structures with their elites and chains of command.[11]

Viewed in terms of North American aboriginal culture areas, these assumptions about Indian violence seem clearly the result of geography, subsistence patterns, and political institutions. In general, true warfare existed in the Eastern Woodlands culture area but was less prevalent in the Far West. The tribes of the Great Basin (Paiutes, Utes, and other small groups), the Arctic and Subarctic (Inuit, Eskimo, and Aleut), and California lacked true warfare. In these areas, because of climate and subsistence factors, the people lived in small extended-family groups lacking well-defined political organization. Since population densities were very low, competition for territories between groups was virtually nonexistent. The tribes of the Northwest Coast (Nootka, Tlinget, Salish), California (Pomo, Hupa), the Plateau (Shoshone, Nez Percé, Flathead) and the Southwest (Hopi, Navajo, Apache, O'Odham, Yaqui) had mixed or weak patterns of warfare. In these areas, although subsistence was difficult, there were higher population densities and agriculture. Raiding was fairly widespread but was carried out on a relatively small scale in organizational terms. True, or well-defined, warfare existed on the Plains (Lakota, Cheyenne, Comanche, Kiowa), the Prairies (Omaha, Osage) and in the Eastern Woodlands (Iroquois, Cherokee, Muscogee,

Delaware, Ojibwa). In these areas, particularly east of the Great Plains, agriculture was extensive and political organization well-defined. Populations were comparatively higher and territorial boundaries were aggressively maintained.[12]

This view of Native American warfare obviously assumes that territoriality and economics were the root causes of aboriginal intertribal hostilities. In areas of low population density, large territories for hunting, fishing, and gathering could be maintained without resorting to war. In other areas, tribal economies required large territories for big-game hunting, slash-and-burn agriculture, and large-scale seasonal gathering. Populous tribes would be forced into political and military organization to protect themselves from even small-scale raids.[13]

The economic hypothesis of Indian warfare, however, has been disputed. Instances of territorial conquest were apparently few and far between in aboriginal North America. Although there were certainly some tribes that possessed power enough to destroy competing tribes, few attempted to do so until after the advent of trade with the Europeans. Given the large number of tribes and the remarkably small number of known military conquests in pre-Columbian times, it seems that warfare for the sake of territorial or economic gain was hardly commonplace.

Some scholars have argued that most hypotheses regarding the motives underlying aboriginal warfare are rationalizations after the fact and that the true origins of Native American warfare lie elsewhere. A few have maintained that aboriginal warfare was the result of cultural diffusion. Others have hypothesized that it was a consequence of Native American nation-building. Several others have argued that, on the other hand, intertribal conflict was simply an activity whereby young males gained status within a group under a strict set of guidelines. From this point of view, Native American warfare and raiding was less a deadly, economy-driven battle for territory and goods than an elaborate game whose players vied to become tribal celebrities and leaders. Pre-Columbian Indian war, as Kirkpatrick Sale puts it, "seems a misnomer for the kinds of engagements we imagine might have taken place, in which some act of bravery or retribution rather than death, say, or territory, would have been the object."[14]

Akin to the idea of Indian warfare as a kind of useful outlet for youthful male energy and exuberance is the notion that warfare is the outcome of the distinct separation, in Native American tribal societies, between female and male physical and spiritual powers.[15] In most tribal societies, female power is associated with the ability to reproduce and nurture. Menses is, in itself, a force that can, according to several tribal legends, block or negate male powers. Women not only gave birth and nurtured children but also among many tribes became the principal sowers and reapers of the soil. In effect, according to Clifton B. Kroeber and Bernard L. Fontana, women "could perform most or even all essential community chores: tend the hearth, bear and raise children, and plant, cultivate and harvest the calories needed to stay alive." As a result the "worth of males, their dignity as human beings, was challenged to the utmost." This "imbalance in the sex division of valued status" led to the establishment in numerous societies of distinct male and female powers: female power was associated with the activities of life (childbearing, cultivation); male power with death (warrior-hunter).[16]

While this view of Indian warfare is primarily cultural and social, another view takes into account two more dynamics in Native American life: kinship and a given tribe's relationship with the spirit world. It has been maintained that many tribes engaged in what has been termed "mourning war." In it, tribal warriors practiced a highly ritualized form of blood vengeance. When a kinsman died or was killed in battle, some groups believed that the clan's, tribe's, or nation's collective spiritual power was "diminished in proportion to his or her individual spiritual strength." Raiding took place to take captives and sometimes to kill a certain number of enemy warriors. Captives, in numerous cases, were simply ritually adopted as replacements for the dead. Killing an enemy or torturing a captive to death was intended to assuage the grief of relatives of the dead tribesmember. Some Native American women literally "dried their tears" with the scalps of slain enemies. All in all, the mourning war kept populations relatively stable (through adoption), promoted group cohesion (through ceremonies associated with warfare), and reaffirmed the tribal sense of superiority over its neighbors.[17]

THE CULTURE OF NATIVE AMERICAN WARFARE: A SURVEY OF TWENTY NATIVE AMERICAN GROUPS

What can be said of warfare in Native North America, with some degree of certainty, is that it was an amazingly complex and varied institution. But to obtain a more precise view of the complexities of American Indian warfare and to understand better the older traditions of Native American Vietnam veterans, I surveyed various cultural features connected with aboriginal warfare in twenty different tribes. I attempted to sort out those features that were part of each tribe's cultural makeup before extensive contact with whites. The twenty tribes were selected on the basis of how well they represented the tribal backgrounds of the Vietnam veterans surveyed or interviewed and the broad spectrum of Native American cultures in the United States. At least one tribe representing every culture area in the United States was selected, and care was taken to include tribes of widely varying aboriginal subsistence patterns. The culture areas represented were the Eastern Woodlands (Cherokee, Creek, Menominee, Mohawk, Ojibwa); the Plains and Prairie (Cheyenne, Lakota, Kiowa, Pawnee); the Basin (Ute); the Plateau (Shoshone); the Northwest Coast (Tlinget); California (Hupa, Pomo); the Arctic (Inuit); and the Southwest (Apache, Hopi, Navajo, Tohono O'Odham, Yaqui).[18]

The tribes were quite varied in subsistence patterns. Among those who practiced extensive farming combined with hunting and some gathering were the Cherokees, Creeks, Mohawks, Hopis, Tohono O'Odham, and Yaqui. The Cheyennes, Lakotas, and Kiowas were big-game hunters who engaged in some seasonal gathering, while the Tlingets largely subsisted on fishing. The Tlingets, like most of the tribes, supplemented their primary food source with game and wild berries, roots, and vegetables. The Shoshone and Utes were basically hunting-gathering groups. Because they lived in perhaps the harshest of climates, the Inuit were almost exclusively hunters of marine animals, including seals, walruses, and whales. Some Inuit groups based their economies on caribou hunting and herding, much like the Sami or Lapps of Scandinavia. The Apaches and Navajos mixed hunting and gathering with small- and large-scale gardening. Later the Navajos developed a pastoral economy based on sheepherding combined with agriculture. Seasonal rice-gathering combined with hunting and fishing sustained the Menominees and Ojibwa, and the Pomo and Hupa likewise fished, hunted small game, and gathered a wide variety of nuts, berries, and other edible plant foods.[19] With reason the Plains and California culture areas were overrepresented in the survey in terms of relative tribal populations. The Plains culture area has heavily affected tribal cultures of the Basin, the Plateau, and the Southwest even before extensive interaction with whites. The Hupa and Pomo of California were definitely overrepresented, but they share a number of common cultural traits with the Northwest Coast and the Basin groups.

In any case, a look at the ethnological literature, the tribal histories, and the information gleaned from a number of tribal elders revealed several special cultural features linked to warfare, raiding, and other forms of organized violence. These features were: (1) specialized regalia, arms, and/or equipment (other than hunting weapons); (2) military sodalities; (3) group ceremonial preparations for battle; (4) specific honors for heroic behavior in combat; (5) cleansing rituals for those who participated in war; and (6) victory or honoring ceremonies following battle. Added to these specific features was the inquiry into why the tribes launched war expeditions, raided, or engaged in some form of group violence.

A glance at Table 1 indicates that a majority of these tribes share a number of features connected with warfare. In the first place, practically all the warriors of the tribes in question carried some special piece of weaponry or equipment into battle or while raiding. A few, like the Tlingets, Hupa, Pomo and, in ancient times, the Mohawk, wore wooden armor. Most of the tribes of the Eastern Woodlands, the Plains, and the Southwest carried war shields into battle, but the protective power usually was perceived to lay not in the rawhide or wood of the shield but in the symbols painted on them. Quite often, warriors carried special war clubs, bows, and lances. Even if their weaponry was not specialized for warfare, most warriors at least wore clothing or accoutrements or amulets that were: medicine bags, bundles, or charms; carved fetishes; headdresses, cloaks, shirts, or pieces of adornment that distinguished them from others on the battlefield; and/or face or body paints. Many of the war-related accoutrements were in fact connected with the individual warrior's spiritual power. Many tribal warriors from the Eastern Woodlands, the Southwest, the Northwest Coast, and the Plains wore tattoos that recounted their honors from previous battles or that symbolized their personal medicine or helping spirits.[20]

Apparently the war parties from the Southeast went on expeditions with more than individualized war medicine. James Adair, the chronicler and observer of southern Indian life in the eighteenth century, noted that war parties always brought an "ark," no doubt a tribal or group medicine bundle continuing numerous sacred objects, with them on large war expeditions.[21]

Most tribes in what is now the United States drew a very rigid line between the activities of war and peace. Some tribes lived under the constant threat of attack by enemies; they felt that unless they placed the military dimension of life in a ritualistic context, it might well permanently dominate all other considerations. War medicine, for these tribes, was an important part of both the sacred and the secular sides of

TABLE 1. Aboriginal Native American Warfare

Tribes (Culture Areas)	Principal Motives	Special Regalia, Arms, Equipment	Military Society	Group Preparation Ceremonies	War Honors	Group Cleansing Rituals	Victory/ Honoring Ceremonies
Apache (Southwest)	Revenge, economic, traditional enemies	*		*	?	*	*
Cherokee (Eastern Woodlands)	Revenge, traditional enemies, captives	*	?	*	*	*	*
Cheyenne (Plains)	Revenge, traditional enemies, horses	*	*	*	*		*
Creek (Eastern Woodlands)	Revenge, traditional enemies, captives	*		*	*	*	*
Hopi (Southwest)	Defense	*	*			*	
Hupa (California)	Revenge, captives, economic			*	?	*	*
Inuit (Arctic)	Revenge, economic, captives, witchcraft				?		
Kiowa (Plains)	Traditional enemies, revenge, horses	*	*	*	*		*
Lakota (Plains)	Traditional enemies, revenge, horses	*	*	*	*		*

Tribe (Region)	Reasons						
Menominee (Eastern Woodlands)	Revenge, traditional enemies	*		*	*		*
Mohawk (Eastern Woodlands)	Traditional enemies, economic, captives	*	*	*	*		*
Navajo (Southwest)	Traditional enemies, economic	*	*	*	*		*
Ojibwa (Eastern Woodlands)	Witchcraft, economic, revenge	*	*	?	*		*
Pawnee (Plains)	Traditional enemies, revenge, horses	*		*	*	*	*
Pomo (California)	Revenge, witchcraft	*		?			*
Shoshone (Plateau)	Traditional enemies, revenge, economic	*		*	*		*
Tlinget (Northwest Coast)	Captives, witchcraft				*		*
Tohono O'odham (Southwest)	Defense, revenge		*		*		*
Ute (Basin)	Revenge, traditional enemies	*		*			
Yaqui (Southwest)	Defense, economic, revenge	*	*	*	*	*	*

tribal life. Other tribes viewed warfare as an abnormal disruption in the natural scheme of things. The Tohono O'Odham, for example, defined war as chaos or a form of insanity. At the same time the O'Odham possessed war medicine. Should the community be embroiled in conflict, the war priesthood, war societies, or individual warriors could use it to combat an enemy. The chasm between the activities of war and peace could only be crossed ceremonially. And the line was so distinct that many tribes even categorized their leadership in those terms. Among the Lakota, the Kiowas, the Menominees, the Creeks, and numerous other tribes, there were "war chiefs" and "peace chiefs," or civil leaders. Although the civil leaders usually had good war records in their respective tribes, their duties often involved attempts to prevent younger men from rashly courting conflict. The Cherokees and Creeks determined clan identification along the lines of "white" (peace) and "red" (war) clans.[22]

Six out of the twenty tribes had well-defined military societies. These societies were typically seen as tribal militias, but their most important function was keeping the community's war medicine—the medicine that not only helped protect the community but moved the society onto a wartime footing. Most warrior societies had supernatural origins and special regalia and accoutrements. Even the Hopis, whose ancient traditions strongly opposed violence in any form, had war priests, warrior societies, and special religious functions tied to warfare.[23] One tribe, the Cherokees, had no historical warrior sodality; but the *gadugi* (the word's root is *gadu*, meaning "bread"), or men's "working group" that still exists today in many Cherokee communities, was organized along the lines of a military command structure, with its chiefs, captains, and little captains.[24] Although it could never be proven, the *gadugi* might have been the remnant of a very ancient war priesthood or society of warriors.

Warrior societies were prevalent and best known among the thirty-five or so tribes that made their homes either on or peripheral to the Great Plains. For these tribes, warrior societies were extremely important religious and political institutions. They did much more, in fact, than simply act as domestic, rival militias. In addition to acting as the keepers of the tribes' spiritual power in warfare, the societies generally kept order during hunts, while in camp, and when the people were on the move. They punished criminals, guarded the villages against surprise attacks, and, when attacked, bought time with their lives, if need be, to allow the women, children, and elders to escape. The societies scouted the movements of the buffalo herds and held ceremonies, Give-aways, and feasts for the social and spiritual benefit of the entire community.[25]

As a consequence of the rigid distinction between war and peace, tribes developed special ceremonies—of which the military society ceremonies were a part—to aid individuals and, indeed, entire communities, in making the transition from peace to war and back again. Warriors were ritually prepared for war and offered protective medicine to assure their safe return to the community. In addition to the preparation rituals for war, many tribes devised purification ceremonies to restore individual warriors, as well as the rest of the community, to a harmonious state. Unless the returning warriors were purged of the trauma of battle, it was felt that they might bring back memories of conflict to the tribe and seek to perpetuate patterns of behavior unacceptable to the community in its ordinary functioning. All of these ceremonies were thought necessary to maintain a tribe's continued harmonious existence with the physical and the spirit worlds. James Adair commented on one such ritual purging among the southern tribes and about the attitudes of the community toward its function:

> Tradition, or the native divine impression on human nature, dictates to them that man was not born in a state of war; and as they reckon they are become impure by shedding human blood, they hasten to observe the fast of three days . . . and be sanctified by the war-chieftain, as a priest of war, according to law. While they are thus impure, though they had a fair opportunity of annoying the common enemy again, yet on this account they commonly decline it, and are applauded for their religious conduct.[26]

War ceremonies were part of a matrix of tribal customs, sacred rites, beliefs, and medicine that underpinned the holistic power and cohesion of the tribe itself. Without warriors there could be no war power. That power, along with other ceremonies, customs, and powers, were the pillars on which a society was built. Remove one and the rest were weakened. Given the organic structures of tribal societies, in which religious practice, a reciprocal economic system, political organization, and territoriality were all interrelated, even the loss of a single aspect of culture could lead to a severe disruption of the whole.[27]

As far as I could determine, all but one of the tribal peoples listed in Table 1 utilized ceremonies to prepare, cleanse, and/or honor warriors.

These ceremonies ranged in form from the simple to the complex. Some, like the one mentioned by Adair, were strictly observed even when the community might have kept the pressure on the enemy. They were time-consuming, costly, and elaborate, yet tradition demanded that they be performed, if for no other reason than the maintenance of the tribe's special relationship with the spirit world. In many cases, a warrior could not perform any other ceremony or even take part in normal daily functions without first being purged of the taint of battle. Some ceremonies honored those who stood in battle and celebrated their successful return. The warrior was, as Adair indicated, always applauded for either his bravery in combat or for his antebellum and postbellum attention to sacred duties. Status, then, was awarded not only for courage but also for remembering, defending, and conforming to the traditional ways and value systems of the community. Several tribes bestowed specific honors for bravery on warriors and, in many cases, looked to these individuals for leadership even in civil affairs. They had, after all, seen life in all of its benign and malevolent facets— from the comfort of hearth and home to the violence and death of the battlefield.

WAR AS TRADITION:
THE MEANING OF WAR IN NATIVE AMERICAN SOCIETIES

As can be seen in Table 1, economic motives were certainly present in American Indian warfare even before extensive trade with whites. When tribes went to war, or raided other tribes, or clashed during chance encounters, one side normally took from the other such goods as clothing, weapons, ornaments, and even sacred objects. Some tribes put a very high premium on the taking of captives or livestock. Sometimes groups battled over hunting and fishing grounds, but rarely did these territorial disputes escalate into wars of conquest. The majority of the tribes in Table 1 gave honors to those who bravely stood to arms against their enemies. It can be said also that warfare was indeed a way for males to gain status and maintain their spiritual powers. There can be no doubt that some tribes fought defensive engagements to protect themselves from being raided by other tribes, and so adapted themselves to the concept and reality of organized violence. Most, however, fought traditional enemies and sought vengeance for the loss of relatives killed in battle. But like nearly everything in Native American life, none of these motives can be singled out as the principal cause underlying Indian warfare. All of these motives—territoriality, ritualism, economics, male status, revenge, religion, the maintenance of tribal identity—were intricately and inseparably bound together. In short, it would be better to explain the warrior traditions of the American Indian Vietnam veteran as a complex set of relationships between these meanings and motives than to search for the single origin of aboriginal intertribal violence.

It is readily apparent that most of the tribes surveyed fought with traditional enemies in order to take revenge on them for relatives lost in previous battles or raids. The need for revenge in these societies can be explained in terms of the mourning war, which was necessary to maintain a stable tribal population and spiritual well-being. Vengeance can be understood in Western military thought as a justification for violence. Indeed, retribution is very much a part of the European sense of justice. The concept of having traditional enemies and remaining in an almost perpetual state of war, however, is a bit baffling in the context of Western military thought. Certainly very long-lasting wars could occur in a cycle of violent reactions to a single act of aggression. But, again in the Western military tradition, one side or another should eventually gain the upper hand in battle, win the war, and impose some kind of orderly settlement to end the cycle of violence. Indeed, the concept of the "decisive battle" is very much a part of European military theory.[28] And, although two groups might maintain traditional enmities toward each other, it would not be rational for them to make perpetual war. One or the other, and perhaps both, would surely suffer social collapse.

On the other hand, having traditional enemies and being involved in a constant state of war with them makes perfect sense if war is seen as a ritualistic act rather than a chance to destroy one's enemy. Historian Gwynne Dyer has argued that "primitive" warfare was, in fact, a rather rational outlet for aggression that, in its ritualistic context, kept tribal societies healthy. According to Dyer, tribal battles were "not lethal, nor even very destructive . . . individuals get killed, a few at a time—mostly young males, who are both biologically and economically the most dispensable members of the tribe—but the society itself survives intact."[29] Perhaps tribal peoples—as closely knit kin groups—intuitively understood that warfare had the potential to become massively disruptive to the societies that overindulged in its practice and therefore rationally placed warfare in a ritualistic context.

There were other practical reasons to participate in ritual, as opposed to predatory, warfare with longtime foes. In the first place, traditional enemies were known quantities. Tribal leaders and warriors, therefore, had little cause to be suspicious of novel tactics, new weapons, or even the size of a given enemy's force. Native Americans faced each other on the battlefield symmetrically armed. Modern militaries, by contrast, have to plan battles on a contingency basis: What kinds of technology in weapons does the enemy possess? Will the enemy use such-and-such a weapon? How will one side counter the effects of a hypothetical weapon, if indeed the enemy has such a weapon? Who will be the next enemy? The consequences of constantly assessing and reassessing ("guesstimating," to use a former intelligence officer's term) an enemy's war-making potential and developing new weapons to counter the potentialities are twofold. "Guesstimating" is excessively expensive and can lead, as we witnessed in the recent Gulf War against Iraq, to a massive, but militarily efficient, overkill. It follows, then, that this kind of war-making can conceivably disrupt the winner's economic base and utterly destroy the loser's society.

For the most part, these two outcomes were absent in aboriginal North American warfare. Ritual warfare with traditional enemies was not all that expensive in terms of either lives lost or the constant search for more destructive weaponry. Tribal warriors equipped themselves or perhaps sought out skilled artisans who fashioned arms. These weapons-makers were believed to perhaps be endowed with magical powers that could be transmitted into their handiwork. In addition, the numbers of combatants in tribal encounters were usually low. Armed with muscle and spiritually powered weapons and fighting in limited numbers, tribal warriors very likely were not, after all, seeking the utter destruction of their traditional foes. In fact, the ultimate annihilation—or even capitulation—of an enemy might very well have been antithetical to the goals of tribal warfare.

Tribal identity, or the notion of peoplehood, is a fabric woven from the yarns of a sacred history, a particular language which is both liturgical and colloquial, ceremonial life, and territory. Tribal lands are home lands and holy lands. Anthropologist Ernest L. Schusky relates a personal experience with the Lakota of South Dakota that captures the essence of the tribal sense of peoplehood and its organic linkage with turf and religion:

The Sioux or Lakota . . . often spoke of the disappearance of their people. When I answered that census figures showed their population increasing, they countered that parts of their reservations were continually being lost. They concluded there could be no more Indians when there was no more Indian land. Several older men told me that the original Sacred Pipe [the focus of the Lakota religion] given the Lakota in the Beginning was getting smaller. The Pipe shrank with the loss of land. When the land and Pipe disappeared, the Lakota would be gone. Discussion of land, and especially its loss, were cast in emotional tones. I have heard similar tones among Iroquois, in the Southwest, and in Alaska when land was an issue. For many Native Americans, an Indian identity is intertwined with rights to land.[30]

Within this context, it would seem that territoriality could have become a strong reason for tribal expansionism and consequent wars of conquest and destruction. But certain factors appear to have been operating in most tribal societies that militated against territorial expansion and actually favored maintaining traditional foes. In the first place, territoriality has a meaning all its own in tribal societies. To be sure, a tribal identity is linked to a particular place with its own sacred features and spirits. The idea of colonizing a strange territory very likely would have been thought of as disrupting the natural order and balance of things. But what, then, could territoriality have meant within the context of traditional tribal warfare?

John Keegan, a British historian who has looked at warfare from just about every conceivable historical angle, gives us some important clues in unraveling this riddle. Basically, he sees tribal warfare as potentially deadly but well-controlled in terms of time, place, and numbers of combatants. Tribes certainly had well-defined and sacred territorial boundaries, but they were also fairly small and probably did not butt up against each other. Territories surrounding these particular lands were shared hunting grounds or ranges claimed by numerous groups. In effect, they were no-man's-land or, more properly, extensive areas that were owned by no one but used by all, in which the tribes hunted, gathered, and warred. These lands were like the air we breathe. Tribal warriors might meet in pitched battles or intercept and ambush enemy raiding parties in these essentially neutral lands. In most cases, war leaders would simply withdraw from the encounter should the number of deaths exceed a certain point or should the battle go badly for them in psychological terms.[31]

Tribal warfare, viewed from this perspective, was indeed territorial, but only within the confines of the battlefield itself. Moreover, Keegan also views these kinds of battles as being primarily psychological or, perhaps, spiritual conflicts, in which warriors experimented with what are known in biology as critical and flight distances. According to Keegan, zoologists have observed that many animals respond to threat according to the "distance at which the threat was offered," and that "[b]eyond a certain distance—which varies from species to species—the animal would retreat [take flight] . . . within it he would attack [critical response]." Keegan writes that within the context of human behavior on the battlefield:

> Soldiers certainly play games with critical and flight distances. The advice of Sun Tzu, the ancient Chinese philosopher of war, that confrontations with the enemy should begin by the donning of fearsome masks and the uttering of dreadful threats, and that only after these preliminaries had failed to put him to flight should recourse be had to the use of weapons themselves, contains an implicit recognition of the critical reaction; and a great deal of primitive warfare . . . takes place safely outside the two sides' critical distance. Indeed, it is probably true to say that the more primitive the peoples involved in warfare, the less they will be prepared to violate critical distances.[32]

Keegan might also have made mention of wearing face paint in battle. For many Native North Americans, war paint was not only intended to frighten the enemy, but also to symbolize the spiritual power of the individual warrior or his military society. In any case, if an enemy could be put to flight without resorting to bloodshed, then the winners of the battle could share in what amounts to a spiritual, ritualistic victory.

Ritual warfare with known, traditional enemies reinforced tribal solidarity. It also reaffirmed the tribe's unique place in the natural order. In the early 1700s, when the whites were urging the Cherokees to make peace with the Tuscaroras, they were told that the Cherokees "could not live without war" and that the nation would be forced to find new enemies.[33] The Cherokees had obviously built numerous customs and traditions around warfare and thought that their unique identity would be in jeopardy if they did what the whites wanted of them. In 1802 Muscogee Creek elder Efau Harjo echoed the Cherokee sentiment and warned the whites not to interfere with traditional intertribal warfare:

> There is among us Four Nations [Muscogee Creek, Cherokee, Choctaw, and Chickasaw] old customs, one of which is war. If the young men, having grown to manhood, wish to practice the ways of the old

people, let them try themselves at war, and when they have tried, let the chiefs interpose and stop it. We want you to let us alone.[34]

Similar ideas are apparent among numerous tribes. Cherokee anthropologist Robert K. Thomas once told me a story he heard while doing research on the Lakota in the late 1950s. Although neither he nor I could trace the origins of the story, it nevertheless neatly illustrates the notion that some tribes reinforce their own group identity by contrasting themselves with traditional enemies. It also illustrates the seemingly unique American Indian outlook toward opposing warriors—a kind of "love/hate" attitude in which a warrior can deprecate a foe yet feel that a given enemy's courage was ultimately what brought honor to individuals on the battlefield. Apparently, an intertribal council was held between some Lakota and Crow elders some time early in this century. The tribes had been traditional enemies, but the United States' reservation system had effectively imposed a peace between them. The men met, exchanged stories, and joked together as only old campaigners could. During the meeting, one of the Crow chiefs remarked that because the Lakota were such great warriors the Crows had actually enjoyed fighting them. The Lakota elders basically returned the compliment by stating that their battles with each other had given young Lakota men the chance to prove themselves great warriors. In short, a lesser foe would not have allowed either side's men to gain honor and carry on their own unique rituals connected with warfare. It seemed clear that both the Lakota and Crows needed each other and would have looked upon the outright conquest and subjugation of the other as nonsensical. In many ways, they defined each other.

Implicit in both Efau Harjo's speech and the dialogue between the Lakota and the Crow was the idea that honor and respect could only be attained by those who followed the old customs. In short, warfare offered a young male the opportunity to demonstrate, by his behavior before, during, and after combat, that he was the embodiment of individual tribal virtue. The warrior did not act out a role in tribal society as much as he developed a relationship with the community that sustained and reaffirmed tribal identity. By participating in preparatory and postcombat ceremonies the warrior demonstrated the proper reverence for the tribe's special relationship with the spirit world. The warrior replaced lost kin and dried the tears of mourning relatives. Equally, the warrior contributed significantly to tribal wealth, prosperity, and continued intratribal harmony. To illustrate: by raiding warriors could accumulate a degree of wealth, which could then be given away to other tribal members. Generosity was a much honored tribal virtue that was ritualized among a number of tribes. The potlatches of the Northwest Coast tribes were formal displays of generosity conducted on special occasions or for particular reasons. Quite often material goods for potlatches were obtained among groups like the Tlingets by raiding enemy villages. The potlatch itself enhanced a family's status because the family always gave to other families, thus promoting an interfamily bond.[35]

Several other tribes in Table 1 practiced ritualized generosity as a part of their warfare complex. Returning Cherokee warriors gave prisoners and booty over to their female relatives. The material goods apparently were, in turn, distributed among needy kinsfolk during the Eagle Dance cycle. In addition, warriors' families normally sponsored a postwar feast for the entire community.[36] Among several Plains tribes, such as the Cheyennes, Lakotas, and Kiowas, traditional chiefs were often said to have been very poor in material wealth because, in their concern for the welfare of their people, they had simply given away most, if not all, of their possessions. Kiowas placed a great deal of emphasis on stealing horses from traditional enemies, as did the other Plains groups in Table 1. Kiowa warriors not only measured their status in terms of horses but habitually gave them away to less fortunate young men. The recipients, in turn, could thus take part in mounted raids on enemy tribes for more horses. They could then pay back their benefactors, raise their status, and become benefactors themselves.[37] It might be mentioned also that nearly every Plains tribe, including the Kiowas, looked upon the stealing of a horse tied to an enemy's tipi as a specific and high-ranking war honor.[38] While the Apaches of the Southwest, unlike the Plains tribes, appear not to have had specific war honors for feats of bravery, they nevertheless honored their warriors for stealing goods and livestock and thus for adding to and continually redistributing wealth within the group. To be sure, Apache warriors were highly regarded because they served a specific economic function. But they were also given respect in stories and song for either their stealth or their extreme valor in capturing livestock or obtaining goods from enemy peoples.[39]

THE SPIRITUAL DIMENSION IN INDIAN WARFARE

As can be seen in Table 1, the issue of witchcraft was a lesser motive underlying warfare. On the other hand, it also appears that individuals launched campaigns against other groups simply to prevent or perhaps put a stop to sorcery. Given the typical tribal reverence for the supernatural (although it could be said that Native Americans rarely, if ever, distinguished the differences between the natural and the supernatural), and the notion that the universe has a natural order, anything evil or malevolently disruptive to the divine system, or to the tribe in its normal functioning, was subject to attack. The Inuit and Pueblos certainly sanctioned organized violence against practitioners of sorcery and witchcraft, and the Ojibwa probably did so as well.[40]

Although combating witchcraft was seemingly not a widespread motive or rationalization for war among the tribes, the spiritual dimension of tribal warfare has not always been properly emphasized. It is very rarely mentioned, for example, that among some tribes, such as the Tohono O'Odham, the reward for victory in battle, according to Ruth Underhill, "was the acquisition of power, not for war, but for curing."[41] Some tribal elders speak of defeating enemies by "capturing their spirits." In practice, this often meant finding a way of humiliating an individual enemy yet leaving him alive to wallow in self-doubt. The humiliated enemy, in turn, would readily join an expedition against his traditional foes to regain both his self-esteem and spiritual power. The cycle of traditional warfare, with its relatively bloodless encounters, could thus be continued indefinitely without the need to destroy an enemy's entire society. The main point, however, is that traditional enemies sought to humiliate each other on an individual, as opposed to a societal, basis. Even though it has usually been associated with a system of graded war honors for acts of bravery, the taking of coup among the Plains tribes was a method of raising warfare to this kind of spiritual level. The object of taking coup was either to touch an enemy with a special coup stick or, for that matter, with one's hand, or to capture an enemy's weapon, or to steal a favorite horse. The actual killing of an enemy warrior was considered to be the least important part of battle.[42] The recitation of a warrior's coups brought honor not just because he exposed himself to danger, but also because he had more truly defeated, in a spiritual sense, an enemy of the tribe. One of the best examples of coup in its spiritual aspect has been recounted in Ernest Wallace and E. Adamson Hoebel's book, *The Comanches*. Although not one of the twenty tribes, the Comanche are representative of other Plains groups, like the Lakota, Cheyennes, and Kiowas, in their idea of coup. During the 1930s, while preparing their study, Wallace and Hoebel interviewed a Comanche elder by the name of Post Oak Jim. Post Oak Jim related to the authors a coup story about a respected warrior who had previously stolen a blanket from the Utes, traditional Comanche enemies. This warrior, along with the then-youthful Post Oak Jim, rode to a Ute village. Then,

> After dark, he drew his blanket over his head and sauntered into the Ute encampment. From within one of the lodges he heard the songs of a hand game in progress. Protected by his disguise, he walked right through the door to join the spectators. Nobody paid any attention to him. Casually and slowly moving about he touched one after another all the Utes in the lodge. When he had touched them all, he strolled out and rejoined his friend. He had counted coup on twenty enemies at once. It was a great deed.[43]

Perhaps the most gruesome and most written about features of Indian warfare were scalping, torturing captives, and ritual cannibalism. These practices, while horrifying, were not the result of a particular lust for the macabre on the part of Native Americans, nor were they always part of Indian warfare. Rather, these practices were ritualized manifestations of deeply held religious beliefs. It must be remembered that on a worldwide basis these kinds of acts in warfare were fairly typical of human behavior in this period, the fifteenth through nineteenth centuries. In Europe, some rulers habitually impaled prisoners of war and tortured and burned heretics at the stake; in Europe, as well as in China, Japan, and the Middle East, heads were taken as trophies of the battlefield. There are numerous legends of pirates who ate the hearts of their victims. All of these acts of cruelty might well have been exaggerated, either by the opposing side to instill hatred for their foes or by the perpetrators themselves to instill fear into the hearts of their enemies. The Dutch and English colonies and several Mexican states in fact helped perpetuate the practice of scalping by offering bounties for Indian scalps.[44] The bounty system produced a number of truly appalling incidents largely perpetrated by whites. Perhaps the most sickening was the story of David Owen, who was married to an Indian woman and fathered her three children. In 1763, Owen:

> when taking a thought that he would advance himself, killed and scalped his wife and children and brought their scalps to Philadelphia, he received no reward only was made ambassador between general [Henry] Boquet and the Indians.[45]

Boquet, it might be added, was the conduit through which General Jeffery Amerst distributed several smallpox-infected blankets and handkerchiefs among the followers of Pontiac in that same year.[46]

Given that tribal societies were kinship based, it would have been highly unlikely that an Indian male would ever have conceived of murdering his own wife and children, let alone scalping them. Tribal warriors, from Maine to Arizona, took scalps to assure kinswomen that their slain relatives had been avenged as part of the mourning war pattern. Some tribes viewed the taking of scalps as capturing the combative essence of the enemy warrior. Among many tribes the wearing of a scalp lock, or long lock of hair at the crown of the head, was symbolic of warriorhood and a challenge to enemy warriors. In this case, the scalp would have been viewed as a symbol of power and thus an object to be obtained if possible. Scalps were widely used in ceremonies. In the ritual cleansing of Navajo warriors, known as the Enemy Way, a scalp is ceremonially shot with an arrow. The Tohono O'Odham preserved and stored enemy scalps for use in some ceremonies. Nearly every tribe in the survey of twenty had, as part of each group's ceremonial cycle, a ritual called, in translation, a Scalp Dance. The Scalp Dance was largely a female ritual in which enemy scalps were carried in triumph, dragged in the dirt as objects of scorn, or used literally to dry the tears of female mourners. All in all, scalps came to be considered sacred objects imbued with the power of the enemy or symbols of captured enemy spirits.[47]

Ritual cannibalism was not as widespread as scalping, but without doubt it did occur in the Eastern Woodlands. Some tribes practiced the ritual on those rare occasions when an enemy was exceptionally courageous or was seen to have had great skill in battle. In such a case, a warrior might ingest the power of his foe by eating a strip of the enemy's heart. The Mohawks apparently ate the flesh of a captive who, while being tortured, displayed outstanding courage in the face of death.[48] Cannibalism was primarily a function of ingesting an enemy's spiritual power on the level of an entire community. As historian Gregory Evans Dowd has pointed out, killing, torturing, scalping, or consuming the flesh of an enemy was not in the strictest sense the same as dehumanizing tribal foes. Dowd shows that Eastern Woodlands tribes classified traditional enemies "roughly parallel to animals." But because the tribes "did not elevate humanity above other creatures," enemies were, like animals, simply other beings with spiritual powers who commanded "ritual attention."[49]

It must be said at once, however, that most tribes surveyed thought cannibalism abhorrent in the extreme: to be called a cannibal would have been considered a terrible insult. But however repulsive cannibalism was, at least some tribal warriors, indeed entire tribal communities, thought that individual medicine power could be essentially increased through these rituals of blood and of the soul.

If we also accept that many tribes went to war for revenge in a cycle of raiding and retribution, then we have to admit that anger and hatred could lead to sanguinary excesses. I know of no references to tribes torturing white females, but the torture of male prisoners, particularly in the Eastern Woodlands, has often been described as exceedingly cruel and gruesome. In general, prisoners were given over to the women, who decided their fate in a test of pain. They might be burned to death or perhaps forced into running a gauntlet. Whatever the form of torment, if the captive was exceptionally strong or courageous during his trial, he could revile his enemies and win everlasting fame as an uncommonly brave foe. His spirit could become part of the community's medicine power. On the other hand, the women could, in these exceptional cases, hand out a reprieve to the captive and adopt him as one of their own kin. That indeed was a female prerogative. Very likely, however, the prisoner would opt for death in order to prove his valor and thus overcome, in a spiritual sense, his tormentors. Dead, the captive helped put an end to bereavement in the community; alive, he replaced physically and spiritually the lost tribe member. It might be noted also that the torture of captives was the ritual by which the entire community participated in the defeat of an enemy.[50]

More often captives were simply adopted without being subjected to torture. There is evidence to suggest that children were captured in fairly large numbers on raids and immediately taken in by childless parents. In some cases, captives were treated as slaves. Slavery was particularly prevalent in the Northwest Coast region.[51] By and large, however, the tribes thought of captives as potentially adding to both the spiritual and physical strength of the community. In regard to warfare and the taking of captives among the Cherokees, James Adair wrote the following:

> [The] old headmen . . . told me that formerly they never waged war, but in revenge of blood; and that in such cases, they always devoted the guilty to be burnt alive when they were purifying themselves at home, to obtain victory over their enemies. But otherwise they

treated the vanquished with the greatest clemency, and adopted in the room of their relations, who had either died a natural death, or had before been sufficiently revenged, though killed by the enemy.[52]

The adoption of captives, children, and adults served an important social function. Captives actually replaced lost members of families and essentially became functional and often permanent members of the tribal community. Ethnologist James Mooney related the story of a Cherokee boy captured by the Seneca:

> Years afterward, when he had grown to manhood and had become a chief in the tribe, he learned of his foreign origin, and was filled at once with an overpowering longing to go back to the south to find his people and live and die among them. He journeyed to the Cherokee country, but on arriving there found to his great disappointment that the story of his capture had been forgotten in the tribe, and that his relatives, if any were left, failed to recognize him. Being unable to find his kindred, he made only a short visit and returned again to the Seneca.[53]

Among the Iroquois, of whom the Mohawks in Table 1 and the Senecas mentioned in the Mooney account above are a part, the adoption of captives seems to have been the strongest of the roots of their Great Peace. The confederacy laid down strict rules of adoption and essentially made it clear that adopted captives were to be treated as Iroquois by birth, provided that an Iroquois clan or family pay the cost of the accompanying ceremonies. According to the nation's constitution:

> Should any person, a member of the Five Nations' Confederacy, specially esteem a man or a woman of another clan or of a foreign nation, he may choose a name and bestow it upon that person . . . When the adoption of anyone shall have been confirmed by the Lords of the Nation, the Lords shall address the people of their nation and say: "Now you of our nation, be informed that such a person, such a family of such families, have ceased forever to bear their birth nation's name and have buried it in the depths of the earth. Henceforth let no one of our nation ever mention the original name or nation of their birth. To do so will be to hasten the end of our peace.[54]

In the Iroquois concept of the Great Peace, the word *peace* was an all-encompassing notion that bespoke of a universal order—a natural law—that provided for justice, harmony, and a group's special place and relationship in the natural and spiritual worlds. Captives were not viewed as "others," nor were they dehumanized in any sense of the word. The more people under the Great Peace the more powerful—or righteous—the cause. And the cause, of course, was the Great Peace. Clearly, the members of the Iroquois confederacy—Mohawks, Cayugas, Onondagas, Oneidas, Senecas, and later the Tuscaroras—saw the spread of the Great Peace as their special mission given to them by the Creator. Other peoples could enter the League freely but there were also provisions in the law to extend the Great Peace by force of arms. In fact, there was a war song composed for this very purpose:

> I am of the Five nations
> And I shall make supplications
> To the Almighty Creator.
> He has furnished this army.
> My warriors shall be mighty.
> In the strength of the Creator . . .
> For it was He who gave the song,
> This war song that I sing![55]

Ultimately, the League's war song was a sacred act to be used in the extension of the Great Peace. It enjoined the "Almighty Creator" and was a vow to perform "supplications" to ensure success in the Iroquois mission. In that sense, it was a holy duty to utilize the song, and most warriors would probably not have gone into combat without it any more than they would have fought without weapons.

War songs, like those of the Iroquois, demonstrate the ritual nature of Native American warfare almost more than anything else. War songs were formulas for personal medicine, and thus the method by which a warrior came in contact with the spirits. Some songs were beautifully expressed lamentations about the cruelty of war. Others summoned a warrior's helping spirit. Most Native Americans did not think of themselves as superior to nature. Human beings, especially men, were born naked and without power. Numerous prayers begin with a listing of those things in which humans are deficient: "The bear is stronger; the deer swifter; the eagle more far-seeing." Powerless, humans have to appeal to the spirit world for help. If the individual or the group does the right things, if they are worthy, then they can expect the spirits or a spirit to give them a ceremony or a song or a special token to help them perform a certain task or accomplish particular goals. This connection with the spirit world was and is reciprocal. Warriors sought help from certain spirits and received special personal war medicines; in return, they were obligated to maintain and keep sacred the ceremonies and objects given to them.

The following four war songs in reality are sacred formulas used to accomplish certain goals. The first two are songs of exhortation very likely composed by an individual who had, after a period of fasting, cleansing, and prayer, received the song in a vision. The first song, from the Crow people, is a personal formula probably given to the warrior by a supernatural being. In a sense, it is owned by the person, who could sell it or give it to someone else.

> Eternal are the heavens and earth;
>> Old people are poorly off.
> Do not be afraid.[56]

The second song is an Omaha song from the Hethushka warrior society. Probably composed for the society by an individual, it was part of the group's particular rituals and could be used by its members only. Members of the society would be obliged to honor the song at all times. Today, when a certain society's song is sung at a pow-wow, members of the society are expected to give something to the drum group that "brought out" the song. No doubt Hethushka society members of 150 years ago had the same kind of obligation. The song contains almost the same message as the personal Crow song:

> I shall vanish and be no more,
> But the land over which I now roam
> Shall remain
> And change not.[57]

The third is a song from the Tohono O'Odham of the Southwest. Because the O'Odham people emphasize peace above all and think of warfare as something well beyond normal human behavior, this particular song is an explanation for the personal involvement of a warrior in combat. It is a saga that reads like poetry and, at the same time, an individual's formula for power in war. It also suggests that to enjoy the good things in life—food, drink, a wife, children—one sometimes has to perform onerous tasks. The lot of the warrior, then, is not enviable but nevertheless noble.

Is it for me to eat what food I have
And all day sit idle?
Is it for me to drink the sweet water poured out
And all day sit idle?
Is it for me to gaze upon my wife
And all day sit idle?
Is it for me to hold my child in my arms
And all day sit idle?
　My desire was uncontrollable.
It was the dizziness [of battle];
I ground it to powder and therewith I painted my face
It was the drunkenness of battle;
I ground it to powder and therewith I tied my hair in a war knot.
Then did I hold firm my well-strung bow and my smooth straight-
　flying arrow.
To me did I draw my far-striding sandals, and fast I tied them.
　Over the first land did I then go striding
Over the embedded stones did I then go stumbling.
Under the trees in the ditches did I go stooping.
Through the trees on the high ground did I go
　hurtling.
Through the mountain gullies did I go brushing
　quickly.
In four halts did I reach the shining white eagle,
　my guardian.
And I asked power.
Then favorable to me he felt
And did bring forth his shining white stone.
Our enemy's mountain he made white as with moonlight
And brought them close,
And across them I went striding.
　In four halts did I reach the blue hawk, my guardian.
And I asked power.
The hawk favorable to me he felt
And did bring forth his blue stone.
Our enemy's waters he made white as with moonlight
And around them I went striding.
There did I seize and pull up and make into a bundle
Those things which were my enemy's,
All kinds of seeds and beautiful clouds and beautiful winds.

Then came forth a thick stalk and a thick tassel,
And the undying seed did ripen.
This I did on behalf of my people.
Thus should you also think and desire
All you my kinsmen.[58]

The last song, from the Cherokees of Oklahoma, can either be sung or simply said as circumstances permit. It can also be written down on a piece of paper and carried as a charm. In other words, it is an intrinsically powerful bit of medicine calling upon the Thunder, or male aspect of the Supreme Being, to turn his blue, or malevolent, side toward the enemy. The warrior himself symbolically and spiritually becomes the Red [war or warrior] Thunder and kills the enemy. This is a universal Cherokee war medicine formula and was carried by Cherokee sheriffs who had war medicine, as well as by warriors:

Now! Blue Thunder, very quickly You have just come to make a
    home.
Now! You have just come to join the body.
Now! Red Thunder!
Ha! You splattered blood.

[From *The Shadow of Sequoyah: Social Documents of the Cherokees, 1862–1964*, translated and edited by Jack Frederick Kilpatrick and Anna Gritts Kilpatrick. Copyright © 1965 by the University of Oklahoma Press.]

These examples of Native American war songs and formulas are often beautifully phrased and powerful in their meaning. They are also perhaps the supreme expression of American Indian spirituality even when confronting the stark realities of war.

TACTICS, WEAPONRY, THE BATTLEFIELD, AND ITS AFTERMATH

Much of what we know about the realities of aboriginal intertribal warfare has to be reconstructed from the writings of early white observers. These observations, however, are clouded by two factors. First, they were written after contacts were established between Europeans and Indians. Consequently, the observers were seeing tribal societies after they had already obtained European goods and even firearms. Second, most of the observations are made in the extensive literature on Indian captivity, which was by and large written for a white audience. These stories were usually extremely lurid tales about Indian depravity told to draw certain moral conclusions. Hence, they tend to emphasize torture, scalping, and other forms of "deviltry" to the point that other aspects of tribal life seem insignificant. Some of this literature, on the other hand, at least makes the attempt simply to describe experiences firsthand and refrain from value judgments. Other descriptions of Indian life come from the published accounts of various explorers. While these seem quite a bit less judgmental than the captivity tales, they tend to view Indian life as a cultural dead end, doomed by the opening of new territory and progress.[59]

This literature, combined with oral traditions and scholarly treatises done on American Indian political organization, can, however, give a remarkably good picture of American Indian warfare in terms of weapons used, preparations for battle, tactics, and the ways in which the tribes handled victory or defeat. One can also deduce what the effects of battle were on the combatants. In most ways actual combat—wounds, death, offense, defense, ambush, concentration of force, the excitement and terror of battle—is universal and much described.

Remarkably, and despite great cultural differences between Native American tribes, the patterns of Indian warfare varied little from tribe to tribe and region to region. With only minor variations, the same kinds of general preparations, weapons, and tactics were used in what is now the state of Washington as were used in what is now Florida:

1. War leaders were followed because they had already proved themselves in combat or had been granted special medicine by supernatural forces.

2. Individual warriors concerned themselves with their personal medicine.

3. The principal weapons of war were clubs and hatchets, bows and arrows, lances, knives, and, later, guns.

4. On the trail, war parties moved silently and utilized various methods of communicating with their comrades.

5. War parties preferred using surprise and the concentration of force.

6. Retreat in the face of superior force was no shame.

7. Warriors of all tribes made every attempt to remove their wounded from the field of battle and to recover their dead.

In general, the tribes decided on the need to mount a war expedition in one of two ways. The most common was when an individual convinced a following of warriors that an expedition was necessary. Usually a leader of some repute literally "sang up" a following. In the Eastern Woodlands an individual hoping to lead a war expedition gathered people around his lodge by singing a war song, accompanying himself on a drum or with a rattle. The leader would then speak to the listening crowd, according to Adair,

> with a very rapid language, short pauses, and an awful commanding voice, [telling] them of the continued friendly offices they have done the enemy, but which have been ungratefully returned with the blood of his kinsmen.[60]

In short, he exhorted the warriors to seek blood revenge. Ultimately the expedition depended on the forcefulness, will, and persuasive powers of the individual war leader. Nearly every tribe whose principal motive for war was revenge began a raid in this manner. Minor variations on the theme occurred: on the Plains a leader might convince a following that they should raid another group for horses; a leader on the Northwest Coast might persuade warriors to put an end to another group's practice of sorcery. In all cases, however, the individual who gathered the group was in complete charge and the entire expedition was instantly dependent on his tactical abilities—his personal war medicine. If the expedition should fail the leader might suffer a grave loss of prestige:

> They reckon the leader's impurity to be the chief occasion of bad success; and if he lose several of his warriors by the enemy, his life is either in danger for the supposed fault, or he is degraded, by taking from him his drum, war-whistle, and martial titles, and debasing him to his boy's name.[61]

At minimum an expedition leader, should his medicine fail, would certainly be unable to raise a following for a second venture into enemy country.

War could also be declared institutionally. Among some tribes the council, ruling clan, or priesthood might decide the need for war. This ruling body would then call upon a tribal war chief to gather a following and lead the expedition in much the same manner described above. On certain occasions battles might even be arranged in neutral territory. Often enough an individual, perhaps with a friend or a kinsman, simply went to war alone to fulfill a vow, to seek individual wealth or revenge, or to follow a vision to go to war. In any case, there seems to be no evidence of forcing individuals to participate in war among any tribal group. Warfare was strictly voluntary.

After a war party was formed most tribes prepared for battle with specialized rituals. Warriors took sweat baths, discontinued sexual relations with their wives, prayed, gathered to be blessed by war priests, and fasted. Some tribes held large preparatory dances. Other tribes left preparation to the individual warrior, who gathered not only his arms but called upon his own helping spirits to protect him in combat.[62]

After the rituals and the taking up of arms, war parties proceeded toward their objectives with great caution—over-cautiously, according to Adair, because war leaders feared for their reputations.[63] Individual warriors usually supplied their own provisions, whether parched corn, cured meat or fish, pemmican, or various dried fruits, depending on the region in which they lived. Whether on foot or mounted on horses, war parties always attempted to deceive the enemy by traveling in single file to hide their numbers, or by making false trails. Some warriors tied buffalo hooves to their feet to conceal their party's presence in enemy country.[64] They also normally put out flank guards and posted sentries and listening posts when encamped. Members of a war expedition were extremely cautious of befouling a leader's or the group's war medicine. While on the trail, most tribes had special taboos that were strictly followed. Some warriors were not allowed to lean against trees; others could not touch themselves with their hands; still others were forbidden certain foodstuffs. Cherokees appointed a "waiter" to accompany war parties. This person served out the provisions and the warriors could take food only from his hands. Most Indian warriors were expected to avoid sexual contact. Consequently, the stories of Indian men raping female captives, particularly in the captivity tales of the seventeenth and eighteenth centuries, are dubious at best.[65]

It was firmly believed that the failure to observe these restrictions could lead to the failure of the entire expedition. Adair's description of a war party on the move is especially revealing:

As soon as they enter the woods, all are silent; and, every day they observe a profound silence in their march, that their ears may be quick to inform them of danger; their small black eyes are almost as sharp also as those of the eagle, or the lynx; and with their feet they resemble the wild cat, or the cunning panther, crawling up to its prey. Thus they proceed, while things promise them good success; but, if their dreams portend any ill, they always obey the supposed divine intimation and return home, without incurring the least censure . . . I have known a whole company who set out for war, to return in small parties, and sometimes by single persons, and be applauded by the united voice of the people.[66]

A famous piece of Kiowa history illustrates the importance of observing sacred restrictions even in terms of tactical necessity. Sometime in 1847, a group of Comanches, who had been at peace with the Kiowas, approached a Kiowa encampment to propose that they go on a joint war expedition against their mutual traditional enemies, the Utes. The Comanches argued that they needed horses and could also capture some Ute women, both of which the Comanches apparently desired. The visiting warriors stressed the idea that a joint undertaking of this kind would solidify the peace between the two peoples. The Kiowas were unwilling to go at first. They had many horses and did not desire to take captive any Ute females. Sitting Bear (one Kiowa man told me it was Stumbling Bear), a Kiowa warrior of high repute, reminded the rest of the village, however, that the Utes had taken the life of one of their own in a recent raid and that this person's death should be avenged. All then agreed to the expedition, made their individual rituals, and set off to attack the Utes. While on the trail, the Comanches killed and ate a bear. This act was offensive to most of the Kiowas because the bear was Sitting Bear's helping spirit and name animal. The Kiowas also had a strict religious injunction against eating bear in the first place. Consequently, Sitting Bear thought it wise to abort the expedition and duly returned home. Other Kiowas, however, continued on with the Comanches. Unfortunately, the joint raid turned out to be a disaster in which most members of the war party were killed by the Utes. Many Kiowas contend, of course, that the expedition was doomed because a taboo was violated. The desecration literally destroyed the group's cohesion and unity of command.[67]

Most non-Indian observers had a remarkable degree of respect for Indian battle tactics. For one thing, Indian tactical knowledge was wholly suited to the environment in which they fought. Native Americans largely adapted hunting techniques to the battlefield and used logic, the correct application of force, surprise, maneuver, communications, and all of those intangibles which contribute to winning victories. In fact, numerous noted historians allude to the idea that Europeans would not have been able to subdue the continent if American Indians had possessed sufficient fighting forces.[68]

From a military standpoint, Native American war parties were all lightly burdened, fast-moving (whether mounted or dismounted), well-organized, cohesive tactical units. Warriors had been trained from boyhood in arms manufacture and usage and had been encouraged to participate in a wide range of physical activities, including long-distance running, ball-play of various forms depending on the tribe, swimming, and other demanding sports. Boys were taught to endure pain and long periods of fasting for religious reasons as well as to build stamina for the hunt. Young men learned a number of different forms of communication that, when used, were designed not to reveal a human presence—hand signs, animal vocalizations, bird calls, mirror flashes, and other signals. They learned the use of stealth not only in the hunt but also in war, and were taught to strike fast and to disappear quickly if overwhelmed. War parties used ambush and infiltration and often sought to lure opponents into traps. All in all, Native American war parties, as light infantry or cavalry, were the epitome of small-unit strike forces.

A war party's effectiveness in combat was dependent primarily on its commander. The party was under the leadership of the person who issued the call to arms, or perhaps a tribal or community war chief. It was *his* undertaking, and because all service in the striking force was voluntary, tribal commanders could count on individuals, in a highly professional sense, to take orders, utilize their weapons effectively and efficiently, and, most importantly, use their initiative on those occasions when the best-laid plans went awry. The war party was dependent on the commander's abilities, topographical knowledge, and tactical expertise—in short, his medicine. Consequently, Indian commanders could assure themselves that their followers would keep silent and fire on command, act willingly as bait for a trap, or hold their ground, keeping a larger enemy force in place with a minimum of force while their main body swept into a flank attack. Tribal battle leaders could also count on their warriors to charge and press an attack or to withdraw in a timely fashion. The hand signals and hunting calls learned in their youth allowed warriors and commanders to act and react almost in "real time" during a battle. Colonel James Smith, a teenager serving in a Colonial militia unit, was captured and then adopted by the Caughnawaga, Mahican, and Delaware tribes of western Pennsylvania between 1755 and 1759. Smith later served in the Revolutionary Army against the British. In 1799, he wrote an accurate and appreciative treatise on Indian modes of warfare.

In a position of favor, Smith was accorded nearly unlimited access to tribal knowledge and war rituals. As a military man, he was especially mindful of and full of praise for Indian tactics and mobility in combat. Smith was probably the first person who urged learning the tribes' art of warfare. As he states in his preface:

> The principal advantage that expect will result to the public, from the publication of the following sheets, is the OBSERVATIONS ON THE INDIAN MODE OF WARFARE. Experience has taught the Americans the necessity of adopting their mode, and the more perfect we are in that mode, the better we shall be able to defend ourselves against them, when defense is necessary.[69]

Smith clearly wrote his treatise as a warning to the Americans. Despite their victory over the British, which Smith attributed to the adoption of Indian tactics in the first place, Americans could be beaten by a more disciplined, mobile, and battle-hardened group—namely, American Indian warriors. Smith plainly scoffed at the idea held by most white military officers of the time, that Native Americans were "undisciplined savages." Aboriginal tactics, he wrote, were superior to those of the Europeans simply because Indians acted in concert and went into battle unencumbered. More mobile and possessing a superior system of communications, Indian war parties could "perform various necessary manoeuvers, either slowly or as fast as they can run."[70] Moreover, "their officers plan, order and conduct matters until they are brought into action, and then each man is to fight as though he was to gain the battle himself."[71] According to Smith:

> The business of the private warriors is to be under command, or punctually to obey orders—to learn to march a-breast in scattered order, so as to be in readiness to surround the enemy, or to prevent being surrounded—to be good marksmen, and active in the use of

arms—to practice running—to learn to endure hunger or hardships with patience and fortitude—to tell the truth at all times to their officers, but more especially when sent out to spy the enemy.[72]

In intertribal warfare where valorous behavior was the norm—some members of particular Plains military societies literally staked themselves in one spot on the battlefield either to turn the tide of battle or to die in place unless specifically commanded by fellow society members to disengage themselves—combat could become bloody but not necessarily protracted or result in great numbers of battle deaths. Weapons, even before the tribes acquired muskets, rifles, and pistols, were deadly. Indian bows, after all, could bring down bears and buffalo. War clubs, lances, tomahawks, and knives could inflict lethal wounds if the victim was struck in the right spot. More often than not, on the other hand, these weapons produced severe but treatable puncture wounds and contusions. If a victim was not killed outright or had not suffered a puncture wound in the abdomen, which could result in peritonitis and certain death, his chances of survival were remarkably good. For one thing, wounded Indian warriors probably were not as likely to suffer infection as Euro-American soldiers. Gas gangrene, which accounted for a very large number of postcombat deaths among whites until twentieth century medical practices and antibiotics prevented its spread, is contracted from debris—bits of microbe-infested clothing and dirt—being dragged into a wound by a projectile or some other weapon. Most tribal warriors, except those who wore some kind of armor into battle, wore little clothing in combat. Thus when struck, they were likely to receive "clean" wounds. In addition, Indian doctors apparently practiced wound debridement—the thorough cleaning of wounds—and used various methods to stop excessive bleeding. Mosses, spider webs, and a number of different herbs which were effective coagulants and antiseptics were placed on wounds. Barbed arrowheads most often had to be surgically removed. A number of tribes actually had specialists in the treatment of trauma. Known as "binders of wounds" in the Eastern Woodlands, they treated not only large, open cuts from edged weapons but also set and splinted broken bones. Indian doctors, unlike white doctors, apparently knew enough medicine not to bleed repeatedly the victims of weapons-produced trauma.[73] Even being scalped was not necessarily lethal, although the victim probably would have preferred death.

Warriors and battle leaders made every attempt to remove their wounded from the field and recover their dead. The wounded were given first aid if there was time and were helped on the road home. Normally, the war party would build litters or sledges to carry the severely wounded. It was a kinsman's obligation—in fact, sacred duty—to spare the wounded from being scalped or taken to the enemy village and tortured. That duty seemed also to have applied to the dead. Several tribes customarily transported bodies in the same manner as the wounded. If hard-pressed, the war party might make a temporary burial place. A number of groups built scaffolds to protect the corpse from animals. Later, when it was thought that the body had decomposed to nothing but bone and it was relatively safe to enter enemy territory, warriors would be sent out to recover a kinsman's remains for proper burial according to custom in the tribal homeland.[74]

But Indian raids and battles apparently were not lethal to great numbers of warriors simply because they were rarely, if ever, telescoped in terms of time and space. Battles were short and compact affairs for several reasons. In the first place, tribes in their home territories had relatively good security. If an enemy war party was in the vicinity, very likely someone would get wind of it and a counterforce would be sent to intercept the foe. If given enough warning, the community might even assemble an overwhelming force and ambush the raiders. Raid leaders, being cautious of their war medicine, would usually order a withdrawal if confronted with disaster. On the other hand, small war parties might go undetected and make lightning strikes against villages. Adair wrote of two Mohawks who had evidently evaded detection in enemy Cherokee country for several months before being caught and tortured to death.[75] Raiders, since they were not concerned with taking a particular piece of land or in conquering the opposition completely, typically retreated after accomplishing the limited goals of revenge, obtaining a few goods, or simply demonstrating their courage. According to Adair, war parties were "usually satisfied with two or three scalps and a prisoner."[76] When routed, the war party dispersed to deceive the enemy and linked up again at a prearranged spot. Interestingly, this tactic was one of the great strengths of the North Vietnamese Army and the Viet Cong during the conflict in Southeast Asia.

Victorious warriors could, for the most part, expect a welcome home of triumphal quality. A war party sent out runners well ahead of the returning force to announce a victory and to prepare the community for their reception. Lakota warriors, when returning from a successful raid, painted their faces black and waited outside the village until someone formally invited them to enter.[77] Several other tribes had similar customs. Scalps were usually stretched on hoops two or three inches in diameter and carried into the village to be ceremonially displayed or used in a Scalp Dance. Women of the community took charge of the trophies or prisoners. After being cleansed of the taint of battle or after being sequestered for a certain period of time, the warriors would be expected to participate in war rituals; dances were held, speeches were made, and gifts were distributed by the warriors.

If a war party had met defeat or if it had lost more lives than necessary, its members would usually return home and reenter the community on an individual basis. Their families would take the responsibility of finding a medicine person to purge them of the trauma of battle and essentially restore them to the community as normally functioning members. Death was mourned, usually by individual families. In some cases, a dead warrior's possessions were distributed among the entire community. Some other tribes customarily destroyed the possessions of the deceased. Ritual mourning took several forms. Widows and bereaved mothers sometimes gashed their arms and legs, or heaped ash and dirt on their heads, or tore their dresses, or amputated fingers in a ritual sacrifice to a husband's or son's memory. Mourning periods varied from tribe to tribe. Whether in defeat or victory, the experience of war was shared at least on an intellectual level by everyone in a tribal community.

Even though with the advent of firearms Indians shifted from muscle power to chemical power in weaponry, tribal battle tactics did not change to a great degree. The horse probably made a greater difference than firearms in battle tactics because of the greater degree of mobility it offered. The notion that Native Americans thought of firearms as supernatural forces or that they were overawed and cowed by guns is wrong. The alacrity with which tribes adopted these new weapons indicates that Indians viewed firearms realistically rather than as products of European magic. Guns were used in ambush and the tribes still used flanking movements and the tactic of luring an enemy into a trap well into the nineteenth century. On the other hand, guns were far more destructive to human flesh and could wound, disfigure, and kill people at much greater ranges.

Although guns certainly gave the tribes more firepower and increased their ability to do damage to an enemy at greater ranges, no practical reason existed to alter tribal battle tactics. At least one recorded attempt made by an Indian war leader to adopt eighteenth century European linear battlefield tactics to the North American setting ended in complete failure. In July 1776, the Cherokee war chief Dragging Canoe led a large body of warriors, apparently in column, to meet a contingent of American militiamen near a place called Island Flats in Tennessee. The Americans were in ambush position in a tree line. Upon seeing the Americans, the Cherokees apparently took station, fired a volley at the militiamen, and charged them, European-style, thinking that the white men were retreating. The Americans, however, were actually deploying in line, and they returned fire with deadly accuracy. Dragging Canoe was shot through both thighs and the Cherokee attack lost its impetus. Historian John P. Brown concluded:

> This serious defeat, early in his career, taught Dragging Canoe a lesson that he never forgot. Thereafter, he did not attempt to "fight in armies" as the white men fought, but employed the old method of Indian warfare; surprise, attack, scalp, and disappear.[78]

Strategically, however, Native American warfare changed a great deal after the appearance of the whites. North American tribes became involved in the series of trade wars fought between the European colonizing powers. Several tribes, caught in the grips of the fur trade, sought to expand their territories by war. Others fought to maintain the boundaries of their homelands. Ritual warfare, it seems, ceased, and the tribes began to fight simply to conquer or to avoid conquest. It was not without reason that, during this strategic shift, warriorhood in Native American tribes took on an even more profound meaning that has lasted and has affected deeply the present-day value systems of our American Indian veterans.

3. WARRIORS INTO SOLDIERS

Euro-American Warfare and the Militarization of Native Americans

Most of my relatives have fought in wars . . . most of my uncles have fought in them from the Civil War to the Cherokee wars . . . there have always been warriors in my family. I have a . . . cousin, in World War II, his name is Jack Montgomery, he won the Medal of Honor in Italy. And I always looked at that picture of him and Roosevelt . . . that was a really great honor.

— CHEROKEE VIETNAM VETERAN,
DISTINGUISHED SERVICE CROSS

One feature of warfare, or perhaps of the psychology of conquerors, is that the victors often endow their enemies with unusual military strengths. The enemy has to be crafty, vigorous, determined, tenacious, cruel, barbarous, bloody-minded, and brave. If the opponent were otherwise, the victor's courageous actions, brutal wounds, and battle deaths would have no significant meaning. A foe would probably be so endowed with these military virtues and outrageously savage behaviors even if he was not particularly adept at soldiering or had no warrior tradition. In a colonial context, economics might dictate why a given nation embarks on such a venture, but colonizers normally justify their actions in terms of bringing progress and civilization to a "savage" indigenous population. A militarily conquered group has often been given a bit more status in colonization. Barbarous but brave natives are somehow more "worthy" of being "civilized." The mythical "martial race," overcome only by military adeptness and tactical genius in the first place, has been invented and reinvented by colonizers throughout history.[1]

European colonizers have accorded Native Americans this dubious status almost from the beginning; but at the same time they have developed a calculated misunderstanding of American Indian tribal values, traditions, and sacred rites. This misunderstanding is especially true of the ways in which tribes viewed warfare and their warriors. Now there is certainly a tendency to view Native American warriors from a simplistic, reductionist outlook. Native American nations did not normally conquer vast territories, engage in the wholesale slaughter of other tribes, occupy enemy lands, or seek decisive victory. The concept of decisive victory is central to the way Euro-Americans fight wars. To them there is no other point to battle. How else can one triumph over one's enemies and insure at least a temporary peace without the utter destruction of the enemy's fighting forces? And since Indian tribes did not usually seek to establish large, predatory empires, their motivation for war must have been based on simple blood lust or utter savagery.

Despite the best scholarly efforts to dispel this simplistic analysis of Native American warfare and the place of the warrior in tribal societies, it is nevertheless still very much alive today. For example, in a *Time* magazine essay entitled "The Warrior Culture," feminist writer Barbara Ehrenreich (who should know better), perpetuates the inaccuracies about Native American warfare and warriors with a vengeance. According to Ehrenreich:

> In what we like to think of as "primitive" warrior cultures, the passage to manhood requires the blooding of a spear, the taking of a scalp or head. Among the Masai of eastern Africa, the North American Plains Indians and dozens of other pretechnological peoples, a man could not marry until he had demonstrated his capacity to kill in battle. Leadership too in a warrior culture is typically contingent on military prowess and wrapped in the mystique of death . . . it was the duty of the Aztec kings to nourish the gods with the hearts of human captives.[2]

Ehrenreich's assertions border on the absurd. In no Northern Plains society did a man have to kill an enemy before he could marry. A man did have to prove his ability to support a wife before a tribal father or mother would allow a daughter to marry him; hence, the prospective husband provided a bride-price of a certain number of horses, or perhaps other gifts, often obtained by raiding. Among the Plains tribes, the highest war honors went to those who counted coup on a live enemy. Killing an enemy was decidedly a secondary concern. Stealing an enemy's horse or horses was viewed as a high distinction. Moreover, according to several tribal elders, men who had skills in the healing arts or who had sacred powers certainly could marry without a single demonstration of the ability to kill in battle. It is clear that Ehrenreich defines *warrior* from a Eurocentric standpoint. To her, a warrior obviously is a mindless male bloodletter. In many tribal languages, however, the word for warrior simply means "one who defends" or "protects." A warrior could be either a male or female—there are numerous examples of warrior women in American Indian history—who was willing to defend the people. He or she did not have to fight because war was always voluntary and linked to medicine and spiritual power, but the warrior was expected, as was anyone, to defend the community if attacked. Leadership was accorded to individuals, again either male or female, on the basis of their experience and ability and not solely on the basis of whether or not a person has killed another human being. Leadership in tribes followed a "traditional authority" model. Age and experience were associated with wisdom.[3] Who better to urge caution in warfare than one who has experience in combat? Equally, who better to call for the taking of a captive to replace dead kin than a woman who has experienced the loss of a loved one?

Ehrenreich's views of Indians are at least as old as the Spanish colonies in the New World. Because they fought well (i.e., savagely), Indians were worthy of being civilized. At the same time, they did not fight for reasons Europeans could immediately understand (i.e., conquest, control of natural resources), and were therefore motivated only by a lust for blood. From the first contacts between whites and Indians, Europeans met resistance to their goal of colonization. The fact that Europeans and later Americans suffered numerous defeats at the hands of American Indian warriors gave rise to a kind of schizophrenic attitude toward the ways in which the tribes conducted warfare and, in the long run, toward all Indians as individuals. Except in a few cases, Indians were never overawed by Euro-American arms or tactics. Indian warriors fought the whites with a tenacity unmatched by other groups. Moreover, the tribes outmatched well-drilled and seasoned troops by using sound tactics and taking the utmost advantage of topography. Whites had to respect Indian abilities in war and, in fact, altered their own tried-and-true tactics along tribal lines. But at the same time, the whites came to detest Indians to the point of dropping any pretensions of merciful behavior in battle. They justified such behavior on the basis that they were simply doing what the Indians did in the first place. And Indians were constantly accused of committing the most horrible kinds of excesses in combat. The warfare between Indians and whites became particularly sanguinary and brutal.

An ironic situation developed. The European powers and later the Americans needed Indian allies to further their conquest of the New World and to aid in fighting among themselves. They needed, indeed were forced, to tap Native American military abilities for their own purposes. Thus, they developed a long-standing policy of actively seeking, at first on a tribe-by-tribe basis and later as atomized individuals, Indian comrades in arms. This policy of militarizing Native Americans led to the development of a secondary military tradition among many Indian people. The older tradition of tribal warriorhood began to mesh with a newer tradition of service in the white man's armies. This newer tradition did not appear overnight. Whites certainly needed Indian allies and, in some cases, Indians sought military alliances with the whites; but the whites always were suspicious of their Native American comrades in arms. Thus, Indians ended up fighting and dying for the European colonizers and their successors without being fully trusted until very recent times and for very complicated reasons.

But to understand better the reasons why Europeans sought to militarize Native Americans in the first place, it is necessary to understand that Europeans developed a particular way of making war and that this methodology was particularly unsuited to waging war in the New World. In other words, an initial look at the evolution of European warfare will give us some insight as to why many Native Americans started on the road toward syncretizing tribal warriordom with becoming soldiers in the service of the whites.

THE WHITE MAN'S WAY OF WAR

European military history is not necessarily a chronology of steady technological development nor of progressively better tactical and strategic thought. It is, rather, a history of long periods of inertia and conservatism punctuated by fits of technological and philosophical change.

In terms of technology, Europeans shifted uneasily from muscle-powered to chemical-powered warfare in approximately the same period in which they began to explore other continents. Yet they seemed to waffle back and forth philosophically regarding the ultimate purpose of warfare.[4]

The classical civilizations of Europe—Greece and Rome—relied on mass infantry formations to solidify their conquests. That they were out to conquer other peoples for political and economic purposes goes without question. Both Alexander the Great and Julius Caesar used light infantry auxiliaries and cavalry to either harass, shock, pursue, or outflank enemy formations. But in their heyday the Greek phalanx and the Roman legion were basically unbeatable because they utilized sound tactics and suitable weaponry. Both the Greeks and the Romans recognized that heavy infantry was needed to take and hold ground.[5]

During Rome's lengthy decline, however, the legions were often being beaten on the battlefield by the more mobile, mounted troops of the nomadic peoples of the eastern steppe. These people invaded Europe in several waves of migration and, in effect, destroyed the Roman imperium. As groups like the Visigoths and Ostrogoths swept westward, solidifying their own conquests, they brought what became a mounted, militaristic aristocracy. After the final fall of the Roman empire, European warfare quickly became a series of clashes between the new mounted feudal lords, each one vying for land, wealth, and position. According to Gwynne Dyer:

> In every society the nomad invaders conquered, they were never more than a minority of the population. [They] constituted a warrior ruling caste that naturally monopolized military power and equally naturally favored the form of military power they knew best, cavalry. Quite apart from the fact that, in Western Europe at least, society had taken such a battering that it probably lacked the social discipline and organizational skills to produce highly trained and highly motivated formations of infantry in the first centuries after the barbarian conquests, it was nowhere in the conquerors' interests to call back into existence a form of warfare that would undermine the primacy of their cavalry formations.[6]

Social stratification based on military prowess, the feudal system itself, and the age of chivalry in Europe were the end products of these nomadic conquests. Mounted knights began to appear, and warfare almost became once again a ritual rather than a form of predation. Society itself remained extremely violent, and deaths on the battlefield were seen as a part of life; but among the knights themselves—who owed their positions to a mastery of arms—combat was a formal culmination of their training and way of life. And, until the sixteenth century, knights, in battles with other knights, looked to capture and ransom their opponents rather than separate them from their heads.[7] Little wonder that most Europeans in the Middle Ages continually looked backward to a more enlightened "golden age." In any case, for more than a millennium cavalry was the "queen of battle."[8]

Infantry began to reappear in significant numbers during the latter part of the fourteenth century, during which Europe was undergoing the protracted bit of carnage now known as the Hundred Years' War. By that time longbows and crossbows had been introduced into European warfare and had been developed to the point that the arrows and iron bolts they shot could pierce the chain mail worn by mounted feudal knights and lords. The knights, in turn, began wearing plate armor with facets and ridges intended to deflect the projectiles aimed at them by, significantly, men of the lower social strata. The knights, however:

> could not protect their horses all over with similar armor; the weight was simply too great. The battles of the Hundred Years' War, like Agincourt in 1415, saw the pathetic spectacle of dismounted knights, wearing about sixty pounds of plate armor each, attempting to charge on foot like infantry. Chivalry, in the most literal sense, was dead.[9]

The battle of Agincourt was significant in more ways than one. First, cannons appeared on the battlefield but were utilized to almost no effect. Second, a genuine sense of nationalism seemed to exist, at least among the English who fought in the muddy, recently ploughed field. Their king, Henry V, was not only present, but also wielded unusual, for the period, tactical control of the army. For the time, the comparatively few Englishmen standing in line at Agincourt were a purposeful, cohesive military unit. The French, by contrast, fought as retainers to the various feudal counts, earls, and dukes present. Finally, the English longbowmen proved to be the group on which the tide of battle turned. Standing amid thickets of pointed stakes pounded diagonally into the ground, the archers launched flights of arrows that provoked a French cavalry charge. The mounted French charge was met with flight after flight of chisel-shaped, iron-tipped arrows—the bodkin point. A few of the French knights who made it through the arrow volleys actually impaled their mounts on the archers' sharpened stakes. The French charge was turned into a rout. As the survivors of the cavalry charge were dashing back toward their own line, their comrades launched a second, dismounted attack on the opposing English knights, rather than on the longbowmen. While the French knights in their heavy plate armor surged at the English men at arms, the archers emerged from behind their stakes and attacked the French flanks. These attacks, carried out in small groups, essentially caused a tumbling effect around the edges of the densely packed French force. This, combined with the fact that the English knights were more than holding their own at the front of the formation, caused the French collapse. The archers tripped up or clubbed down the heavy-laden French knights and simply skewered them through the joints in their armor. It was almost unprecedented. Knights, who owed their status to a lifetime of training with the sword and the lance, were slaughtered like sheep by their social inferiors.[10]

Europeans learned the lessons of Agincourt. Eventually the knights and nobles became commanders in state armies over lower-class pikemen and, when gunpowder began to be used effectively, over arquebusiers. It is interesting to note that the age of gunpowder did not really enter European warfare with a bang. Arquebuses were smoothbore, muzzle-loading weapons that were fired by touching a slow-burning match mounted on a lever-like hammer to the gun's touchhole in the barrel. The packed powder charge in the barrel would ignite and send a round piece of lead toward the target. Arquebuses were big, clumsy, inaccurate weapons that were difficult to load and had to be rested on a forked stake when fired. Artillery—smoothbore, heavy cannons—were not much better for use in a tactical situation. It took a large number of horses to move these lumbering weapons around, not to mention the cost of providing enough fodder to keep the animals going in the first place.[11]

Because the arquebuses and cannons had such slow rates of fire, an opposing infantry or cavalry force had only to sustain perhaps one volley or salvo before being able to charge and overrun an enemy firing position. Hence, arquebusiers were placed within formations of pikemen for protection. The Spanish first organized these pike and arquebus formations into squares, with the arquebusiers at the corners and, in a very shallow line, along the four faces of the square. Thus the terms *standing in square* or *fighting squares* describe an important tactic of European heavy infantry units. Later the Spanish would develop the idea of volley-firing by training a line of arquebusiers to fire, then countermarch to the rear of a formation, thus allowing a second firing line to volley while the first reloaded.[12] Cannons were placed either in front of a formation of pikemen or along their edges so that the artillerymen could retreat to safety within the square. The French developed the idea of hiding groups of arquebusiers within a pike formation. When charged, the arquebusiers would emerge suddenly and deliver a volley of fire into the square's attackers.

As better firing mechanisms were developed, the protective pikemen became less and less necessary. The arquebus gave way to the lighter but more expensive wheel lock and finally to the fusil, or flintlock musket. Each of these tentative steps in the evolution of military weaponry stemmed from the need to find a fast-loading, reliable infantry firearm. When the socketed bayonet was invented, the need for pikemen disappeared completely. Remarkably, cannons changed little in more than four hundred years after their appearance on the battlefield. Light, more mobile artillery pieces were introduced in the seventeenth century, but they still had to be unlimbered and fired from set positions. The best thing about lighter cannons was that they required fewer horses to pull them, thus cutting the cost of their operation. Smoothbore cannons, both light and heavy, were still in use as late as the American Civil War.[13]

The Spanish, Dutch, English, and French all brought pikemen and arquebusiers to aid in each nation's attempt to colonize the New World. And the colonial experience greatly affected the course of European military history. Colonies, it seemed, brought new wealth to these imperial powers. With newfound wealth, the monarchs of the Western world were able to expend vast sums in maintaining standing armies. Warfare between these powers became almost inevitable both in the New and Old Worlds.

Between 1618 and 1648, Europe underwent a bloodbath known as the Thirty Years' War. Although its immediate causes seem to have been rooted in obscurity, it nevertheless first engulfed Italy, then flared up in France and Holland, and finally spread its horrors to Germany and Bohemia. The war was singularly predatory in nature—villages and towns were pillaged, fleeing soldiers were hunted down, prisoners of war were routinely executed, and noncombatants were tortured, enslaved, or simply killed. The new weaponry—firearms, mostly arquebuses, were commonly used on the battlefield by that time—seemed to make these horrors just that much easier to manufacture. Armies carried disease far easier than they transported their weapons and left the populations of the German states decimated. All in all, the Thirty Years' War was one of the most gruesome conflagrations in European history.[14]

Significantly, Europeans recoiled in horror at the carnage, rethought the underlying reasons for warfare, and changed the rules under which nations clashed on the battlefield. Monarchs held both their strategic aspirations and the size of their armies in check. Wars were to be fought in border regions, and the goals of warfare were limited to taking or re-capturing an odd province or two. Generals could be decisively beaten on the battlefield, yet rarely forced into an unconditional surrender. A balance of power was established so that no single nation would be al-lowed to become so strong as to replace completely the government of another state. Armies carried their own supplies with them, fought dur-ing certain seasons of the year so that fodder for the pack animals would be plentiful, built magazines and depots, and, generally, left the noncombatant population alone. So long as the European monarchs agreed to continue limited warfare, they could assure themselves of be-ing able to stay in power. As a consequence, warfare in Europe developed into a kind of formalized bloodletting that preceded a negotiated peace.

After the Thirty Years' War, battlefield tactics of nearly all European armies were of the same stamp. By 1700, soldiers carried flintlock mus-kets into battle and used essentially the same linear tactics. The basic idea underlying European warfare was to deliver a concentrated volume of fire on an enemy position in the hope that the opposing force would eventually break and run. When and if they did, cavalry could then pur-sue and kill these routed soldiers at will. Relatively inaccurate weap-onry was compensated for by the volume of fire a regiment could ex-pend. European infantry formations were closely packed groups of men, standing in square, who had been trained to load and fire their weapons on command. Although more accurate rifled weapons were available, the smoothbore flintlock remained the infantry's weapon of choice be-cause it could be loaded and fired more rapidly. Besides, pinpoint accu-racy in this kind of combat was less important than having the fusiliers firing at the same time in the same direction. Artillery, usually placed in front of infantry formations, delivered canister shot and grapeshot into the ranks of the enemy.

The end result of musket volleys and cannon salvoes shot at close range could be devastating to an opposing line. In effect, a European in-fantry regiment sent a fairly solid wall of lead balls at an enemy posi-tion. Of course, the distance at which the volley was fired made a great deal of difference in the effectiveness of the fusillade. The closer an enemy position, the more likely the shot would take its toll. The impact of a volley at close range would have an immediate and telling effect. Flintlock muskets fired a solid, three-fourths-inch lead ball at subsonic speed. The impact of such a projectile on human flesh and bone was appalling. Large chunks of flesh and bone could simply be blown away. Cannon rounds, whether solid, canister, or grapeshot, would, of course, create an even greater and more devastating effect on opposing formations. Artillery could tear great, gaping holes in enemy lines, causing a formation to lose its cohesion and thus its fighting effectiveness.[15]

Limited, formal warfare in Europe ended for a time with the French Revolution and the rise of Napoleon. The French introduced the concept of a nation in arms and conscripted the largest fighting forces seen on European soil since Roman times. They overran other states with rapidity and without remorse. Despite the fact that the balance of power doctrine reasserted itself and eventually won out over Napoleon in 1815, the ideas underlying his military conquests prevailed in the long run. A comprehensive theory of total war had not yet been developed by the time of Napoleon's fall, but his general notion that armies, used correctly, could be used to dominate other states formed the basis for fully modern warfare. But then again, this central idea had seemingly always prevailed in Europe's overseas colonies.

EUROPEAN WARFARE IN THE NEW WORLD

The whites came to the New World during the period in which they were undergoing the gunpowder revolution. The early explorers from Spain, England, and Holland brought pikemen, arquebusiers, artillerymen, and cavalry with them to deal with native opposition to their new territorial claims. As more and more European powers became infected with the colonial imperative, warfare spread and nearly became total. A new kind of warfare was introduced to Native North America in which the tribes were forced to fight simply to survive as distinct, independent peoples. And American Indians were never really subjugated by force of arms. The tribes might very well have been lacking firepower at first, but through trade and alliances with competing European colonial powers they obtained enough of the white man's weaponry to more than hold their own in war. In addition, the tribes had a knowledge of the environment in which they fought, while the whites' conventional battle tactics were ill-suited for warfare in the mountains, deserts, and forests of North America. It is apparent, in fact, that were it not for either using Indian allies or adopting unconventional (from a European standpoint) tactics, the whites might have lost every single engagement with Native American warriors, including those they fought against the supposedly pacifist Pueblo tribes of the Southwest.

Since the Napoleonic era, a number of military thinkers—including Henri de Jomini, Carl von Clausewitz, Charles Ardant du Picq, Dennis Hart Mahan and Alfred Thayer Mahan, and Alfred von Schlieffen—have attempted to develop a theory of war. In effect, one of Napoleon's legacies has been the idea that warfare might very well be a science rather than an art. In any case, all of these important philosophers of combat have boiled down military efficacy to nine basic principles of war. These principles, while not foolproof, as Clausewitz pointed out in his discourse on the "frictions" of war, can provide a basis on which winning and losing on the battlefield can be analyzed regardless of time period or technological development. Even though they might not have spelled them out or completely understood their meaning in combat, ancient warriors, such as Alexander the Great and Genghis Khan, certainly practiced the following basic tenets:

1. *Objective*. Military operations at all levels must have defined, decisive, and attainable goals.

2. *Simplicity*. Clear and uncomplicated plans must be prepared in order to insure understanding and thus execution.

3. *Unity of Command*. Unity of command results from simplicity. An army must be well coordinated and lower-echelon commanders must know about and agree to a given plan of action. Commanders at all levels must accept and execute orders from higher command.

4. *Offensive*. Commanders must take the initiative in battle and seize a given opportunity to attack. Exploit a weakness.

5. *Maneuver*. Commanders must place an enemy in a disadvantageous position so that an attack can be carried out in the most effective manner.

6. *Mass*. Commanders should concentrate force through maneuvers at particular and decisive times and places.

7. *Economy of Force*. To achieve mass at a critical point during a battle, commanders must be able to reduce strength at less vital positions. Typically, this means keeping a superior enemy force occupied while in a defensive position.

8. *Surprise.* Commanders should strike an enemy when and where he least expects an attack. Enemy troops, caught off-guard, lose the initiative immediately and often become demoralized.

9. *Security.* In order to take the initiative in battle or to attain surprise, commanders must be able to keep the enemy ignorant of his plans, positions, and strength. Conversely, commanders must seek, through the use of spies, scouts, and/or special reconnaissance units, information about an enemy's plans or positions. Good intelligence is in itself a security measure.[16]

Because these principles can be applied theoretically to all battles, except some ritual engagements, we can analyze with some degree of confidence why American Indian methods of warfare were often extremely effective against standard European battlefield strategy. Even though the Europeans understood the principles of war, they often failed to recognize that their Native American opponents understood them as well. As can be seen in the following two early examples of European-Indian warfare, Spanish and British-American military commanders apparently underestimated tribal abilities in warfare or wrote off Indian commanders and warriors as undisciplined barbarians who lacked military skills, tactical knowledge, and strategic insight. These two examples are but brief outlines of European-Indian encounters and perhaps are atypical of all the battles fought between Native Americans and whites, but they certainly illustrate Indian strengths in developing strategy and using tactics. These were major defeats for the whites, but luckily for them, and to the detriment of the tribes, the overly confident, ethnocentric, militarily conservative white commanders who were defeated in these engagements were relatively few in number. Most white military leaders eventually heeded the lessons learned in these and other engagements and adapted their battle tactics to the American environment. Finally, Euro-American military elites began to recruit American Indians openly. Those who refused to do so often paid the price for their overconfidence or conservatism or racism in blood.

THE PUEBLO REVOLT. In 1680, a number of Pueblo tribes rebelled against the Spanish colonists in New Mexico. According to most sources, the causes of the Pueblo Revolt were many and complex. Basically, however, the various tribes simply rebelled against the Spanish policies of conscripting laborers from the tribes and of overtly attempting to stamp out traditional religious practice.

The root causes of the revolt aside, it appears that the Pueblos' overall strategic plan had been in the making for a number of years. It was not a spontaneous uprising. One of the leaders of the revolt, Popé, a war captain of San Juan Pueblo, had been arrested in 1675 for fomenting rebellion among the Tewa of northern New Mexico. After being punished for his alleged crimes, Popé began to talk of expelling the Spanish from all of Pueblo territory. He organized a loose confederacy of several tribes and won over a number of other prominent war captains-priests. Popé's plan of action was carefully crafted and won the approval of the various warrior sodalities. According to Joe S. Sando:

> First, [the Pueblos] would cut off the capital, Santa Fe, from the outlying Spanish settlements and farms, thus leaving these without leadership and, therefore, easy to overcome. Second, the other messengers from the planning group would send word to the settlements south of Santa Fe that the capital had fallen, and to the settlements north of Santa Fe that the Pueblo people were in control of the south. This would confuse the Spaniards and weaken their confidence.[17]

Finally, the attack was to be timed immediately before the appearance of the three-year Spanish supply caravan. Popé predicted that the caravan would be late and, sure enough, the supplies had been held up by inclement weather.

On August 10, 1680, armed with bows, throwing sticks, slings, and warshields, the Pueblos launched well-timed and coordinated attacks on outlying Spanish settlements. Using surprise and taking the utmost advantage of terrain, the warriors swept south from Taos and west toward Zuni. Approximately four hundred Spaniards were killed. Spanish refugees apparently were allowed to filter into Santa Fe, where the basis for a siege operation had already been laid. The initial Pueblo attacks had cut the Spanish fighting forces into two major groups. The first, under Governor Antonio de Otermín, was to bear the brunt of the siege operation against Santa Fe. The other force, under Alonso García, captain-general of the Rio Abajo settlements and Otermín's appointee, was attempting to regroup at Isleta. Both Otermín and García were desperately trying to contact each other in the hope of consolidating their forces for a counterattack.[18]

The information about the success of the Pueblo attacks, spread by tribal runners, however, severely crippled Spanish reactions. Unable to communicate with each other, both Otermín and García very likely thought the other destroyed or at least severely weakened. Consequently, they both began to think of retreat. On August 11, a day after the initial Pueblo offensive, García formed a makeshift advisory council from local military and religious leaders to advise him on an immediate course of action. The majority of the council urged García to retreat to El Paso, or at least as far as it would take to rendezvous with the delayed supply caravan coming from Mexico. A few military men wanted García to split his forces, leaving a group to protect Isleta and sending the other to aid in the relief of Santa Fe. García was apparently uncertain about splitting his own forces in two or as to whether or not there was still a garrison to relieve at Santa Fe. If what intelligence he could obtain was correct and he split his force (usually a risky military decision in the first place) to relieve a nonexistent Santa Fe garrison, his command, along with the entire Spanish community, would have been placed in dire jeopardy. On August 14, García ordered a retreat south toward El Paso.

Otermín in Santa Fe was facing the same dilemma but with less freedom of action. Santa Fe was cut off. The Pueblo army controlled the water supply, encircled the town, and had massed forces at possible sally points leading out of the besieged fortress. The Spaniards suffered for several days under the hot August sun. Otermín, unsure about the possibility of relief and fearing the worst, was desperate. He finally ordered a breakout on August 20. There is some debate as to whether or not the Pueblos simply let the Spanish escape the siege. According to one source, Otermín's forces attacked a "complacent and careless" Pueblo position and forced a breakout.[19] Joe S. Sando, on the other hand, suggests that the Pueblo aim in the war was to drive the Spanish from New Mexico and that they simply allowed Otermín, his garrison, and the Spanish clerics and civilians to escape. The Pueblos certainly made no effort to destroy either Otermín or García after they began their retreats. In any case, both Spanish forces linked up in the south and retired to El Paso. The Spanish were unable to retake the territory lost in the Pueblo Revolt for at least another eleven years, and even then they did so only with the aid of other Indians and some Pueblo turncoats.[20]

In the final analysis, the Pueblos used surprise and misinformation to great effect. Neither Otermín nor García, it seems, realized that the Pueblos were other than docile subjects of the Spanish Crown. Both were obviously torn by their conceptions of Indians and Spanish power. On the one hand, they found themselves in grave military situations and were forced to acknowledge, grudgingly, that the Pueblos had launched a successful military operation and that the Spanish were on the brink of destruction. On the other hand, they could not really admit that the theretofore peaceful Pueblos had the wherewithal to plan and coordinate such an attack. The Spanish might have cursed the Pueblos as treacherous and deceitful people; but deception, along with maneuver, mass attack, the division of an enemy's force, and economy of force were and are vital parts of war-making.

BRADDOCK'S CAMPAIGN. In 1753, the French established a garrison at Fort Duquesne at the junction of the Allegheny and Monongahela rivers, thereby staking a claim to the Ohio Valley. The British and the American colonists viewed this move as a threat to their own plans for expansion into the area. The establishment of Fort Duquesne is seen more often than not as being the incident that precipitated the French and Indian War one year later. The French were acting from a position of strength. They had numerous Native American allies and knew it would take a large British force operating on extended supply lines to force a French withdrawal. Not that French security rested on a significant number of regular army personnel—the garrison itself was very small—but they could count on a number of tribes to come to their aid. The French, of course, had been trading with the Great Lakes and Ohio Valley tribes for years.[21]

Despite the known difficulties inherent in a campaign to dislodge the French, Governor Robert Dinwiddie of Virginia nevertheless ordered a force of Virginia militia to take Fort Duquesne. This force, under the command of George Washington, invaded the Ohio Valley, established a makeshift base of operations, and launched a short campaign using the tactics of European limited warfare. Washington's force was poorly supplied for such a campaign and eventually was defeated and compelled to withdraw from the area of operations. The British government became aware of the French threat and in 1755 dispatched two regular regiments from England under the command of Major General Edward Braddock. Braddock augmented his force with both Virginia and North Carolina militiamen, trained them in close order formations and volley firing, and set out in June of 1755 for Fort Duquesne. Braddock's force numbered more than two thousand.[22]

Braddock moved westward in column clearing a roadway as he went. The British-American force included, because of the known logistics problem, a remarkably cumbersome baggage and supply train. Of course, Braddock, very much like Washington before him, intended to conduct a campaign in the European manner, establishing supply depots and magazines and finally maneuvering the French into a fatal decisive battle. Because he had to make a number of river crossings, Braddock eventually decided to let the baggage train follow as best it could, while he proceeded at greater speed with about thirteen hundred troops. He also proceeded with caution and, in fact, decided to cross the Monongahela twice to avoid what he thought were potentially dangerous ambush positions. After making the second crossing on July 9, Braddock ordered Lieutenant Colonel Thomas Gage to take an advance guard and scout ahead of the main column. Within a mile of the river crossing, Gage was taken under fire by a relatively small group of French and Indian musketeers. Gage immediately fell back on Braddock's position. Meanwhile, the main body of opposing Indian warriors infiltrated the forest on either side of the British-American force. They began to pour well-aimed fire into Braddock's command. The U.S. Army's volume on American military history describes the battle:

> None of the training or experience of the Regulars had equipped them to cope with this sort of attack, and Braddock could only exhort them to rally in conventional formation. Two-thirds of his officers fell dead or wounded. The militia, following their natural instincts, scattered and took positions behind trees, but there is no evidence they delivered any effective fire, since French and Indian losses for the day totaled only 23 killed and 16 wounded. The few British cannon appear to have been more telling. Braddock, mortally wounded himself, finally attempted to withdraw his force in some semblance of order, but the retreat soon became a disordered flight. The panic-stricken soldiers did not stop even when they reached the baggage wagons many miles to the rear.[23]

Assigning blame for this remarkable setback to British and American arms has become fairly commonplace in the literature. Some writers have criticized Gage for not simply charging through the French-Indian line that opposed his passage. It was a very small force and not all that effective in terms of inflicting casualties. If Gage would have forced the passage, it presumably would have given Braddock more freedom of movement and would not have allowed the tribal warriors time to conceal themselves on Braddock's flanks. Others tend to blame Braddock's own overconfidence in regular British troops and his conservatism in attempting to utilize European tactics in forest warfare. Both arguments smack of ethnocentrism, because they imply that the British-American force would have certainly carried the day had it not been for two simple but costly errors. Putting the blame on Gage and Braddock avoids admitting that the Indian commanders—most scholars do admit that the French had no tactical control over the tribesmen and were not the real authors of the victory—simply outgeneraled and outfought Braddock's command.[24]

The battle tactics used against the British-American force on that day were simple and the result of adapting traditional tribal techniques to new weaponry and the situation at hand. Braddock's force clearly was not ambushed in the usual sense of the word. He had proceeded with caution, using an advance guard to seek out enemy ambush positions. Braddock most certainly had a plan of action if and when his advance guard found the enemy. Very likely Gage was under orders to fall back once he was engaged. If so, Braddock could proceed in attack column toward the enemy and use the superiority of British volley fire and light cannon salvoes to break the French-Indian force. It seems that some modern scholars assume that the Native American commanders had no battle plan and had simply gotten lucky, catching Braddock in a place where he could not maneuver.

What actually happened to Braddock, of course, was that he was outmaneuvered, contained in a large killing zone, and broken by well-concealed, accurate fire. The Native American plan of action anticipated the light infantry, nonlinear, infiltration and skirmishing tactics adopted later by every major European army. A small force was utilized either to hold the enemy's vanguard in place or compel it to fall back on its own main force. Meanwhile, the Native American main body split into two attack groups to circle around and strike at the flanks of the British-American regiments. To avoid the impact of concentrated fire on a massed body of warriors, the tribesmen moved singly or in small groups using both cover and concealment to optimum firing positions. The warriors brought a steady but well-dispersed fire upon the enemy. Caught in a crossfire, the British attempted to return the fusillade with a solid wall of lead. Their volleys were ineffective because they simply could neither see the enemy nor concentrate their fire on an opposing concentrated force. The Indian firing positions were scattered all over the high ground flanking both sides of Braddock's force. Had they been in even a concealed line on either side, the British could have at least concentrated fire at a particular elevation and done a great deal of damage to the tribal force. As one British veteran of the battle put it, "Scarce an officer or soldier can say they ever saw at one time six of the Enemy and the greatest part never saw a single man."[25] Its officers dead or wounded, caught in a pocket of white smoke discharged by hundreds of muskets, the air seemingly filled with lead projectiles, and unable to see its enemy, Braddock's command simply lost its cohesion, turned into a mob, and fled the field.

INDIANS AS A "MARTIAL RACE"

Indian victories, like the successful Pueblo campaign against the Spanish and certainly like Braddock's defeat, implanted forever in the Euro-American mind-set the idea that Indians were particularly adept in the art of war. In 1799, Colonel James Smith published his treatise on Indian warfare to not only explain Anglo-American defeats, like that of Braddock's, at the hands of Indian warriors, but also to spark interest in permanently changing Euro-American battle tactics and institutionally adopting Indian methods in combat. In addition to listing the attributes of Indian warriors, he also produced a lengthy list of Native American military successes between the years 1755 and 1791. Smith, who was a captive of one of the tribes involved in Braddock's demise, flatly asserted that Indian tactics were solely responsible for the English general's defeat. "I know it was the Indians," he wrote, "that laid the plan, and with small assistance put it into execution."[26] Smith went on to enumerate Indian victories with the intention of proving that, without adopting "the Indian mode of warfare," the Americans would have had not a chance of victory against either the British or the tribes themselves:

I am of the opinion that from Braddock's war, until the present time, there never were more than three thousand Indians at any time, in arms against us, west of Fort Pitt, and frequently not half that number. According to the Indians' own accounts, during the whole of Braddock's war, or from 1755, till 1758, they killed or took fifty of our people, for one that they lost. In the war that commenced in the year 1763, they killed comparatively few of our people, and lost more of theirs, as the frontiers (especially the Virginians) had learned something of their method of war: yet, they in this war, according to their own accounts, (which I believe to be true,) killed or took ten of our people, for one they lost.[27]

Smith went on to list the great British and American losses in "blood and treasure that was spent in opposing, comparatively, a few Indian warriors":

> Additional to the amazing destruction and slaughter that the frontiers sustained . . . the following campaigns were also carried on against the Indians—General Braddock's, in the year 1755; Colonel Armstrong's against the Cattanyan town, on the Allegheny, 1757; General Forbes's, in 1758; General Stanwick's, in 1759; General Monkton's, in 1760; Colonel Boquet's in 1761—and 1763, when he fought the battle of Brushy Run, and lost above one hundred men; but by the assistance of Virginia volunteers, drove the Indians; Colonel Armstrong's, up the west branch of the Susquehanna, in 1763; General Broadstreet's, up Lake Erie, in 1764; General Boquet's, against the Indians at Muskingum, in 1764; Lord Dunmore's, in 1774; General M'Intosh's, in 1778; Colonel Crawford's, shortly after his; General Clarke's, in 1778–1780; Colonel Bowman's, in 1779; General Clarke's, in 1782—against the Wabash, in 1786; General Logan's, against the Shawanees, in 1786; General Wilkinson's, in ———; Colonel Harmar's, in 1790; and General St. Clair's, in 1791; which in all, are twenty-two campaigns, besides smaller expeditions—such as the French Creek expedition, Colonels Edward's, Loughrie's, &c. . . . When we take the foregoing occurrences into consideration, may we not reasonably conclude, that they are the best disciplined troops in the known world? Is it not the best disciplined that has the greatest tendency to annoy the enemy and save their own men? [28]

American Indian tactics continued to win victories until well into the nineteenth century. Between 1835 and 1842, the Seminoles carried on an effective guerrilla campaign in Florida. The Seminoles' hit-and-run tactics, combined with the rigors of campaigning in the swamps, forced the Americans, weary after seven years of war, to cut their losses and simply discontinue the war.[29] In the late 1860s, the Lakota Chief Red Cloud forced the United States to withdraw from its forts along the Bozeman trail. It was during Red Cloud's war that Crazy Horse planned and executed an elaborate ambush of Captain William J. Fetterman's command.[30] A few years later, the Modocs of Oregon and California engineered a brilliant defensive action against American forces in the lava beds of Tule Lake in California.[31] In 1876, George Armstrong Custer's Seventh Cavalry was caught in an extraordinarily large Lakota and Cheyenne L-shaped ambush at the Little Big Horn River.[32] A year later, the Nez Percé under Chief Joseph conducted a well-coordinated fighting retreat that is still used in military history texts as an example of how such a campaign should be executed.[33]

The kind of combat fought in North America had a great impact on Euro-American fighting forces. The Indian wars gave birth to American frontier militia. These citizen soldiers were rarely organized or trained as regulars. Military hierarchy was not emphasized and the militia members commonly picked their own officers. Normally they supplied themselves and were much more adept at foraging than their regular army counterparts. They were also quite differently armed, which in turn affected their tactical use in combat.

The mainstay of European weaponry from the latter part of the seventeenth century until the early part of the nineteenth century was the flintlock smoothbore musket. Because it was not rifled—that is, it lacked a set of grooves cut in the barrel that gave its projectile a spin as it exited the muzzle—the flintlock musket was not very accurate at ranges above 100 yards. A rifled musket, on the other hand, was accurate from more than 200 yards but also more time-consuming to load than the English Brown Bess or the French Charleville military muskets. The Pennsylvania and Kentucky flintlock rifles used by the American frontiersmen were light, very accurate weapons primarily used for hunting game. They were also preadapted for use in nonlinear, small-unit warfare, where more emphasis would be placed on the individual acting independently, rather than for use in the closely packed fighting squares of European-style heavy infantry units. Frontiersmen could conceal themselves and deliver highly accurate but slow fire on the enemy. They were thus employed more often than not as sharpshooters and scouts. But some special frontier units were formed and especially instructed in American Indian tactics. James Smith himself formed one such unit during the American Revolution, going as far as dressing his troops in Indian clothing either to frighten their British adversaries or perhaps to trick the British into thinking that some of their Indian allies had betrayed them.[34] It is interesting, but highly speculative, to note that the renewed and effective use of light infantry skirmishers, normally operating in front of heavy infantry units in European battles, coincided with the extensive European use of frontier militia and Indian allies in North America. Perhaps it is not unreasonable to surmise that the French, who made the most effective use of skirmishers in European combat, relearned the tactic as a result of their North American colonial experience.

But even if the colonial experience did not in any way influence militaries on European soil, American Indian warriors themselves certainly became valued, but not completely trusted, allies and recruits in colonial armies. They also became part of overall Euro-American expansionist strategies. Were it not for their Pueblo and other Indian allies, the Spanish would have had almost insurmountable difficulties in recovering New Mexico eleven years after their eviction. The French made extensive use of Native American allies during their frequent and bloody colonial wars with Great Britain. The English, in turn, actively courted a number of tribes in an effort to counterbalance the French-Indian alliances. The question, of course, is, Why would Native Americans fight for any colonizing power, especially when the obvious goal of colonialism is the exploitation of tribal lands? Indeed, this very question was and is often asked of American Indian veterans of the Vietnam War. Nearly all Native American veterans of the Vietnam War have been confronted with the notion that they were duped into becoming lackeys of American "imperialism" in Vietnam. How have they coped with this accusatory question?

Cynthia H. Enloe, in her insightful 1980 study entitled *Ethnic Soldiers: State Security in Divided Societies*, goes a long way toward explaining this perplexing problem. As part of a larger hypothesis, Enloe suggests that militaries not only provide security for the horizontal *nation* against outside threats, but also are the principal agents that protect hierarchical *state* apparatuses. Additionally, Enloe demonstrates that state elites—those in control of the autonomous structure of public authority—normally have a clear idea of "what pattern of interethnic relations best insures the state's survival." The state elites, both in uniform and out, do not ignore ethnicity within, nor do they strive to insure that militaries reflect a given nation's ethnic mix. In effect, state elites judge a group's military *and* political reliability and assign minority troops to military occupations according to these criteria, thus assuring that those groups satisfying both criteria are given greater military roles. Unreliable troops, either from a military or a political standpoint, are controlled, given "safe" occupations, or are forbidden to carry arms.[35]

Historically, nearly every multiethnic empire or "settler state"[36] military has operated in much the same manner. They have conquered an indigenous group or groups which have been considered "warrior" or "warlike" societies—the Sikhs, the Maoris, the Zulus—in large part because these societies have put up a stiff resistance to colonization.

These empires and states normally have a high regard for the military abilities of the indigenous group and attempt to utilize these so-called martial races to their own benefit. The Roman military had French and German auxiliaries; the British formed Gurkha, Welsh, and Scottish military units; the Russians had Cossacks; and, as recently as World War II, New Zealand formed an all-Maori combat battalion.[37]

Because the various North American tribes put up a great resistance to the Spanish, French, Dutch, and British empires and the settler states of Mexico, Canada, and the United States, Native Americans are known as tenacious, well-disciplined, courageous, and knowledgeable fighters. The Pueblo Revolt and Braddock's defeat certainly demonstrated to the Spanish and the British-Americans that Indians were more than capable strategic and tactical thinkers. But more than anything else, the whites, especially the Americans, began to add an almost superhuman dimension to their imagery of Native American warriors.

First and foremost, whites began to see warriors as being courageous in battle beyond reason. James Smith was, as were other military thinkers of his time, clearly interested not only in tactics but also in the "will to combat" or the ability to stand in battle. As a product of black-powder warfare, in which armies armed with muskets marched to within fifty yards of each other to pour lead balls into the opposite side's closely packed ranks, Smith was especially concerned with the psychology of courage, to use terminology that is perhaps anachronistic. The willingness to stand and fight in European armies of the period was linked to a number of different factors. Professionalism, religious faith, personal honor, the desire to remain in good stead with one's peers, the excitement of battle, simple coercion, and certainly nationalistic sentiment all contributed to keeping men in the ranks while engaged in desperate armed struggle. Even alcohol played a part. One of the heroes of Waterloo has been described as having been "fighting drunk" and "running amok" rather than being simply courageous. As John Keegan has pointed out, the military formations and drills of Smith's period gave the men a sense of security. They held together—and lived and died—as a unit.[38]

Warfare in North America was a different proposition. Neither the Spanish pike and arquebus *tercios* nor the British fighting square were particularly effective against American Indian warriors. When militia—actually borrowed Native American—tactics began to be adopted, Euro-American commanders had to rely more on the individual acting independently rather than on the unity and command structure of the column, line, or square. Individual courage, and with it military reliability, counted for a great deal in any battlefield situation; but it seemed of paramount importance in the kind of combat then being fought in North America.

In Smith's view, the military reliability of American Indians was unquestioned because Indian warriors had courage that did not need to be reinforced by coercion, strong drink, a particular formation, or, for that matter, heroic leadership. To counter any notion that Indians were overly cautious in battle, he attributed the Indian willingness to retreat in certain combat situations to tactical flexibility and intelligence rather than to cowardice. Indeed, Smith related the following anecdote, which he saw as being typical of Indian behavior in combat, to put to rest any lingering doubt of Native American military competency and individual valor in battle:

> If they are surrounded they will fight while there is a man of them alive. When Colonel John Armstrong surrounded the Kittaning town, on the Allegheny River, Captain Jacobs, a Delaware chief, with some warriors, took possession of a house, they defended themselves for some time, and killed a number of our men. As Jacobs could speak English, our people called on him to surrender. He said, that he and his men were warriors, and they would all fight while life remained. He was again told that they should be well used if they would only surrender; and if not, the house would be burned down over their heads. Jacobs replied, he could eat fire; and when the house was in a flame, he, and they that were with him, came out in a fighting position, and were all killed. As they are a sharp active kind of people, and war is their principal study, in this they have arrived at considerable perfection.[39]

Smith attributed Indian martial proficiency to learned behavior. He wrote, after all, that "war is their principal study." Since Smith's time, however, whites have developed a mythology built around the idea that Indian adeptness in combat had an almost mystical character. In combining the idea of Indians as a fierce and courageous martial race with the notion that Indians were the ultimate practitioners of woodcraft, as depicted in novels like those of James Fenimore Cooper, whites have more or less become infected with what can be called the "Indian scout syndrome." This mentality attributes to Indian warriors the ability to detect the presence of an enemy from a bent blade of grass or to hide themselves in an open field. Not only that, but some whites seem to think that these attributes are genetically acquired rather than learned.

By the time of World War I, the idea that Indians had special inherited propensities for warfare and scouting were firmly entrenched in the American psyche. When the United States entered World War I, a large and vocal group of whites bent on the assimilation of Indians into the American mainstream argued that Native Americans should be integrated into white regiments and treated like any other soldiers. Indeed, numerous whites and more than a few military elites saw military service as a "civilizing" agent, where Indians could learn the values of American citizenship.[40] Yet *The Indian's Friend*, a newsletter dedicated to the assimilation policy and the integration of Indians into white regiments, proudly but more than a bit ironically reported that "Indians in the regiments are being used for scouting and patrol duty because of the *natural instinct* [emphasis added] which fits them for this kind of work."[41] It was obvious that their commanders in the trenches believed, as did the white assimilationists in their more comfortable surroundings, that Indians were more stealthy, attuned to their environments, and had better eyesight than their non-Indian comrades in no-man's-land. Either that, or their commanders were simply using them for cannon fodder. Whatever the case, Indians in the trenches of World War I found themselves in a situation that would have been ludicrous had it not been so lethal. During World War II, the media exploited the Indian scout syndrome for propaganda purposes. A number of national magazines reported that Indians were crowding into their agencies, which conveniently also served as recruiting stations and draft boards, begging for the chance to fight the Germans, Italians, and Japanese.[42] Even Harold Ickes, the secretary of the interior during the war years, stated in an article written for *Collier's* that Indians were "uniquely valuable" to the war effort because they had:

endurance, rhythm, a feeling for timing, co-ordination, sense perception, an uncanny ability to get over any sort of terrain at night, and better than all else, an enthusiasm for fighting. He [the Indian soldier] takes a rough job and makes a game of it. Rigors of combat hold no terrors for him; severe discipline and hard duties do not deter him.[43]

The Indian scout syndrome seems to have followed Native American soldiers throughout World War II and into Korea. As Jack Miles, a Sac and Fox-Creek infantry veteran of the Korean War, once recalled:

In Korea, my platoon commander always sent me out with our patrols. He called me "Chief" like every other Indian, and probably
thought that I could see and hear better than the white guys. Maybe
he thought I could track down the enemy. I don't know for sure, but
I guess he figured that Indians were warriors and hunters by nature.[44]

As we shall see, Native American soldiers in Vietnam were placed in
dangerous situations as a result of the Indian scout syndrome and more
often than not accepted the fact that they would be so treated as simply
a normal consequence of American military service.

THE QUESTION OF INDIAN POLITICAL RELIABILITY
AND THE USE OF AMERICAN INDIAN TROOPS

Given these images of Indian warriors, as well as their very real tactical
skills in combat against the whites since 1492, it becomes easy to understand why United States military elites have, through time, actively
attempted to obtain the use of Native American allies. But while the
question of Indian military competence had certainly been resolved
very early, whites, of course, remained extremely doubtful as to whether
or not Native Americans could become reliable enough in a political
sense not to turn their weapons on their white counterparts or allies in
American uniforms.

It must be remembered that the United States, despite an extremely
violent history, really does not have strong military traditions. The
American Revolution was fought with an army made up of ill-
disciplined, poorly equipped irregulars, who were probably more adept
behind a plow than a musket. Although George Washington was no
doubt an inspiring leader, his skills as a general officer were question-
able. He had, after all, been beaten by Native American and French
forces in his 1753 expedition against Fort Duquesne and was a Virginia
militia officer in Braddock's ill-fated command. A large number of commanders on the American side during the revolution—von Steuben,
Kościuszko, Pulaski, Lafayette—were not only foreign-born but also
had learned their military skills in Europe. The newly declared independent colonies sunk deeper in debt and were wary of maintaining a
standing national military force. In many ways, the new nation dealt
with other nations—both Native American and non-Indian—from a
position of military weakness.

Although the Continental Congress had, in 1775, assumed direct responsibility for Indian affairs and continued throughout the Revolution to court Indian allies to join the colonial war effort, most of the tribes sided with the British. It was not until three years into the war that Congress finally signed a mutual aid, peace, and friendship treaty with the Delawares.[45] Eventually Washington was "empowered to employ a body of 400 Indians," and thought that they would be of "excellent use as scout and light troops mixed with our own parties."[46] This was the first of several Native American contingents to serve as allied nations in the American cause.

Following the war with the British for independence, the Americans found themselves in an extremely difficult position. On the one hand, they had grave financial burdens as a result of the debts incurred paying for the war and were still not wholly convinced they needed a standing army. Thus, the United States in the early national period was both ideologically and economically unable to maintain a large enough military force to protect itself from outside aggression and, at the same time, police the frontier, for, incredibly, given the nation's limited resources, the new government had made territorial expansion state policy. Indian tribes, into whose lands the Americans came in droves, could hardly be expected to bow humbly to United States aggression. Wars broke out between tribes and confederated Indian groups and the United States with increasing frequency. Since it was obvious that the Americans could not simply beat the tribes into submission by force of arms, the government continued seeking tribal allies and played on intertribal enmities to carry out expansion.[47]

By 1790, it dawned on American officials that the out-and-out military conquest of Native American tribes was not in any way a pursuable goal, as it could not be accomplished without great bloodshed and further indebtedness. Consequently, Secretary of War Henry Knox, ostensibly to quiet the violence on the frontier, formulated a policy which in theory would allow American expansion in an orderly fashion. The federal government, in a series of Trade and Intercourse Acts, decreed that Indian land would be obtained only by the federal government through treaty, traders would be licensed, whites would be punished if they committed crimes against Indians and vice versa, boundaries would be maintained between the races, and the government would do all it could to promote "civilization" among the tribes. The burden of enforcing the new policy rested on an understrengthened and underfinanced military.[48] The military, unable or unwilling to enforce the new policy in its entirety, did not stop the violence. Warfare continued unabated and the United States was handed a series of defeats on the northwestern frontier. The worst single disaster to American arms up until the Civil War, eclipsing anything that occurred at the hands of the British during the Revolution, took place in 1791, when a confederated Indian army routed General Arthur St. Clair's command north of the Ohio River, inflicting more than nine hundred casualties.[49] The defeat convinced military commanders that the utilization of intertribal enmities, rather than sending out all-white armies to be slaughtered, was the best way to serve American expansion. Subsequently, when General Anthony Wayne defeated the same Indian confederacy that had earlier routed St. Clair's army, he brought along and utilized as scouts and light infantrymen a contingent of Chickasaw and Choctaw warriors.[50]

Between 1790 and 1861, extensive use of troops supplied by allied Indian nations was made against other Native Americans. At one time or another, Cherokees, Choctaws, Chippewas, Osages, and Pueblos fought side by side with the whites in battles with the Creeks, the Shawnees, the Lakota, the Apaches, the Cheyennes, and many other tribes. Most of the treaties made during the period were not only land cessions but also military and political pacts which obligated the tribes to ally themselves with the United States in time of war.[51]

Although they might have had their own battle leaders, allied Indian troops were usually placed under the overall command of a white army officer. It was not until the Civil War that an Indian officer had white troops under his operational control. In general, white officers had a grudging respect for Indian soldiers but did not seem to want Indians attached to their commands for extended periods of time. Indian "political reliability" had not yet been proved in the eyes of the whites. Andrew Jackson's attitudes toward his allies, the Cherokees, during the Creek War of 1814, were probably typical of other army officers' views. When Jackson attacked the Creeks at Horseshoe Bend he had six hundred Cherokee warriors under his command. Although Jackson had personally recruited the Cherokees and told them that they were "all fighting in the same cause," he nevertheless wanted them to return to their homes as soon as their usefulness was through. Jackson complained that the Indians had to be fed from his own provisions and wrote to Thomas Pinckney:

> The very moment I can rid myself of them . . . I shall certainly do so. At Emuckfaw [a battle at which the Cherokees helped avert a white rout] I must find or make a pretext for discharging the greater part of them; and perhaps the whole except my guides.[52]

When the Civil War broke out, Union military commanders and politicians, concentrating on winning (but mostly losing) battles in the east, assigned to Indian affairs a low priority on the national agenda. Northern negligence largely forced the tribes of the Indian Territory, now Oklahoma, into pacts with the Confederacy. Although the Five Civilized Tribes—Cherokees, Creeks, Chickasaws, Choctaws, and Seminoles—were deeply divided themselves over the political ramifications of the war, most of their members actually wished to remain neutral. Pressured by the South and virtually ignored by the North, however, tribal leaders eventually signed treaties with Confederate agent Albert Pike. The tribes raised regiments, which were supposedly to be mobilized only in the Indian Territory for defense, and several Indians received commissions in the Confederate Army. But very early in the war, several Indian units were in fact ordered into battle outside the Indian Territory, serving notably at Wilson's Creek in Missouri and at Pea Ridge in Arkansas. Stand Watie, a Cherokee, became a brigadier general and at one point was given operational control over white troops.[53]

In spite of Union attitudes and Confederate blandishments, many Indians in the Indian Territory decided to remain loyal to the treaties made with the United States. Opotheleyahola, a Creek chief, led a large party of his people out of the Indian Territory into Kansas seeking sanctuary and the protection of northern arms. Later, an entire Cherokee Confederate regiment deserted en masse and fled to Kansas. After suffering through a winter of disease, famine, and privation, the Union Indian loyalists formed regiments and returned to fight in the Indian Territory. When the war ended, the tribes were forced to undergo a period of reconstruction, despite the fact that nearly half of the tribal membership had remained on the Union side.[54]

Nearly twenty thousand Native Americans served in the Civil War. In addition to the Five Civilized Tribes, the Osages provided a few warriors for Southern service. A large contingent of Eastern Cherokee also joined the Confederate cause. But the North too, had a large number of Native Americans under arms. In addition to the loyalists from the Indian Territory, Lieutenant Cornelius Cusick, a Tuscarora from New York, raised an Iroquois company for service in the 132nd New York State Volunteer Infantry. Cusick, promoted to second lieutenant, took part with his fellow tribesmen in the fierce fighting around New Bern, North Carolina, in 1864. But perhaps no Indian unit saw as much action in the Union cause as Company K of the First Michigan Sharpshooters. With the exception of some white officers, the entire company was made up of Chippewa volunteers. Most did not speak English, "which made it," according to one officer, "very hard to drill them." The Sharpshooter regiment had been raised in 1863 and did not see much action until transferred to the Army of the Potomac the following year. By then General Ulysses S. Grant had taken command of the Union armies and had launched his historic drive toward Petersburg. The Chippewas fought in the battles of the Wilderness, Spotsylvania, and Cold Harbor, and finally took part in the siege of Petersburg itself. During the siege, Company K was one of the units ordered into the disastrous battle of the Crater.[55] Later the Chippewas would take part in the capture of Petersburg and Grant's pursuit of Lee's army, which culminated in the Confederate surrender at Appomattox. It was at Appomattox, of course, that Grant's Seneca adjutant, Colonel Ely S. Parker, wrote out the document of surrender.[56]

The Civil War created widespread disruption among Indian tribes and even more conflicts in the Far West. When federal troops were pulled out of many of the frontier posts, state and territorial militias assumed the duties of both pacifying and protecting Indian nations under federal treaty obligations. It seems that none of these militias was interested in upholding treaty obligations and all failed miserably in keeping the peace. The Hopis and other Pueblo groups were left without protection from Apache raids. In Minnesota, the Sioux were engaged in a desperate war largely because zealous whites were determined to rid the state of the tribe. In the end, 303 Sioux men were convicted by a military court martial of complicity in an uprising against the United States and sentenced to death by hanging. Abraham Lincoln eventually commuted the sentences of all but thirty-eight.[57] In Arizona and New Mexico, whites embarked on a crusade that eventually led to the confinement of nearly eight thousand peaceful Navajos at Bosque Redondo.[58] In Colorado, the territorial militia massacred a Cheyenne and Arapaho encampment at Sand Creek almost immediately after the two tribes had signed a peace and friendship treaty with a regular army officer representing the United States government. The massacre at Sand Creek touched off an extended period of carnage that lasted on the Great Plains for years following the Civil War.[59]

As was usual in the aftermath of American warfare, Congress began to cut military spending to the bare bone. Demobilization severely tapped the manpower of the Army, which was meanwhile involved in reconstructing the southern states and fighting a series of wars against Indian tribes on the Plains, in the Southwest, and in California. Badly needing personnel knowledgeable of the land and of the hostile Indian nations, the Army pressured Congress into passing an act in 1866 providing for the establishment of an Indian scouting corps. The scouts, as enlisted personnel, were paid as regular soldiers. In some instances, scouts, being highly mobile and largely operating independently of logistics and other support units, were utilized as strike forces. Colonel Frank North's Pawnee Battalion, for example, was used to respond quickly to raids on the transcontinental railroad by Cheyenne and Lakota warriors.[60] Mixed-blood Seminole-black scouts saw extensive service in the Indian wars in Texas, and Apache scouts were used throughout the Southwest to track down other Apaches who had left the reservations in defiance of United States policies. The Indian Scouting Service was always limited and usually formed on a piecemeal basis whenever an emergency situation demanded it. The Army appropriations bill for 1877, passed on July 24, 1876, for example, provided payment for only three hundred Indian scouts.

Less than a month later, on August 12, Congress repealed the limitation. The year 1876 saw numerous outbreaks of hostilities between the United States and the Lakotas and Cheyennes on the Plains and the Apaches in the Southwest. Obviously, Congress was forced to increase the number of scouts, in spite of its inclination to get as many of them off the government payroll as it could. The military record of the Indian Scouting Service is without parallel. Between 1872 and 1890, sixteen American Indian members were awarded Medals of Honor for bravery in action. The service was not disbanded until 1943. The previous year, the Army Special Forces adopted the scouts' crossed-arrow insignia. The last scout, Sergeant William Major, an Apache, retired from the Army in 1948.[61]

By the 1890s, some members of the American military elite had become convinced that American Indians were not only adept soldiers but also were reliable enough politically to be enlisted as regular troops rather than as scouts in the Army. In 1891 a bill was introduced in Congress providing for the reorganization of the infantry and artillery services. If passed intact, a section of the bill would have authorized the Army to enlist two thousand American Indians. After a tortuous journey through both House and Senate committees on military affairs, a committee of the whole, and a conference committee between both houses of Congress, the bill was finally defeated in the House of Representatives by a few votes.[62]

Secretary of War Redfield Proctor, however, was convinced that Indian troops would become an enormous asset to the military service. He was also somewhat of a reformer and evidently thought that military service would aid the federal government's policy of assimilating Indians into mainstream American society. Since at least the 1870s, federal officials had been convinced that the only way to solve the "Indian problem" was to reorient Indian life. Toward that end the federal government prohibited Indians from conducting some of their traditional religious ceremonies, carried on extensive campaigns to convince Indians to adopt "civilized" dress and hairstyles, changed Indian names, and exported thousands of Indian children from their homes on the reservations to distant boarding schools in order to give them the benefits of the white man's knowledge. In 1887, president Grover Cleveland signed the Dawes General Allotment Act into law. The act provided for the president to survey and divide tribal lands into farm-sized allotments to be deeded to individual tribal members. It was thought that the ownership of private property would immediately make Indians into competitive farmers whose interests would be naturally tied to the stability of the federal government. In short, the assimilation policy was a detribalization process under which Indians would loose their tribal identities and institutions and become American citizens. The "Indian problem" would simply vanish because Indians would "vanish" into mainstream American society.[63]

On March 9, 1891, Proctor issued an order authorizing the enlistment of one company of American Indians for each of the twenty-six regiments of non-Indian cavalry and infantry serving west of the Mississippi River. No doubt the ratio had something to do with having enough white and black troops around should the Indians decide to rebel and use their Army-supplied weapons. But, according to Proctor, he made the decision "after careful inquiry into the conduct in the past of Indian scouts and police employed in a military or quasi-military capacity." Proctor thought that a stint of military service would certainly help the process of assimilation:

> The primary object, fully justifying the experiment, in my judgment, was to give employment, in useful and legitimate channels, to a considerable number of Indians of the warlike tribes. Having been deprived, by the extinction of game, of both employment and means of subsistence, they can not be changed at once from nomads to quiet and successful farmers. Incidentally it was hoped that the habits of obedience, cleanliness, and punctuality, as well as of steady labor in

the performance of both military and industrial work inculcated by service in the Army, would have a good effect on those who might enlist, and also furnish an object lesson of some value and exert a healthy influence upon others of their tribes.[64]

There was one note of difference between Proctor's ideas about assimilating Indians and those of other government officials. The reformers who advocated Indian assimilation in the late nineteenth century normally thought of the process as a quick solution. Once Indians were exposed to American culture and education, they would immediately throw off the last vestiges of their traditional ways. Proctor, however, thought of assimilation as an evolutionary process and believed that Indians needed a period of transition to acclimate them to the "civilized" way of life. What better institution than the Army, with its discipline and orderliness, to accomplish the task of transforming noble tribal warriors into soldiers of high quality? What better way of legitimizing Indian citizens than through service in the nation's armed forces? Proctor wrote that his experiment had turned out:

very satisfactory. Seven companies, three of cavalry and four of infantry, have been recruited to their full complement, and even others partially, and the reports indicate that the organization of these will be completed at an early day. I have had an opportunity to personally inspect some of these Indian cavalry troops, and have received full reports showing the condition of others. In good conduct, drill and military bearing, attention to duty, observance of courtesies, and care of horses, arms and equipment, clothing, barracks, mess rooms and kitchens, they are at least equal to soldiers of other races of no greater experience.[65]

Despite the secretary of war's commitment to the project, it ultimately failed. One by one, the Indian companies were disbanded until, in 1895, the last Indian enlistee was mustered out of the Army. The reasons for the demise of the project lay primarily with the attitudes toward Indians within the officer corps. Apparently, many officers thought that the Army was no place for social experiments and that serving with Indians would prove to be a detriment to careers. General Hugh L. Scott, who had fully backed the idea and did much to aid in the success of the Indian companies, wrote later:

It seems a remarkable thing that British officers could make efficient soldiers of Egyptians, who have been slaves for three thousand years, but American officers could not make soldiers out of Indians, who had fought us successfully for a long period, and who when suitably armed and mounted were the best lighthorsemen the world has ever seen. The truth was that the army was angry at Gen. Scholfield for mustering out the white men of the two troops in each regiment, and did not want the experiment to succeed. Innumerable obstacles were thrown in my way by unthinking officers, and support in Washington was withheld by a change of the Secretary of War.[66]

The main underlying obstacle to the Indian companies was racism and distrust. Jack D. Foner, in his book *The United States Army between Two Wars, 1865–1898*, presents evidence that many white officers thought that Indians were nothing but "savages" and "barbarians," and that Indians did not have the aptitude for regular military service. This obvious hatred, probably the result of having been in battle against the tribes only a few years before, underscored the senior officers' apparent belief that "savages" were not trustworthy enough to arm.[67]

After the turn of the century, white attitudes toward Indians became rather confused. Indians had neither disappeared into the American mainstream nor completely abandoned their cultures or identities. Moreover, many whites in the period began to look favorably on the idea of preserving particular aspects of tribal societies. It was thought that certain attributes or characteristics were praiseworthy and should therefore be integrated into a new American culture. There was a widespread effort to preserve Indian arts and crafts and what were seen to be some of the more colorful tribal ceremonies. At the same time, it was thought that Indians were well on the road to disappearance—hence the effort to preserve particular features of Indian life—and were no longer threats to American civilization.[68] Almost overnight, Indians became a "safe" minority because they had neither the population nor the wherewithal, in terms of political organization or military armament, to menace American citizens in their everyday lives. Only two small armed engagements between Indians and whites occurred after the turn of the century—the Smoked Meat Rebellion in Oklahoma in 1909 and the Ute uprising in 1915. Both of these incidents were put down in relatively short order.[69]

World War I neatly resolved the issue of whether or not American Indians were politically reliable enough to become good American soldiers. Officials in the Indian Office (later known as the Bureau of Indian Affairs) wanted Indians to be integrated into white regiments. From their standpoint, the war offered the opportunity to place Indian males in the military, where they would learn English and discipline, and, at the same time, utilize their "warlike" propensities toward making the world safe for democracy. If Indians served in the trenches they would legitimize themselves as true Americans, worthy of citizenship and respect in the United States. "I hope and confidently believe," wrote Commissioner of Indian Affairs Cato Sells in 1917, "that the native American soldiers will equip themselves with credit to the noble ancestry of their race." The secretary of war allowed the various Indian agencies to act as recruiting and induction centers. Moreover, all Indian Office personnel "were required to serve as registrars and as members of the registration board without compensation."[70] Some Indians were even "told" by zealous white officials with the agencies that they had to volunteer for military service.[71] In the end nearly seventeen thousand Indians served in the military during World War I. Put in terms of the relative Indian population at the time, Indians volunteered and were inducted at a rate nearly twice as high as the rest of the American population.[72]

Although several Native American leaders called for separate Indian units and a few tribes declared war on Germany independently of the United States, the Army, at the urging of the Indian Office, did not officially create separate Indian units. Once in France, however, Indian troops were immediately separated by race and presumed ethnic characteristics and given duties befitting their supposed "natural instincts." General John J. Pershing, commanding the American Expeditionary Force, brought the Apache scouts, with whom he had previously worked while in pursuit of Pancho Villa in Mexico, to France and organized them into a separate scouting unit. In addition to the Apache scouts, Company E of the 142nd Infantry was composed entirely of Indian soldiers. Several other units, like the 358th Infantry, contained large numbers of American Indians. Before long, white military commanders found another way to utilize Indians in war. In 1918, a number of Choctaws and members of several other tribes were placed in the telephone service to confuse German intelligence operations. Choctaws spoke to other Choctaws over the telephone, transmitting orders in their tribal language, and so invented a new "code" which the Germans were unable to decipher.[73]

If there were any lingering doubts as to the political reliability of American Indians, they seem to have been left in the trenches in France. Indians were only a small portion of the population; they had been stripped of many of their traditional tribal customs and institutions; and yet they served the cause of peace and democracy. Even those who had retained their languages in the face of government policies to eradicate native languages had been of great aid in the war effort. They fought bravely and well. The conferring of American citizenship on American Indian veterans in 1919, and on all other noncitizen Indians in 1924, was not necessarily a reward for Indian loyalty. Rather, it simply was acknowledgement that Indians were no longer threats to the American polity.[74]

THE "NEWER" TRADITION OF AMERICAN MILITARY SERVICE

The history of European warfare, its modification in the New World, and America's use of Indian troops is the story of the development of a peculiar nexus between many Native Americans and the United States military. It has been assumed often enough that dependency is ultimately the reason underlying this bond. American Indian tribes joined with the whites to make war on other colonial powers or on other Indian tribes to gain certain favors or for economic reasons. For example, the fur trade pitted the British and their clients against the French and theirs. As the whites moved westward, they displaced a large number of tribes. These dispossessed groups, in turn, warred with other tribes into whose territory they had been forced. The whites essentially took advantage of this domino effect and aided "friendlies" against the "hostiles," to use nineteenth-century terminology.

Since that time, according to the dependency hypothesis, Indians have joined the military in an effort to legitimize themselves first as American allies and then as American citizens. In other words, they have internalized colonization, lost their autonomy, and been deprived of political experience and are presently seeking entrance into the larger American polity. Today, Indians join the military to escape the grinding poverty of the reservations and inner-city enclaves to raise their social standing and gain a certain amount of economic independence. From the viewpoint of dependency analysis, American political and military elites have accepted Indians as being politically reliable because they have supposedly adopted the same basic value system as whites in order to gain greater benefits from the state—either in terms of limited economic opportunity or a degree of social, cultural, and/or political autonomy. The militarization of Native Americans then can be seen as the result of a continued colonial process. And, since World War I, Indians have become a reliable or "safe" minority. Hence, Indians can now even become part of elite military units, operate the most sophisticated weaponry, and occupy an important place in American military tradition and folklore.[75]

The only wrinkle in this kind of smooth explanation for militarization of Native Americans is that it is perhaps too simplistic. In 1919, Commissioner of Indian Affairs Sells complained about the fact that many Indian veterans had returned from the trenches in France and had counted coup, taken part in victory dances, watched as their sisters, mothers, and wives performed Scalp Dances, and had been ritually cleansed of the taint of combat by medicine people.[76] There can be little doubt that the veterans' separation pay or their pensions helped finance these rituals. Some veterans were allowed entrance into rejuvenated warrior societies. In several tribes the status of an Indian veteran of World War I equaled that of a warrior who fought against the whites one hundred years before. He had done the right things. He had fought well, survived, and abided by the treaties signed between his people and the federal government; most importantly, he had taken part in those time-honored tribal traditions linked to warfare. In short, he was a warrior and, whether clad in traditional dress or in olive drab, he had reaffirmed his tribal identity.

The question of why Indians seem to enter military service in relatively large numbers turns out to be very complex. Has the military truly adopted Indians? Or have Indians adopted the military to suit their own purposes? Is Indian service simply an attempt to legitimize themselves as Americans? Indian veterans usually see their own service in a different light. Few, if any, say that they entered the armed forces to gain acceptance in the white world or to better substantially their socioeconomic status in the larger American class structure. None would say that they share the same values as American state elites. Rather, it seems that they have given military service meaning within the context of their own tribal social structures, beliefs, and customs. What more than anything American Indians have done in regard to military service is syncretize it with their own systems. This process is well known and essentially means that, in many cases, humans adapt certain alien institutions and forms by filtering them through their own matrix of cultural practices. It does not necessarily follow that, just because a group accepts a new form, it will accept a completely new value system to go along with it. In effect, many Indian people have come to view military service as a family or perhaps a tribal tradition. This is certainly the case with American Indian Vietnam veterans, 75 percent of whom said they volunteered or submitted to conscription because they thought of military service, especially in time of war, as a family and/or tribal tradition. Their great-grandfathers fought the Americans, their grandfathers fought the Germans in the trenches, and, most importantly, their fathers and mothers had given their all in World War II. Not only that, but all of these forebears were honored for having done so.

4. A LEGACY OF WAR

The American Indian Vietnam Generation

The large majority (83 percent) of the Native American veterans of the Vietnam War who took part in the Readjustment Counseling Service's survey were born between 1944 and 1952.[1] Of course they, and their entire age cohort of late war babies and early baby boomers, were at the right age for military service during the Vietnam War. Since they were the military target age-group in the first place, their total number holds no great significance. What is significant about them is the time period in which they were born and grew up. Even if they were born after the guns of World War II had been silenced, their entire generation was profoundly affected by the American war effort against the Axis powers. In fact, the war arguably caused an upheaval in Native American communities that has yet to be fully comprehended. American Indian Vietnam veterans were literally born to a legacy of dislocation and turmoil.

THE EXTENT AND LEGACY OF AMERICAN INDIAN PARTICIPATION IN WORLD WAR II

In 1942, the *Saturday Evening Post* informed its many readers that a Nazi propaganda broadcast had "predicted an Indian uprising in the United States" should American Indians be "asked to fight against the Axis."[2] If quoted correctly, these German statements were not made without a certain degree of logic. The United States had not exactly treated the Indian nations within its boundaries fairly or with a great deal of respect. "How could," Radio Berlin was reported to have asked, "the American Indians think of bearing arms for their exploiters?"[3]

The extent of Native American participation in World War II, however, surprised and satisfied white officials in Washington. Although there were some American Indians who protested conscription and "fighting a white man's war," by and large Indians flung themselves into the war effort. It was reported that large numbers of men reported to their agencies, rifles in hand, demanding to be shipped overseas at once. According to John Collier, then Commissioner of Indian Affairs, there were 7,500 American Indians in the armed forces as of June 1942, less than six months after the attack on Pearl Harbor.[4] By October of that year, another observer reported that the number of Native Americans in the military had risen to well over 10,000.[5] By 1944 almost 22,000 Indians, not counting those who had become officers, were part of the United States armed forces.[6] At the war's end, there were over 25,000 Native Americans scattered throughout the military services, with the bulk of them in the U.S. Army.[7] "While this seems a relatively small number," wrote Commissioner Collier, "it represents a larger proportion than any other element of our population."[8]

As did Commissioner of Indian Affairs Cato Sells during World War I, Collier authorized the tribal agencies and the Indian boarding and day schools to serve as draft boards and enlistment stations. And, despite the fact that questions of authority developed between the Bureau of Indian Affairs, the Selective Service, and the Justice Department, "Native Americans responded with a one hundred per cent registration rate, setting the standard for the rest of America."[9] On the other hand, many American Indian nations maintained their autonomy and sense of identity even when their young men and women were putting on the uniforms of the white people. A number of tribes, including the Osages, Poncas, and Lakotas, declared war on the Axis. In addition, as historian Jere Franco has pointed out, Indians continued to cross the line between war and peace ceremonially, using ancient traditions to make the war their own:

Native Americans certainly stood ready to "fight the White man's war," but they went to war on their own terms. Nationwide, tribes delivered war messages and prepared military ceremonies for departing servicemen. Zuni medicine men gave their draftees the *eutakya*, a brief blessing ceremony for the protection of warriors. Using corn pollen, the staff of life, and holy water, the Navajo performed the Blessing Ceremony for their inductees. In Wisconsin, the Chippewa held "Going Away" and "Chief" dances to honor their enlistees and ask the guardian spirits to aid and protect them overseas. Tribes honored women as well as men. When a young Sioux woman joined the Women's Army Auxiliary Corps, her family arranged a "Give Away" ceremony, in which the family gives presents to other tribal members, to show their gratefulness for her new stature.[10]

Not only did Indians throw themselves into the war effort and become soldiers in "greater proportionate numbers than any other race," but they also seemed to draw some of the worst wartime assignments.[11] The stereotype of the Indian warrior held, and American Indians were used as scouts on long-range reconnaissance missions and in commando-type units. They were also heavily represented, perhaps overly so, in infantry and marine divisions. Altogether, American Indians received two Medals of Honor, several Distinguished Service and Navy Crosses, a number of Silver and Bronze Stars, and literally hundreds of Purple Hearts. The danger of their assignments led to the large numbers of awards and, unfortunately, to heavy casualties. The Lakota people alone had more than three hundred men killed and wounded during the conflict.[12]

The military also revived the use of tribal languages for communications. Ernie Pyle, the noted war correspondent, reported that the Forty-fifth Infantry Division in Europe regularly communicated in Navajo during the long struggle up the Italian peninsula.[13] Pyle was mistaken. The Forty-fifth did indeed have a large number of Native American soldiers in its ranks, primarily because the division was from Oklahoma. But the Army Signal Corps in Europe utilized Comanche code talkers who had been recruited especially for this duty in January 1941, twelve months before the war began.[14] Navajo did, however, become the code language of the Pacific theater. In 1942, the Marine Corps recruited and trained a number of Navajos for specific duty in communications. Their mission was a tightly guarded secret: the Navajo marines had created a voice code that defied decoding.[15] Cozy Stanley Brown, one of the first Navajos recruited for the duty, explained the process of creating the Navajo voice code:

The main reason for us Navajos was our language. They like to use our language in war to carry messages. So we were taught to use the radio. We had to do that in a hurry at that time. I guess that was why they forced us to complete the training in eight weeks. Then we got together and discussed how we would do it. We decided to change the name of the airplanes, ships and the English ABC's into the Navajo language. We did the changing. For instance, we named the airplanes "dive bombers" for *ginitsoh* (sparrow hawk), because the sparrow hawk is like an airplane—it charges downward at a very fast pace. We called the enemy *ana'i*, just like the old saying of the Navajos. The name *ana'i* is used in the Navajo Enemy Way ceremony. We changed the English alphabet to the Navajo language, like for the letter "T" we used *tashii* (turkey), *tsin* (stick), and *tliish* (snake) in Navajo. We usually used the harmful animals' names that were living in our country for the alphabet. Then a name was written on a piece of paper. Some words were marked off and some were accepted.[16]

The American Indian contribution to the war effort was used very effectively for propaganda purposes, as well. The entire media coverage of Indians in the war was geared to give the impression that Native Americans were standing shoulder-to-shoulder with the whites against Nazi oppression.[17] The outpouring of Indian patriotism, duly reported in the nation's press, seemed to validate the American sense of mission. Indian tribes, despite being dispossessed of land and stripped of tribal institutions by the American government, were, according to the press, totally committed to the crusade against the Axis. Native Americans danced and sang for war bond rallies, and tribal elders posed for photographs with young men in their new, crisp American uniforms. Native Americans were not only lauded for their sacrifices in combat but also for sacrifices on the home front. Several tribes gave up more lands to the federal government for use as military training sites and authorized the secretary of the interior to purchase war bonds from tribal trust funds.[18] One Japanese American internment camp was located on an Indian reservation.[19] Some tribes made presentations of war bonnets to Allied political and military leaders like Douglas MacArthur, President Franklin D. Roosevelt, Joseph Stalin, and even Wendell Wilkie.[20] On the reservations, which by 1944 had become critically short of a male work force, Indian women accounted for much of the production of food. They drove heavy equipment, repaired tractors, and herded cattle. Principally because of Native American women, the production of

Indian livestock doubled in the ten years between 1933 and 1943. Agricultural output greatly increased as well, accounting for a significant rise in the standard of living on many reservations, compared to the truly appalling conditions during the years of the Great Depression. By 1945, it was estimated that nearly 150,000 American Indians—more than half of the total Native American population—directly participated in the industrial, agricultural, and military aspects of the war effort. More importantly in the long run, more than 40,000 Native Americans had left their home communities to work in war-related industries in the cities. John Collier called this particular movement "the greatest exodus of Indians" that had ever taken place.[21] It mattered little what Indians actually believed or fought for, because the fact that a nonwhite minority had so unflinchingly thrown itself into the war effort gave the American cause moral legitimacy.

The upshot of these Native American sacrifices to the American war effort was a renewed white movement to "amalgamate" Indians into mainstream American society. Many whites took the Indian war effort as a sign that Native Americans were attempting to legitimize themselves as American citizens, gain entrance into the American mainstream, and share economically in the great victory over totalitarianism and oppression. In a 1944 article for *Christian Century*, Oswald Garrison Villard authoritatively outlined this idea and essentially made the case for Indian amalgamation. Villard assured his readers that the thousands of Native Americans fighting overseas and working in war industries were in fact striving to "be awarded citizenship like other Americans . . . a citizenship unhampered by restrictions which do not apply to everybody." Although he sought "to break up no reservation," Villard's entire discourse on what he presumed Indians really wanted advocated that very goal. He argued that Indian ceremonies, arts, and indeed all aspects of tribal cultures were doomed to extinction and that Indians had grown weary of being "circus exhibits" and of being imprisoned in "yesterday's culture."[22]

There were others of Villard's sentiment. O. K. Armstrong, who claimed to have interviewed Indians in all parts of the United States, offered a similar argument for Indian amalgamation in a 1945 article for *Reader's Digest*. Armstrong unequivocally stated that he had found that Indians possessed an "unmistakable determination" to "demand full rights of citizenship." Those Indians, he assured his audience, who "return from the service will seek a greater share in American freedom." Moreover, those Native Americans who had labored in the factories and "tasted economic opportunity for the first time" would not be satisfied, as Armstrong put it, "to live in a shack and loaf around in a blanket."[23]

Armstrong saved his heaviest ammunition for an attack on John Collier's administration of the Bureau of Indian Affairs. In the twelve years since Collier had taken office, Indian policy and the bureau had undergone great change. Since the passage of the Indian Reorganization Act of 1934, tribes had been able to form governments, allotment of Indian lands had ceased, a revolving loan system had been set up to aid in the establishment of tribal businesses, and, in general, the policy of trying to destroy tribal cultures had been curbed. In Armstrong's eyes, the entire reversal of the movement to assimilate Indians under John Collier had been a serious mistake, if not an outright denial of the promise of American democracy. According to him, the Indian New Deal had forced "a collectivist system upon the Indians, with bigger doses of paternalism and regimentation." Under John Collier, bureaucracy had grown to unwieldy proportions and with that growth a greater burden on the taxpayer. After attacking the Collier administration in conservative terms as befitted the period following the war, Armstrong continued the assault in a liberal tone. Since 1934, according to Armstrong, the Bureau of Indian Affairs had allowed the perpetuation of the reservation system and thus had maintained a policy of "racial segregation."[24]

As the postwar period progressed and the Cold War grew in intensity, it became increasingly obvious that more and more white policymakers began to share Villard's and Armstrong's opinions. As Donald L. Fixico skillfully points out in his book on federal Indian policy between 1945 and 1960, the government concocted "termination" to end the federal trust relationship with the tribes and "relocation" to urbanize Indians on an individual basis. Until termination and relocation, Indian policy fluctuated back and forth between dealing with Indians as members of larger polities (tribes and nations) and treating Indians as backward individuals to be incorporated into the American mainstream. The new policy was to be a grand one-two punch that not only got the federal government out of the Indian business, but also moved Indians as individuals away from their home communities to a "better life."[25] Thousands of Indian people were given vocational training and resettled in urban areas to join the already relocated World War II Indian factory workers. Little follow-up was done to see how these relocatees from reservations or nonreservation rural areas were adapting to the cities, or if, indeed, they had found "better" lives. In any case, by the late 1960s almost half of the entire Native American population had been urbanized. The termination edge of the new policy's sword cost a few tribes their reservation land-base and the security of their trust relationship with the federal government. It was into this period of political, social, and economic change that the majority of Native American Vietnam veterans were born.

THE AMERICAN INDIAN VIETNAM GENERATION

Instead of creating a large, urbanized, and stable Native American middle class, the termination and relocation policies created a large, more physically—as opposed to economically and socially—mobile Indian underclass. About the only thing that it effectively accomplished was to establish pan-Indian ghettos in cities like Chicago, Dallas, Los Angeles, and Denver, and set up a situation that encouraged supratribal amalgamation. This, combined with the social and cultural influences of the Indian boarding school system, which emphasized intertribal relationships among students and their parents, profoundly affected the ways in which Native American Vietnam-generation youths lived and viewed themselves. The RCS survey of Native American Vietnam veterans revealed that the 170 veterans who answered the questionnaire represented 77 tribes or combinations of tribes. Of the group, 59 claimed affiliation with two or more tribal groups. This figure means that their parents, or even their grandparents, had married outside their own tribes at a rate of over 30 percent. In addition, there were very likely some of those who only claimed one tribal affiliation but whose parents or grandparents had married non-Indians. Admittedly, most of those who claimed multitribal affiliations were born of marriages between individuals who were located in close geographic proximity or from major culture areas: Creek-Cherokee (Eastern Oklahoma); Colville-Yakima (Washington state); Kiowa-Sioux (Plains culture area); Navajo-Hopi (Southwest culture area and geographic proximity). The out-marriage rate seems very high for that period given that Indian Vietnam-generation parents were more often than not products of tight-knit tribal communities. What made the difference, perhaps, were the Indian boarding schools and the massive dislocation of American Indians during and immediately after World War II. Several Native American veterans of multitribal affiliations stated that their parents had met in Indian schools. Others said that their parents had met as a result of their fathers being stationed in the military near Indian reservations or near cities with urban Indian populations. Some claimed that their parents had met as a result of the federal relocation programs. This situation would probably only apply to the very few younger veterans born after 1953. Random mixing of tribes and of Native Americans with other groups was, of course, part and parcel of the new Indian amalgamation policy.

It is apparent that, as children, the Native American Vietnam generation was exceptionally mobile. There is a tendency to think of American Indians as being isolated and geographically fixed on reservations, in rural nonreservation areas, or in inner-city Indian ghettoes. The majority (57 percent) of those who took part in the RCS survey of Indian Vietnam veterans stated that they had indeed been born and had grown up in reservation or nonreservation rural communities. These communities were "communities" in the strictest sense of the word. Generally, they had very small populations with extensive kinship networks in which everyone had a place and worked, worshiped, and socialized together. On the other hand, fully one-quarter of the RCS informants admitted that much of their childhoods had been spent moving back and forth between large urban centers and these small Native American communities. Often enough, they returned to their home communities either when their parents ran out of work, or when a family crisis arose, or, in some cases, when a tribal ceremony required their presence. Several others spent summers or oftentimes longer periods away from the cities simply to be with their grandparents or other relatives. A number of Indian veterans stated that they had been reared by their grandparents in small Indian communities because their mothers and fathers had either found jobs in the city and did not want their children to move with them or had become so burdened with financial problems that it was economically beneficial to send their children to live with other relatives. This practice is not child-abandonment; instead, it is a sign of the strength of Native American extended families and kinship networks. For the veterans, whether living on a reservation or moving back and forth between the city and the country, there was always a home community filled with caring relatives. Very few of the veterans spent their entire periods of childhood and adolescence in the cities.

The era of termination and relocation, however, resulted in a severe loss of the veterans' tribal languages. All of the respondents to the RCS questionnaire had attended either public or Indian schools and, consequently, were fluent in English. Those who were affiliated with two or more tribes indicated that English served as the common language in their homes. Even in small, relatively tight-knit, isolated Indian communities, English was used extensively to communicate with merchants, schoolteachers, nontribal law enforcement officers, tourists, politicians, and government officials. Eighteen percent of the RCS respondents were completely fluent in their native languages—a figure, according to Tohono O'Odham linguistics professor Ophelia Zepeda, that would be expected given their age-group and period of childhood. Despite the pressures not to use or learn their own native tongues, however, well over half of the veterans said that they had picked up a great deal of their tribal languages in words and phrases.

In spite of some vocational training under the relocation programs, the Native American parents of the Vietnam generation did not always find well-paid jobs in the cities. Practically every one of the urban Indians interviewed told of living in impoverished neighborhoods and attending substandard schools. Some dropped out of school to enter the military service. Life in rural areas for Native Americans during the 1950s was not any better in economic or educational terms. Some reservations then, as now, reported almost unbelievably high unemployment rates and education well below high school levels. Most of the RCS respondents reported relatively high educational levels—some with college degrees—but these levels, they admitted, were primarily attained after their military service.

The Vietnam veterans as a group displayed a marked disenchantment with federal policies toward Native Americans and the grinding poverty of both the inner city and the reservation and rural areas in which they grew up. The "economic opportunity" of the relocation programs helped create, rather than alleviate, Indian problems. According to one Indian veteran:

The system's wrong, man. I lived in Milwaukee when I was a kid. My parents worked hard but the bills piled up. They started drinking . . . I hit the streets. It's a bullshit system.

The streets where a number of them grew up were often lined with winos, pimps, hustlers, and thieves rather than with the gilded economic opportunity the Bureau of Indian Affairs had promised. "I grew up in a pretty tough area," said one man. "There were fights all the time . . . The cops always liked pushing Indians around." Another man from a different city likened his neighborhood to a "battle zone," where Indians clashed with other ethnic youths on a day-to-day basis. "Seemed like I'd get into a fight every day," he said. Others were constantly singled out as being different and subjected to the prejudices of their non-Indian neighbors. Several mentioned that stereotyping and hatred followed them everywhere: schoolmates called them "redskins"; neighbors called them "dirty Indians"; the police called them "drunks"; teachers called them "backward." One man remembered walking home from school through a group of white children who all "put two fingers up on the back of their heads and whooped with their hands over their mouths . . . you know, like the movies." He took it for a short time, then "one of them got in my face and I hit him." He was eight years old at the time.

In rural Indian communities the poverty was equally evident. A Cheyenne veteran, who was brought up in a rural area in western Oklahoma, related:

> Before the white man we had everything. There was buffalo and elk and water in the streams. We lived together and prayed together. Now look. We've got nothing. Indians are spread out on farms. A lot of them just lease their land and hand it over to some white man. Some of us have a few cows but it's no big thing.

In addition to the poverty, Indian Vietnam veterans from both urban and rural areas shared other experiences which were disillusioning at best. Every one of the veterans interviewed expressed distaste for the educations—or lack thereof—they received while growing up. A common complaint was not about the lack of schooling they received but its complete lack of relevance to their experiences and heritages. White educators compartmentalized subjects and did not demonstrate the interrelationships between humans, animals, plants, and entire societies as did their relatives in tribal stories and songs. Moreover, their own histories and cultures were generally ignored, even in the Indian schools. "I heard about the Pilgrims," said one man, "but I didn't hear shit about Indians." All in all, the Indian Vietnam generation spent its childhood and adolescence outside of the prosperity of America in the 1950s and early 1960s.

Over the last twenty years or so a number of scholars have begun to take an interest in the study of generations. These scholars seek to understand how and why some generations in some societies become bonded together and often collide politically with a previous generation. According to Richard G. Braungart and Margaret M. Braungart,

two leading political sociologists and scholars of life-course and generational politics:

> Age is one of the most basic social categories of human existence.
> The truest community to which one belongs . . . is that defined by
> age and experience. In almost all societies, age is a primary factor for
> assigning roles, granting prestige and power, and influencing the in-
> dividual's attitudes and behavior.[26]

There can be no doubt that the period of American history now
known as the Vietnam era was rife with domestic factionalism, conflict, and extreme politicization. White middle- and upper-class youths
protested the war, the exploitation of the environment, and the ill-
treatment of women and racial minorities in the United States. Many
of them formed what one author called a "youthcult," which was, ostensibly, the social and cultural opposite of the status quo. "Don't trust
anyone over thirty" became a phrase of both protest and alienation, as
students verbally and sometimes physically attacked an indefinite but
decidedly older group known as the "establishment."[27]

Although more attention has been given to intergenerational conflict
among whites, several other American racial and cultural groups also experienced similar internal strife, indicating that minority groups were
not immune to the social upheavals of the period. There were certainly
indications of conflict among American Indian people in the late 1960s
and early 1970s. For example, the takeover of Wounded Knee, South
Dakota, in early 1973 was an expression of youthful Native American
outrage against federal Indian policies (directed by non-Indian members
of the age-group 30–65) and the handling of the Oglala Lakota tribal government (operated primarily by Lakota men also of middle age).[28]

On the other hand, there are equally strong indications that many
American Indian youths of the period (the Indian Vietnam generation)
formed an intergenerational bond with the most senior Native American generation. In the case of the Wounded Knee protest, Indian youths
identified with and were joined by a number of traditional elders in opposition to the political dominance of the middle-aged generation of
federal and tribal officials. The protesters' concepts of authority demanded that they defer to the most senior Lakota generation when traditional values and the tribal identity itself became important in the
controversy.[29]

If seen from German scholar Karl Mannheim's perspective on generational politics, the American Indian Vietnam generation's bond with the most senior Native American generation seems clear and understandable. Although Mannheim's theories are somewhat complex, they account for several conditions characteristic of the American Indian experience during the Vietnam era. In essence, Mannheim argues that the simple fact of birth does not automatically make for intragenerational unity, nor does it inherently create a willingness to challenge and displace the middle, or next, generation. Young people make, according to Mannheim, "fresh contacts" with ideas, customs, and political institutions. They may develop unity as a result of these contacts within the context of their social conditions and the historical period in which they live. Intergenerational conflict occurs after the youthful generation develops a historical identity, unity, and its own style or spirit, or in Mannheim's terms, its own "entelechy."[30]

The Vietnam generation of American Indian youths was born, as we have seen, in an extremely disruptive period in Native American history. Within this historical context of turmoil, rapid change, and extreme geographic mobility, it can be justly said that their "fresh contacts" with urban and rural poverty and the federal policy of amalgamation in general were typically unsatisfactory. Many of these young men and women developed, perhaps in acute identity crises, a new understanding of and appreciation for—a rapprochement with—their grandparents who, by definition, were closer to traditional tribal lifestyles and value systems. Tribal traditions offered personal identity, an almost organic affinity with a geographic place (homeland/holy land), and social controls not found in the seemingly chaotic lifestyles of a large urban setting. They turned to tribal traditionals (or traditionalists) for religious guidance, tribal identity, and a more satisfactory outlook on life. Native American elders, in turn, hoped that the younger generation would retain tribal traditions in spite of the unfavorable social and political climate.

The Native American veterans of the Vietnam War who responded to the RCS survey have a marked affinity for tribal elders. The great majority of them view the members of the most senior generation as teachers, persons of authority, and living history. They feel that younger people and especially the present tribal governments tend to ignore tribal elders much to the detriment of everyone's well-being and self-esteem. Many feel that their tribal elders should have more say in tribal political decisions. In fact, almost 60 percent stated that their particular tribal governments ignored traditional tribal elders. This is not to say that American Indian Vietnam-generation youths developed an entelechy or distinct generational unity. They were unable to form an entelechy because of the accelerated tempo of change that occurred during their first twenty-five years or so of life. Mannheim mentioned this problem:

It is conceivable that too greatly accelerated a tempo might lead to mutual destruction of the embryo entelechies . . . we can observe . . . various finely graded patterns of response of age groups closely following upon each other and living side by side; these age groups, however, are so closely packed together that they do not succeed in achieving a fruitful new formulation of distinct generation entelechies and formative principles.[31]

Mannheim's idea can be easily extended to the experiences of the Indian Vietnam generation. Changes in federal Indian policies and programs took place with remarkable rapidity between 1950 and 1965. The relocation programs and termination policy began to be modified and/or deemphasized within a span of approximately seven years after their implementation. Tribal relations with the federal government were focused on again, and the government instituted a new policy of educational and welfare programs for Indians. The early 1960s saw the rise of new Native American militancy against the termination policy as well as demands that tribal rights be recognized.[32] The conditions under which the Vietnam-generation youths were born were markedly different from those of other Indians born just a few years later. In addition, the Vietnam War itself created ambivalence within their biological age cohort. The rapprochement with the most senior Indian generation, however, offered the generation a set of interpersonal relationships, well-defined identities, and cultural heritages to rely on instead of impersonal institutions and disruptive policies. Mannheim explained the process of intergenerational rapprochement in this way:

Such generations, frustrated in the production of an individual entelechy, tend to attach themselves, where possible, to an earlier generation which may have achieved a satisfactory form.[33]

Or, as one Indian veteran put it:

> Our elders know the true ways. They teach us to be reverent to life
> and to be generous. They know the ceremonies and the medicine
> that heals us and makes us better people. If it wasn't for them, we
> would have nothing.

Little wonder that most of the veterans interviewed and surveyed by
RCS claimed to have been brought up in more or less a "traditional"
manner. Even those who had been reared in urban environments managed to find a way to assert their "Indianness." They all felt good about
participating in traditional ceremonies whenever and wherever possible. Most, in fact, thought of themselves as being tribal in outlook and
worried about the maintenance of tribal traditions and their tribe's special relationship with the spirit world. It is safe to say that the Native
American Vietnam generation was and is very conscious of having membership in a larger Indian identity as well. Indeed, their allegiance and
orientation is primarily toward the tribe and secondarily toward Native
Americans as a kind of collective political entity. They reflect what
is important in their own tribal communities—even if they reside
someplace else—whether it be the maintenance of harmony with the
environment, the protection of sovereign treaty rights or preconstitutional aboriginal rights, or the preservation of tribal customs, values,
and ceremonies.

The orientation of the Native American Vietnam generation, especially that of Vietnam veterans, calls into question the concepts of marginality and acculturation. In his classic 1937 study, Everett Stonequist
theorized that marginality occurs basically when members of a group
"divergent in race or possessing distinct cultures" attempt to adjust
themselves to a dominant society.[34] The "marginal man"—or woman—
is acculturated or assimilated by the dominant group, but only to a certain extent. The individual is trapped on the periphery of both societies,
because he or she is neither exactly the same as the rest of the subordinate group nor completely accepted as a full-fledged member of the
dominant group. Change in a subordinate group seems always to imply
that the group is being acculturated to the dominant group's customs,
behavior, dress, economic practices, and/or religion. It is also assumed
that the marginal person who undergoes acculturation attaches the
same meanings and usages to the technologies, practices, and patterns
that he or she has adopted in the effort to adjust to the dominant group.

But there seems to be a conservative tendency in human beings who adapt certain features of a dominant society's culture to make, at the same time, those features uniquely their own. Various communities might syncretize their own traditional religious rituals with those of another society. They might attach a meaning to a certain adapted form that is quite different from its original meaning. In short, acculturation is mitigated, or made less severe, by syncretism. And no society is completely static in the first place; syncretic change can take place on a given community's own terms, even when that community is in a subordinate position. If an individual member of a community undergoing change remains oriented toward it, he or she cannot really be considered marginal, but simply part of a dynamic society. If an individual's orientation shifts toward the dominant society, then he or she could be considered marginal. The variable seems to lie in how much social and cultural autonomy the community has.

In any case, it appears that since the American Indian Vietnam veterans are oriented toward their home communities and dedicated to preserving tribal traditions even in modified form, they cannot be considered marginal, totally assimilated, or completely acculturated. Despite the fact that their entire generation was encouraged to integrate socially with non-Indians, join the ranks of the larger American working class, and leave their communities for a "better life" in the cities, they have remained strongly tribal, or at least "Indian," in outlook. Throughout their lives they continued to socialize with other Indians, marry other Indians, attend Indian functions, involve themselves in tribal and supratribal politics, and communicate with relatives in their home communities. All this has continued in spite of the transitory nature of their upbringing. Truly they grew up in an era of change and turmoil, but it was also one in which they found their true identities.

ENTERING MILITARY SERVICE

Given their orientation, then, why did members of the Native American Vietnam generation enter the military in numbers nearly as great as those of their fathers who fought in World War II? Were they striving to be accepted in the larger American polity? Had they been "Americanized" to the point that they accepted military service as a responsibility of citizenship? Was their entrance the result of the circumstances of second-class citizenship and economic poverty?

It is quite apparent from the information gathered in the RCS survey and from their own words that Indian Vietnam veterans did not enter military service to prove themselves "good Americans," gain a degree of economic status, or become accepted by whites. Rather, according to the veterans themselves, they enlisted or accepted induction because they were patriots in the tribal sense of the word. To them, military service was part of an honorable family and/or tribal tradition. They wanted to be warriors—to protect their land and their people. And, in the tribal tradition of reciprocity, they wanted to gain respect from other Native Americans.

Table 2 lists the reasons that 170 veterans gave for entering military service, as well as their relative importance, as recorded in the RCS survey. Their reasons for entering the service varied (20 percent of the veterans were drafted), but their motivations seem to differ from those reasons commonly thought to have prompted minority enlistment in general. For the most part, scholars logically conclude that members of peripheral minority groups enter a dominant society's military to gain status, improve their financial condition, and/or legitimize themselves as members of the larger polity. Native American Vietnam veterans, however, saw military service in a somewhat different light. While half of them did think financial reasons were somewhat or very important in the decision to enter the service, a greater number (61 percent) felt that the possible respect gained from the non-Indian majority in the rest of society for entering the military was not important to them.

Duty, honor, country, and family and tribal traditions, however, were thought to be somewhat or very important reasons for entering military service by over three-fourths of the veterans who responded to the RCS survey. Those veterans interviewed responded in much the same manner. A number of them stated that they felt honor-bound and obligated legally to defend the country not because they were citizens of the United States but because their individual nations had signed treaties with the whites. According to one man, "My people have always honored our treaties, even when the whites haven't. I went in because our treaties say that we're allied to the U.S." Another stated:

I went to Vietnam, was wounded twice and won the Silver Star, not because I have any particular loyalty to the United States, but because I have loyalty to my own people, my own tradition. We are pledged by a treaty to provide military assistance to the U.S. in times of war. I know that the U.S. has broken its part of the bargain with us, but we are more honorable than that. If we respond in kind, we

TABLE 2. Native Americans' Reasons for Entering Service, Percentages

	Very Important	Somewhat Important	Not Too Important	Not Important at All
Duty, Country	44.1	31.2	13.5	11.2
Financial Reasons	20.6	29.4	27.6	22.4
Respect from Indian People	35.3	27.1	17.6	20.0
Respect from Non-Indians	15.3	23.5	25.3	35.9
Family Tradition	51.2	24.1	11.8	12.9
Tribal Tradition	43.5	31.8	12.9	11.8

are no better than they are. The point is, we are better than they; we honor our commitments, always have and always will. Even the ones which are inconvenient or unpleasant. So, it was my obligation to do what I did, even though I didn't really want to.

It must be noted that this particular man carried the tradition of honoring his tribal nation's treaty with the United States to the extreme. He served in the U.S. Army's Special Forces—the Green Berets.

If the tradition of honoring treaty obligations prompted some to enter the military during the Vietnam War, then a tradition of another kind prompted others. The older tradition of warriorhood had its effects. A number of Indian Vietnam veterans more or less explained that they had wanted to follow in the path of the old-time warriors: to gain respect from their own people for having done what young men have always done in times of conflict and by taking part in the traditional ceremonies of warfare reaffirming the tribal identity and special relationship with the spirit world. Many grew up hearing stories of courage and self-sacrifice in battle. Many more had seen as children the rituals used to honor and cleanse their relatives who had returned from World War II and Korea. Others noted that their people often deferred to those who have experienced combat and have seen the other side of life.

Often as not, the veterans simply pointed out that their fathers and grandfathers had fought in wars and that, like their fathers, they were carrying on a family tradition. It must be remembered that kinship was and is an important dynamic in tribal Native American societies. Several of those interviewed mentioned that their relatives almost expected them to follow in their fathers' footsteps and enter the service. At least two men, one a Hopi and the other a Cherokee, said that their respective maternal grandfathers had essentially selected them individually, out of all the other young men in their families, to become warriors. It was apparent that the newer tradition of service in the United States armed forces had, at least in some Native American families, taken a very strong hold.

But there are reasons to believe that the motives underlying Indian enlistment during the Vietnam War were as complex as those that motivated their ancestors in ritual tribal warfare. Economic motivation certainly played an important role in prompting enlistment, but it was particular to the communities from which the veterans came. A brief look at the way traditional Cherokee communities in Oklahoma function might help to explain the complexities involved in why young Cherokee males enter military service. In these communities, mature men and women, those forty and over, are the breadwinners and political leaders. They more or less control the life of the community. Younger men, especially those between eighteen and twenty-five, have little if anything to do with the community's economics, politics, social life, or religious functions. As anthropologist Albert L. Wahrhaftig writes:

> Looking at Cherokee men in terms of different role expectations appropriate to different age groups of men, two things about the young are readily apparent. There is no niche for them within the institutional structure of a Cherokee settlement; and furthermore, the processes of Cherokee socialization operate to pull Cherokee men out of the settlement even as the absence of structural niche and social reward conspire to push them out.[35]

Younger men are almost expected to leave the community for a time, and most often they either find jobs in urban areas, do migrant farm labor, or enter the military. When they return (some never do), they are resocialized into the Cherokee pattern of behavior, bringing with them information and experience useful to the community. Some return with military pensions or retirement benefits that contribute in a great way to the community's economy. It seems that the retirees or pensioners are rewarded with a degree of status for their monetary contributions to ceremonials, churches, or the general welfare of the settlement. In short, military service can provide, as it has historically, an outlet for younger males and an economic benefit to the community.

To a great extent the Cherokee example applies to a number of Native American communities and even to urban Indian enclaves. As a Navajo man put it, "There wasn't anything else, man; no jobs, I was too young to sit down and learn things in the old way. I was done with school. I just went in and signed up." His military pay, however, benefited his family appreciably. "I had an allotment taken out of my check for my mom. My dad was able to fix the pickup and get a few things. I was in 'Nam, didn't need money." Another Native American Vietnam veteran who was brought up in Minneapolis said half-jokingly, "The Army got me off the streets." Literally dozens of Indian veterans said essentially the same thing: the military gave them something to do, and at least some of their pay, in one way or another, found its way back to their home communities. "It was just like in the old times," said a Chippewa veteran, "the young men went to war." Perhaps military service (the newer tradition) did fill the gap left when the tribes were compelled to abandon ritualized warfare (the older tradition). Native American males gained experience outside of the community, contributed to the general welfare, and expectantly returned to a degree of status.

This is not to say that Native American communities were solidly in favor of the Vietnam War or of sending off their young men to fight in a foreign war. As they did during World War II, a number of Indians objected to fighting the white man's battles, especially if Indian rights were ignored and Native American communities were living in dire poverty. As one man wrote to the *Navajo Times*:

> A yellow lowdown, cowardly Navajo you may think about me, but you are wrong. *As a man*, I look at the Vietnam conflict as a senseless war in which Americans have been fighting the Vietnamese for over fifteen years . . . *As a Navajo*, I look at war as if fighting alongside the whiteman, who tried desperately to annihilate the American Indians (Navajo) fighting for what was once ours and now to protect what is no longer ours.[36]

Despite these reasonable objections, Indian communities did not join in a wholesale effort to dissuade their young men from joining the military. In many Native American communities, there was a remarkable ambivalence toward the war, or, at least, a tendency not to view the conflict in political terms. Several individuals were warned that the military might be wrong for them personally. A number of fathers, uncles, and grandfathers with military experience themselves told some of their younger relatives exactly what to expect in the military. "I remember my dad told me that I'd have to take orders all the time and dress up like everybody else," said one man. Another man stated that his grandfather admonished him that he should go to college because he "could do better than that" (i.e., military service). But even if most of the veterans were not exactly encouraged to enter military service during the war, they were at least given tacit support after they enlisted. They had made their personal decisions and it was the duty of their families to continue to love them and back them up. In short, warriors were more important than the politics of the war. Or, from a more negative viewpoint, as one Lakota woman stated, "Most people here don't like the war at all but they don't like those Indian boys who are draft dodgers either."[37]

We can assume that whatever their motives were for accepting military service or however their communities viewed the war, that Native Americans entered the United States military during the Vietnam War in proportional numbers nearly equal to those of their fathers between 1941 and 1945. They certainly did not have to endure the media hyperbole that sent their fathers off to World War II; by the 1960s the United States apparently did not have to validate its sense of mission by propagandizing the fact that Indians were being sent to Southeast Asia in large numbers. In any case, the Veterans Administration reported in 1980 that there were 62,100 Native American Vietnam-era veterans; 58,200 of them with no service during the previous Korean conflict era.[38] As stated before, approximately 42,000 Native Americans served in Southeast Asia during the war.

The above figures notwithstanding, there is very little chance of obtaining a truly accurate count of Native American veterans of the Vietnam War. Enlistment contracts and draft papers of the period contained no racial category listing of "American Indian," and apparently recruiters habitually and simply assigned racial categories to individuals based on appearance. Consequently, only sixty-eight, or 40 percent, of the American Indian veterans surveyed for the RCS study reported that they had been enlisted as American Indians. Thirty-three of them had no idea what racial category the recruiters or selective service personnel assigned them to. The rest of the enlistees were placed in various other racial groups: fourteen were listed as "other"; two as "Mongolian"; one as "Negro"; four as "Latin" or "Spanish"; and forty-eight as "Caucasian." All were enrolled members of Native American tribes in either the United States or Canada. This information suggests that those who processed the armed forces contracts and selective service papers assigned racial categories in more or less an arbitrary manner. The "other" category was simply a catchall assignment for those individuals who were not visibly "Caucasian," "Negro," or "Mongolian." At one time anthropologists believed that everyone could be assigned to one of these three racial groups and that American Indians "naturally" fell into the "Mongolian" category. This idea, while completely out of date even then, probably accounts for those two individuals who were listed as "Mongolian." The forty-eight listed as "Caucasian" were probably designated as such either because their surnames were not "typically Indian" or because they had certain degrees of white ancestry. The "Latin" or "Spanish" listings are fairly easy to explain. Many Apaches, Navajos, O'Odhams, Pueblos, and Yaquis from the Southwest have Hispanic surnames but are, of course, tribal Native Americans. The single individual listed as "Negro" probably had some African American ancestry and the armed forces entrance and examination personnel assigned him to the category on the basis of physical appearance. Either that, or the "one drop rule" of the nineteenth century still applied for African Americans within the United States armed forces. That rule held that even a drop of black ancestral blood meant that the person was considered all black, regardless of actual skin color.

Even if the number of American Indians who served in Vietnam is accepted as 42,000, it is nevertheless exceptionally high. During the Vietnam War the total Indian population of the United States was less than one million persons. American Indians thus made up nearly 1.4 percent of all the troops sent to Southeast Asia, while Indians in general never constituted more than 0.6 percent of the total population of the United States in the same time period. Approximately one out of four eligible Native Americans served in military forces in Vietnam, compared to one out of twelve in the general American population.[39] In other words, Native Americans, like other members of racial minority groups in the United States, bore a disproportionate share of the fighting in Southeast Asia.

BECOMING SOLDIERS

Before they could become full-fledged warriors, however, they had to undergo a transition from civilian to military life. Basic training is universal. Every nation's military force puts its recruits and conscripts through a period of learning military customs, tactics, weaponry, and discipline before they go on to learn their specific military occupations. Some militaries send their recruits directly to their units for training; others have specific depots from which recruits are assigned to units after an intensive training period. The United States armed forces follow the latter method of transforming civilian youths into soldiers, marines, sailors, and airmen.

In the 1960s, basic military training was a fairly short, intensive period of physical and mental stress. Although recruits were subjected to great doses of patriotic rhetoric and symbolism to "motivate" them to do battle, military elites understood that these abstractions were not enough to enable a recruit to cope with the realities of combat. Basic training was, and is, really intended to sever a recruit's bond with everyday civilian life, instill in him or her a notion of belonging to a separate, very distinct group, and inculcate in the recruit a desire to obey orders instantly and without question.[40] (In the Vietnam era basic training for women was radically different than it was for men, as there were no combat roles for women.)

Basic training then began by breaking a recruit's ties with everyday life and lowering the individual's sense of self-esteem as a civilian. "My drill sergeant called me everything in the book," said one man, "from slimy civilian to maggot." Ethnicity was attacked as well. According to a Muscogee Creek veteran of the Marine Corps, "My drill instructor called me a blanket-ass and several other things, including chief," but the combat recruit was informed, also in no uncertain terms, that once boot camp was over with he would be first and foremost a Marine. The recruit's head was shaved, he was given a uniform, and he was made to walk, talk, and even eat in a so-called military manner. Most recruits were forced to send the clothing and personal effects they carried with them home to their families. If anything, the initial phase of basic military training was the ritualized severance of family bonds, something that Native Americans found difficult to understand in light of the traditional warrior's relationship with the community.

After degrading all aspects of the recruits' lives other than their membership in the military, the drill instructors attempted to instill in them a sense of self-pride and unit pride. Physical training—running long distances, doing endless push-ups and squat-thrusts, and negotiating obstacle courses—actually gave the recruits a series of small triumphs. They found they were becoming stronger and had more endurance. They began to negotiate the obstacle courses quicker and more easily. Those who failed some of the physical tests were told that they had failed their entire units. For some Indian recruits the physical training was fairly easy. A number of them had been high school football players, wrestlers, and runners. But there was also a certain idea among several of those who trained them that Indians were naturally athletic and tough as a result of their backgrounds of poverty. As one man recalled, "My drill sergeant would stand me in front of the platoon and say: 'Look at chief here, he's a born hardass and can take anything.'" Drill instructors seemingly viewed their Native American recruits as being uncomplaining and stoic regardless of the physical and mental abuse they endured. According to one man:

On graduation day, my senior drill instructor called my name out and told me that I was an 03 [infantry military occupation specialty]. Then he told the whole platoon that I had been one of the best privates because I didn't complain or cry or anything. He said that the best privates were the ones that just blended into the platoon and didn't screw up.

The key phrase this man's drill instructor used was "blended into the platoon." Basic training's ultimate purpose for combat recruits was to create a bond, a "brotherhood," among these young men and instill in them the notion that individual self-pride derived from being part of a collective fighting force. Basic training, then, imparted a value system that emphasized the idea that self-esteem was connected with the military unit to which one belonged. According to Gwynne Dyer:

What really enables men to fight is their own self-respect, and a special kind of love that has nothing to do with sex or idealism. Very few men have died in battle, when the moment actually arrived, for the United States of America or for the sacred cause of Communism, or even for their homes and families; if they had any choice in the matter at all, they chose to die for each other and for their own vision of themselves. . . . The way armies produce this sense of brotherhood . . . is basic training; a feat of psychological manipulation on the grand scale which has been so consistently successful and so universal that we fail to notice it as remarkable.[41]

Although military recruits and conscripts of the 1960s received instruction in military history, the care and use of small arms and various pieces of equipment, first aid, the military code of conduct, and numerous other details of military life, the real centerpiece of basic training was, and is, drill. The practice of drill (marching in step, staying in line or column, the manual of arms) seemed archaic, particularly during the Vietnam era. Warfare had changed a great deal since Alexander the Great marched his phalanxes into the Persian masses and the British stood in square, shoulder to shoulder, at Waterloo. The war in the rice paddies and jungles of Vietnam was being fought by relatively small groups of men operating in scattered formations, if one could call them formations at all.

But drill had its purposes, even in training modern armies. Probably its first real purpose was to move large masses of spear-toting young males from one place to another. Soon it was discovered that concentrating a mass of spearmen and moving it directly at another force was the best way to win battles. When gunpowder came on the scene, drill was utilized not only to concentrate firepower on an opposing force but also to automate the loading and firing of the guns themselves. Loading and firing a musket was a rather complicated sequence of measuring and pouring powder, ramming a projectile into the breech, and priming the firing mechanism. The sequence of steps had to be followed so that the gun could be fired at all. Constant drill with their weapons fine-tuned the firing sequence and, perhaps more importantly, cut down the number of accidental firearm discharges and woundings within the ranks.[42] During the American Civil War it was discovered that the weaponry had gone beyond the tactic of mass concentration of fire, but this discovery did not by and large affect field strategy. Civil War–era muskets were more accurate and had longer ranges that could decimate mass formations. By the end of World War I, commanders had finally realized that scattering their troops would save lives and win battles. Moving large, massed bodies of men around the battlefield was an exceedingly dangerous maneuver. In addition, the sequence of loading and firing a rifle had become much simpler. By the time of the Vietnam War, all a soldier needed to do to fire the weapon was to insert a preloaded magazine, pull an operating rod handle to the rear, and squeeze the trigger.

By the time Native American Vietnam veterans entered the military service, drill was used for several different purposes. In the first place, it taught military bearing as a form of martial aesthetic and increased the recruit's pride in wearing a uniform, displaying military carriage, and participating in a precisely choreographed team effort that was pleasing to watch on parade. Perhaps drill—even more than qualifying at the rifle range or learning a firearm's internal mechanism—fostered a real familiarity with the basic weapon. The soldier got used to feeling a rifle's weight and its contours by handling it and moving it to positions in cadence. "We were supposed to sleep at attention with our rifles," said one man. In addition, the constant drilling was intended to teach an unqualified and instantaneous obedience to command.

Most of the Native American Vietnam veterans emerged from basic training with a great deal of pride in having survived its rigors and with a marked sense of being distinguished as members of a particular branch of the military service. As a former Marine put it:

Boot camp was a bitch, but you came out feeling good and looking good. We all knew that the DIs [drill instructors] were brainwashing us, but we loved it. You were part of the Green Machine. You felt you could kick anybody's ass and that all the girls would just jump all over you.

A Cherokee said:

When I got out of basic, I knew I was going to jump school [parachute training] and all that. I was going for the Rangers [a very specialized Army combat training school]. One day I was going to wear the badge, the beret, and the jump boots. Man, that felt good.

They went on in the military to various schools and training programs. By and large they ended up in combat military occupations as infantrymen, combat engineers, artillerymen, tank crewmen, or parachutists. Although their rather low educational levels probably would have placed them in nontechnical military occupations anyway, many volunteered for combat duty and hence drew assignments to particular military specialties. "I wanted to go airborne all the way," said one man, "get into combat, man, that's all I could think about." Another stated, "I went eleven-bravo [Army infantry] so's I could get into the war. I wanted to be a warrior." Still another stated that "the grunts was the best way to go, I thought. They teach you how to fight." The Indian veterans of the Vietnam War who were interviewed repeatedly stated that they had gone into the military to be warriors and that a soldier could not be a warrior while "sitting behind a desk or cleaning latrines."

It could be argued that the members of the Native American Vietnam generation were prime candidates for military service. Since American Indians as a group were a relatively young population, it follows that they would have a proportionally higher number of young males than other older groups. In the 1960s, there were no combat roles for females, although numerous females, especially nurses, found themselves in combat zones. The combat military occupations were exclusively male and the armed forces at the time were perfectly satisfied to keep it that way. Young males were and are highly desirable recruits. Normally they are exuberant, tend to bond with each other easily, and readily submit themselves to authority as a result of peer pressure. They also seem to have a clear vision of manhood as being a blend of rugged individualism, group cooperation, and casual indifference to pain and suffering. American Indian males were highly desirable recruits—perhaps more desirable to the military than other groups—for a number of reasons. As a group they came from poverty and presumably were therefore seeking a form of economic security. Recruiters, drill instructors, and others in the ranks often assumed that poverty breeds toughness or the ability to cope with adversity. In addition, it was widely assumed that Indians, as tribal people, tended to perform various activities very well in groups. The Indian scout imagery no doubt enhanced the desirability of Native American recruits in the eyes of military elites. Perhaps these assumptions and attitudes on the part of military personnel explain why several Indian Vietnam veterans mentioned that they and their friends and relatives were heavily recruited. "When I told the recruiter that I finished high school," said one man, "the guy nearly shook my hand off and almost cried with joy."

If anything, however, American Indians had a slightly different vision of themselves than did the military recruiters. The turmoil and poverty in their early lives seemed to foster in them the desire to maintain their distinct identities as tribal Native Americans. Many of them truly wanted to be warriors in the older tradition and keep those ceremonies connected with warfare alive. Some of them thought that by becoming soldiers in the newer tradition, they could form a link to their warrior ancestors. Others looked upon military service as an honorable method of gaining respect within their home communities. The recruiters and draft boards signed them up and sent them off to learn the basic arts of soldiering. Basic training made them into soldiers; next it was time to become true warriors and see the other side of life on the battlefields of Vietnam.

5. "INDIAN COUNTRY"

When I got to the bush, my platoon sergeant tells me and the guys I came in with that we were surrounded. He said: "The gooks are all out there and we're here. This is Fort Apache, boys, and out there is Indian country." Can you fuckin' believe that? To me? I should have shot him right then and there. Made me wonder who the real enemy was.

— SENECA VIETNAM VETERAN

Nearly every Native American veteran of the Vietnam War has, at one time or another, echoed the irony, sentiment, and depth of outrage in this statement. Yet, like the individual who made it, they all stayed and fought and, in many cases, watered the soil of this Southeast Asian "Indian country" with their own blood. Instead of shooting his platoon sergeant, the latter-day Iroquois warrior was wounded twice in firefights and won a Bronze Star for valor in action against the North Vietnamese Army and the Viet Cong. The war was like that for many Indian veterans. They came to hate war, the Vietnam War in particular, but would not have missed the experience of combat if they had it all to do over again. For many of them, the war became one of those life experiences that seemed to overshadow nearly all others. They felt that their combat experiences had given them knowledge and abilities over and above those of their nonveteran peers. They had seen death and destruction. They had possessed the means to take human life. Moreover, they had survived the conflict while others had not. "Being in the war," said one man, with a certain amount of guilty pride, "taught me how to survive."

A DIFFERENT KIND OF WAR

It can be said with a great degree of certainty that simple survival was of paramount importance to the average combat soldier in Vietnam. "After we got there," one veteran said, "all we did was try to make it back to the 'world' alive." Their mission, combat or otherwise, had very little importance except in terms of carrying it out with the least possible number of casualties. Some individuals were reckless, to be sure, and seemed not to fear the horror of being maimed or killed, but the average combat soldier in Vietnam wanted only to return home alive and physically whole. But, for the most part, it was remarkably difficult to avoid becoming a casualty, especially if one was "in the bush."

No war, of course, is easy on combat troops. But Vietnam seems to have been unique in American military history, yet not because of the terrain, flora, weather, or even the nature of the enemy. It was unique in the way it was fought.

Over the years, a remarkable amount of scholarly debate has developed over the exact nature of combat in Southeast Asia. In strategic and tactical terms, the debate seems to center on whether or not the United States military should have fought a conventional, as opposed to a guerilla, war. One side maintains that by the time American ground forces were committed in Vietnam, the North Vietnamese had gained operational control over Viet Cong guerilla forces, dictated the political meaning of the war, and had switched from guerilla to conventional battlefield tactics. Although military commanders in Vietnam recognized the change, government officials and Pentagon bureaucrats in Washington clung to the idea that the war was still a counterinsurgency operation. The other side of the debate argues that the war was really a revolutionary struggle for independence and that military commanders failed to recognize this most basic and important fact. The commanders in Vietnam have been faulted for using the "World War II model" to fight an unconventional and unpredictable enemy. One side basically argues that the United States could have won the war but for political considerations, while the other side maintains that the war was not winnable in either political or military terms.[1] Colonel David H. Hackworth, a genuine American military hero and very able field commander during the Vietnam War, has basically argued a middle position in the debate. Hackworth, a critic to the end of American military bureaucrats, maintains that counterinsurgency tactics actually worked and that the North Vietnamese and Viet Cong could very well have been beaten at their own game.[2]

Since the Civil War, military elites have developed what has become an American doctrine of war. Americans have put warfare on an industrial basis. Theoretically, to win a war, an armed force must destroy or disrupt an enemy's military and/or industrial base, all the while assembling an overwhelming technological superiority. When the enemy's economic infrastructure has been disrupted to a certain point, the assembled superior force then invades and occupies the enemy's territory, defeats his weakened military forces, and imposes or negotiates peace. But in Vietnam, the North Vietnamese had no industrial infrastructure to speak of and their military was highly mobile. Since the North Vietnamese Army (NVA) relied on imported arms and other war materials, the United States could not really disrupt its military economy without risking war with North Vietnam's suppliers, the Soviet Union and the People's Republic of China. Invading North Vietnam would also have entailed a serious political risk. Consequently, the United States military settled into a conflict that was really a combination of traditional American war doctrine and counterinsurgency tactics. Very likely the scholarly debate over the nature of the war stems from this war-making dichotomy.

Interestingly enough, Native American veterans of the war were curiously split along the same lines as the academicians over the nature of combat in Vietnam. Some stated that they took part in what were basically counterinsurgency operations. A few were in Special Forces teams. One man said that he participated in some Phoenix assassinations aimed at Communist subversives which were planned by the Central Intelligence Agency. Most other veterans stated that their combat duty was essentially conventional in that they served in regular infantry, tank, artillery, or other units against main force Viet Cong or regular NVA troops. The difference between conventional and counterinsurgency combat, it seems, largely had to do with the kind of unit or area in which the troops served. The NVA, a conventional force on the surface, often fought its battles in a decidedly unconventional manner. For example, a Cheyenne veteran who served with an infantry battalion in the Iron Triangle north of Saigon, then the capital of the Republic of Vietnam (RVN, or South Vietnam), maintained that he fought against the NVA and encountered literally hundreds of booby traps and was involved in numerous small-scale, hit-and-run type ambushes. The kind of warfare he described is typical of guerilla operations. It avoids the great losses possible in direct confrontation with larger, better-armed conventional forces, buys time for the guerilla force, and, at the same time, makes the opposition bleed. This kind of warfare presumably aids the guerillas' political aims. When a guerilla force is able to disappear quickly, its opposition tends to become more suspicious of the local population it is supposed to protect. In theory, the opposition becomes more and more oppressive until finally the local population rises up and joins the insurgent guerilla force. The locals become the enemy. As this particular Cheyenne veteran said, "Something would happen almost every day." His unit took large numbers of casualties from booby traps, sapper attacks, snipers, and small ambushes from spider holes (fighting holes fitted with camouflaged trapdoors that could be raised or lowered). "The little kids would be out there setting traps or sniping at you," he said. What this meant was that his battalion's large number of casualties was spread out over a relatively longer period of time.

On the other hand, a Marine whose unit operated very near the demilitarized zone in the far north of the RVN made it clear that his battalion only encountered regular North Vietnamese regiments in fairly large-scale battles. "We might not see any gooks for weeks," he said, adding that when his unit took casualties they came in "big bunches."

The key word in understanding both of these views of the ground war in Vietnam is *encounter*. By the time the majority of Native Americans were deployed in Southeast Asia, the war had settled into the distinct pattern of military police actions. When American ground troops were committed to Vietnam in 1965, they were ostensibly to be used to guard air bases, thus relieving the South Vietnamese Army (ARVN) of this particular burden. The ARVN, in turn, could then launch all-out campaigns against the VC and NVA troops operating south of the 17th parallel. The avowed American policy was to protect the South Vietnamese government and thus contain communism without crossing the demilitarized zone at the 17th parallel or into neutral countries like Cambodia or Laos. Military commanders, at least until various strategic incursions were made to halt traffic on the Ho Chi Minh Trail or attack NVA staging bases in Laos and Cambodia, were to conduct the war on the strategic defensive.[3]

By the end of 1965, two schools of thought had developed about how to pursue the war on this basis. The first idea was to emphasize mobile operations from forward bases. American troops could not only go to the aid of ARVN units but also could carry out their own search-and-destroy missions on the tactical offensive. The second plan of action, to use Marine Corps General Edwin H. Simmons' terminology, was the "inkblot" strategy. This idea held that American troops should establish strong coastal enclaves and gradually extend their tactical areas of control outward in a series of clear-and-hold operations, seeking, as it were, to flow outward in no particular pattern. These ideas were debated thoroughly in the press, but as Simmons has pointed out, neither was mutually exclusive and both ideas were adopted to a certain extent. The federal government, however, reckoned the inkblot plan as being too costly in political terms. It would have necessitated an immediate commitment of large numbers of troops rather than the incremental increase in manpower the Johnson administration was willing to make.[4]

The consequences of search-and-destroy and clear-and-hold missions were nearly the same. Forward combat bases were established in likely areas of enemy activity and operations were conducted to clear large areas of territory around coastal population centers. Military commanders also launched pacification programs to "win the hearts and minds" of the Vietnamese in the countryside. What it all boiled down to, however, was the practice of simply assigning tactical areas of responsibility to different commands to police. At the battalion or even regimental levels, this meant sending troops on tactical missions in particular zones of operations. The pacification of the countryside involved setting up either Special Forces teams or, in the case of the Marines, special platoons that would work directly with the Popular Forces (called PFs, they were the South Vietnamese equivalent of the National Guard). Army medics and Navy corpsmen went out on "medcaps" (Medical Civic Action Program Missions) to give shots, treat infections and wounds, and generally provide medical services to Vietnamese villagers within certain tactical areas. Some American troops were assigned the task of providing security for local harvests and moving Vietnamese civilians to secure areas. There was really no such thing as taking and holding territory in the usual sense. To take and hold ground in the accustomed manner would have forced the federal government to send even more troops than it was ultimately willing to do. That meant that the armed forces had to establish bases of operations, or forward combat enclaves, rather than become a complete occupation force. Generally, American military enclaves were of three types. The largest were the main air bases which were more or less permanent and built close to fairly large population centers. These bases, like the ones at Tan Son Nhut, Da Nang, and Chu Lai, could land and launch nearly all types of aircraft, including ground attack jets, resupply transport airplanes, and even civilian transportation craft that flew the troops in and out of Vietnam. The great B-52 bombing raids were usually flown from Thailand or from bases in the Pacific. The second type of base was smaller but usually had some kind of landing strip that could accommodate transport aircraft, helicopters, and light fixed-wing planes. The third type of base was called a firebase, or simply an LZ (for landing zone), and usually could accommodate only helicopters flying resupply and medical evacuation missions. These bases, along with the other two, had artillery, recoilless rifles, mortars, tanks, and other types of more mobile heavy weaponry. The firebases were the least permanent of the three. Of course, helicopters operated in the field away from specifically cleared landing zones and were utilized to insert and extract combat troops, provide fire support and, most importantly, evacuate the wounded. The combat bases and firebases were established not only in areas of enemy activity but also were arranged so that they could lend combat support to one another as well as to the soldiers in the field.

Base camps and firebases in certain areas, after enemy activity had fallen off, were of little value. The Khe Sanh combat base, which had an airstrip that could accommodate aircraft as large as a C-130 cargo airplane and which had survived a heavy siege operation by the NVA during the Tet Offensive of 1968, for example, was abandoned later that same year in favor of establishing another base in a more strategic area. Combat troops could be shifted from one zone to another as the need arose. According to one veteran: "All we did was walk around looking for trouble."

Eventually the policy of a strategic defense and a tactical offense led to the creation of free-fire zones. Ostensibly, free-fire zones had been cleared of "friendlies" as a result of either uprooting local peasants and moving them to relocation villages or simply declaring that certain areas were already under complete enemy control. Basically, free-fire zones were exactly and aptly named. Other than ARVN troops, any Vietnamese within these zones could be considered enemy soldiers or sympathizers. Because American troops were neither taking nor holding ground in the classic military sense, there was no way to measure combat effectiveness in other than base attritional terms—numbers of enemy dead or captured and number of enemy weapons taken. The body count thus became practically the only—as well as the most unbelievable—means of measuring success in ground operations.

This is not to say that American combat units simply went around these free-fire zones killing people and destroying property. On a tactical level, American troops maneuvered to attack known enemy positions, reconnoitered and patrolled particular areas, set up ambushes, conducted mine-sweeping operations, established and maintained mutually supporting firebases or combat bases, and set up community action projects. The classic Vietnam encounter or battle was a short, violent firefight usually started by one or the other side in ambush or as a result of a sweep operation. If and when the Americans could, they utilized hammer-and-anvil tactics in combat. In this type of operation, the enemy was driven by assaulting troops and supporting weaponry toward a blocking force so it could be ground up between the two.[5] Combat troops interacted with various tactical and support units, including tanks, engineers, artillery, helicopter and fixed-wing air squadrons, naval gunfire, and riverine patrol boats. In short, the American military forces attempted to fight, as much as possible, a modern, mechanized war in Vietnam. At the same time, however, the circumstances of combat—the terrain, the politics, and the ability of the enemy to disappear quickly and quietly from a battlefield—forced American commanders to modify and even discard traditional tactical doctrine.

Robert L. O'Connell, in his fascinating book *Of Arms and Men*, points out that, often as not, military history is a matter of fits and starts rather than a progressive and steady sequential evolution of technology and tactical innovation. For the most part, warfare is made between two or more forces that are roughly symmetrical in terms of arms and tactical knowledge. Alexander the Great's Macedonian army used practically the same arms and understood the same tactics as the Emperor Darius' Persian army at Gaugamela; and so did the Carthaginians and Romans at Cannae; the British and French at Waterloo; the Russians and Germans at Stalingrad. That the Macedonians, Carthaginians, British, and Russians won their respective battles had to do with strength of numbers, superior leadership, use of a particular topography, timing, luck, and/or any one of a number of intangibles common to armed struggles. Occasionally, however, forces that are asymmetrical meet in war. Historically, this situation forces one side or the other either to play catch-up in terms of technology or to alter their proven tactics to attain symmetry again. As we have seen, conventional European tactics in North America during the colonial period were mostly inappropriate for the terrain and the weaponry used by Native Americans. American Indians had to play catch-up in terms of military technology, while the Euro-Americans had to play catch-up in a tactical sense.

In Vietnam there was very little symmetry between the opposing forces. The Americans and the South Vietnamese held most of the cards when it came to weaponry. The United States absolutely controlled the skies over South Vietnam, and the American military reigned superior in numbers and types of arms. The North Vietnamese and the Viet Cong, on the other hand, used tactics that, while extremely inefficient in a military sense, were ultimately effective.

The North Vietnamese relied heavily on human resources and human motivation rather than on innovative tactics or weaponry. They carried ammunition and supplies on their backs or on reinforced bicycles. The Ho Chi Minh Trail was hardly a major highway. Even if North Vietnam had possessed a large fleet of supply trucks, convoys would have had little chance of negotiating the bomb craters and undergrowth that dotted the route. They infiltrated troops and supplies rather than trucked them into South Vietnam. On occasion, they carried in heavy weapons piece by piece on the backs of the so-called peoples' porters. The North Vietnamese had sanctuaries in both Laos and Cambodia.[6] Vo Nguyen Giap, the North Vietnamese defense minister and principal architect of the war effort, knew perfectly well that virtually his only natural war-making resource was human.[7] Consequently, he spent human beings as other generals would spend bullets. The entire North Vietnamese military effort was a synthesis of different strategies that was geared toward outlasting its enemies rather than gaining a decisive victory on the battlefield. Between 1965 and 1975, Giap launched at least four major and several minor offensives which were simply crushed by American military might. The most famous, the Tet Offensive of 1968, almost destroyed the Viet Cong main forces. The war-winning 1975 North Vietnamese offensive was met with half-hearted resistance and very little American aid. South Vietnamese troops, after years of fighting, had simply been worn out. The Americans were already gone. Had Giap been an American commander, said General William C. Westmoreland, not without justification, he would have been "sacked overnight."[8] It was not really a guerilla campaign in the strictest sense of the word, but neither was it a conventional war from the standpoint of traditional American military doctrine.

NATIVE AMERICANS IN VIETNAM

It can be said with a great deal of certainty that the individuals who responded to the RCS survey served in nontechnical military occupations and in combat units in disproportionate numbers. As Tables 3 and 4 indicate, Native Americans seem to have been assigned military occupations that almost insured their direct participation in battle. Most apparently served in units corresponding to their military occupations; while in Vietnam, some 38.5 percent of the men had infantry specialties and 41.8 percent served in infantry units. Obviously, there were men with military specialties other than infantry who served in infantry units. Not only that, but more than 80 percent of them saw some kind of combat duty, as Table 5 indicates. The measurement of combat—light to heavy—was judged in terms of length of time in the field, numbers of encounters with the enemy, whether or not the veterans were wounded or saw others (American, ARVN, NVA, VC, and Vietnamese civilians) killed or wounded, and/or actually fired a weapon in combat.

Essentially, Native Americans performed the same kinds of duties as their non-Native peers in these units, except that they were often singled out for some perilous jobs simply because they were Indians. The deeply ingrained white stereotypes of Indians incredibly gave Native Americans a degree of status within the military, but it also endangered their lives. The Indian scout syndrome was very much alive among

TABLE 3. Native American Vietnam Veterans: Military Specialties

Specialty	Percentage
Infantry	38.5
Artillery	7.7
Special Forces	2.8
Airborne	8.4
Armor	3.5
Aviation (helicopter)	7.7
Aviation (fixed wing)	4.9
Ship	3.5
Gunboat	2.0
Medical	5.6
Combat Engineer	4.2
Other[a]	11.2

[a]Includes clerical, mechanical, motor transport, intelligence, supply, armorer, communications, and heavy equipment operators.

TABLE 4. Native American Vietnam Veterans: Units in Vietnam

Unit	Percentage
Infantry	41.8
Airborne	8.2
Artillery	8.2
Aviation (fixed wing)	5.0
Aviation (helicopter)	7.7
Tanks	5.1
Communications	4.0
Engineer	3.0
Medical	3.0
Ship	3.0
Other[a]	11.0

[a]Includes Special Forces, classified, Rangers, Seabees, Intelligence, and logistics units.

company and platoon level commanders. Indians seemed to walk point more often than others and be assigned to long-range reconnaissance patrols and killer teams with great frequency. In fact, American Indian Vietnam combat veterans, almost to a man, feel that they were given these kinds of duties more often than their non-Indian comrades and that most of the time these assignments were racially motivated.

Almost as soon as the soldiers landed, the reality of Vietnam assailed their senses. "It was beautiful—I mean the land," said one man. Another also noted the beauty of the physical setting in Vietnam but quickly added, "I saw hundreds of Vietnamese rooting around in a garbage pile when I came in country. Damn, it looked like flies. They'd been driven from their homes." The smells, the sights, the noises were like nothing else in their experience. Everything was foreign and potentially deadly. "I was scared as soon as I got off the plane," according to one man. Several of the men remembered being told that snipers lurked near the airstrips, sometimes picking off newly arrived soldiers as they emerged from the airplanes. As one said, "I think all those stories about guys getting hit as soon as they landed and, you know, mortar rounds hitting latrines, made everybody paranoid."

After a certain period of time they were sent to their units and assigned the duties they would perform throughout their tours in Vietnam. Many units had an orientation period for newly arrived troops in a rear area (usually one of the larger combat bases) before sending them into the bush. Several of the men, in fact, got their initial taste of warfare while in rear areas awaiting transportation to their units in the field. "We got rocketed the first night I was at An Hoa. Scared the shit

TABLE 5. Native American Vietnam Veterans: Types of Combat Experience

Type	Percentage
Heavy	36.5
Moderate	27.6
Light	18.8
None Claimed	17.1

out of me. If it was like that in the rear, it was going to be even worse in the field," one man recalled. When they were issued their combat equipment and had been assigned to a particular company, battery, or squadron, they reported to their field commanders, who, in turn, settled them into particular jobs and routines. Most carried their fears with them for a time, but the routine—the daily grueling job of simply being in a combat zone—seemed to settle them into a curious state of acceptance and fatalism. As one man said, "For about a month I carried my rifle around at high port. Then I just carried it around on my shoulder. When I got short [nearly completed a tour of duty in Vietnam] I went back to high port."

The state of accepting their fate might also be called a middle passage during which they fitted themselves into the abnormality of combat and became fully evolved warriors. Being a warrior in Vietnam involved performing a large number of duties, as well as numbing oneself to the overwhelming fatigue, the drudgery, the almost unbelievable filth of living in the bush, the shock of seeing horrible wounds and looking upon dead bodies, and one's own fear of becoming a casualty. But numb themselves they did. And they quickly learned, at least subconsciously, that their ancestors had been correct in viewing warfare as a mysterious disruption in the natural order and that without proper spiritual preparation, the horrors of war would certainly scar their very souls forever. The military certainly attempted to prepare them physically and emotionally for combat. It also drilled them, as armies have been drilled since the days of Alexander the Great, in the use of their weapons and equipment. But, as more than one veteran has intimated, military training had not really prepared them for the total experience of Vietnam.

It must be said at once that not all Native American Vietnam veterans were infantrymen. As Table 3 indicates, some of them were clerks, engineers, tankers, helicopter door-gunners, medics and corpsmen, military policemen, artillerymen, and truck drivers. The fact that some of them were stationed in rear areas, however, did not remove the elements of fear, fatigue, and the dangers of combat from their experiences. Rear areas were subject to raids and to rocket, mortar, sniper, and artillery attacks. Many of the men performed regular duties during daylight hours and then served as line fillers on the base perimeter at night. Unlike the infantry men, they certainly were not out "looking for trouble," and they enjoyed an occasional shower in makeshift shower stalls and daily hot meals, but they were often attacked by an unseen and often unexpected enemy. Truck convoys could be ambushed or could run into mines. Engineers did not just put up prefabricated buildings and bridges; they also traveled with the infantry to clear mines and detonate booby traps and unexploded bombs—a distinctly dangerous occupation. Artillerymen not only fired harassment-and-interdiction and fire missions, but were sent out as forward observers to help find and fix the enemy and correct artillery bombardments on enemy positions. As time went on, tanks, once thought unusable in the rice paddies and jungles of Vietnam, were utilized to their fullest capacity. The men who operated them not only fought in them but also had to keep them in working repair. And tanks, despite their rugged, sturdy appearance, seemed to be in need of almost constant maintenance. All in all, there were probably ten to fifteen men in logistical, clerical, medical, and tactical support units for every "grunt" (combat soldier) in an infantry platoon.[9]

The harshness of life in an infantry unit in the field (or, for that matter, even in the rear), even if there had been no fighting, seemed to steel the men; it made them miserable and often turned them into coldly calculating, cynical professionals. Few of the men talked about actual living conditions in the field or the rear, even though how they lived from day to day certainly affected how they performed their duties in general. In many ways, their living conditions then also affect their attitudes and lives today. There is a notion that combat troops in Vietnam—infantrymen, tank crews, artillerymen, engineers and others—stayed in the field or went out on patrols for fairly short periods of time and then returned frequently to rear areas to enjoy the comforts of tents, showers, hot meals, and alcohol. Such an idea is completely dismantled by the testimony of most of the men who served in combat units. Some stated that they had spent more than a month actually in the field without a single day's rest in a rear area. One man said that in his company, the only way to get to the rear was to be wounded or given a job in the company mail room. Others said that they left the field only to go on R & R (rest and relaxation) or to rotate or DEROS (date of estimated return from overseas) out of Vietnam. Another man, an Oklahoma Cherokee, added that the more time a person spent in the field, the more the rear area seemed like a "Disneyland," as he put it, or at least like an adult version thereof, where a man could relax, drink, see a movie or a USO show, get clean, and even obtain for a few dollars the company of a prostitute. More than a few claimed that the military police ran makeshift brothels in bunkers at the larger combat bases. Many of the men worried about venereal disease, especially the legendary form of syphilis that was said to be impervious to penicillin. In addition, there were numerous stories floating around about Viet Cong prostitutes who inserted razor blades in their vaginas with the single-minded and suicidal purpose of emasculating young American G.I.'s. Of course no one completely believed this rumor. Even if the rear had its dangers, however, most of the combat soldiers tended to view it as a sanctuary—a place of rest and of relative comfort.

LIFE IN THE BUSH

If the rear seemed like an adult Disneyland with tents for shelter, baths, and hot food, what was it like in the field? First and foremost, a soldier in the bush was subject to the vicissitudes of the Vietnamese climate. During the summer months, the heat and humidity could become almost unbearable. "You could sit still in the shade and sweat," said one man. It could also create casualties. One Cheyenne-Arapaho, who served with the Marine Corps in 1965, told about a case of heat prostration that occurred while his platoon was on a patrol outside of Da Nang. The stricken man

> was just walking along and then just dropped. The corpsman came up but the guy was already gone. He wasn't dead but his brain had been cooked. The doc said he probably had a temperature of over 110 degrees. He died later on.

The summer rains were deluges that soaked equipment and clothing and, in some areas, flooded trails, roads, fighting holes, and bunkers. Rain-soaked canvas equipment simply added more weight to the already heavy loads each man had to carry. The dirt and the mud meant that the men had to spend more time and effort simply to keep their weapons clean and in operating condition. Sometimes the rain left the men chilled; at other times it simply added steam to the already oppressive heat. When the rains stopped the only thing the men could be certain of was that buzzing clouds of mosquitos would descend upon them. "I think the bug juice [insect repellent issued to the troops in the field] attracted them," said a Navajo. "They [the mosquitos] probably ate that shit," replied another. The insect repellent smelled bad and stung the skin; sometimes the men were caught in the dilemma of deciding which was worse—the repellent or the mosquitos.

Insects of all species plagued them during the spring and summer months. Leeches lived in nearly every place where there was even a hint of water. The troops continually suffered from what were called "fevers of unknown origin," which were probably mild viral or bacterial infections acquired from insect bites, poorly prepared rations causing food poisoning, or tainted drinking water. The heat and humidity caused almost monumental thirst and many men did not take the time to treat chemically the water they drank from streams and ponds. As a result several men picked up intestinal worms. Malaria was rampant in Vietnam and the medical units supplied two kinds of antimalarial pills for the troops. The soldiers claimed that one of the pills induced diarrhea, while the other was an experimental drug for which they were being used as guinea pigs. As a result of the rumors, a large number of the men said that they simply stopped taking the pills. Some were infected with malaria.

As if the mosquitos, worms, leeches, and various forms of bacteria were not enough, the troops also had to contend with several species of stinging ants, exceedingly large centipedes, snakes that sought warmth at night, as well as any number of biting beetles, arachnids, and flies. They were also plagued with a formidable form of fungus or jungle rot widely known as "gook sores." The painful lesions were raised circles on the skin that crusted over with leaking serum. They usually appeared on the arms, feet, legs, and sometimes on the buttocks. Almost constantly on the march, the soldiers suffered through painful blisters, plantar warts, and emersion foot. Almost any cut or abrasion was soon infected.

Clothing and materials sometimes rotted in the steamy heat of summer. A Choctaw soldier told a story about how the stitching of the trousers worn by a member of his platoon had simply rotted and finally split through. The unfortunate soldier's pants literally fell apart, yet he had to wait for a resupply helicopter to fly in a new pair. Because the men rarely wore underwear for fear of jock itch or chafing in the groin area, the storyteller related that his unit "had to see his bare ass for a week." Dirt and body oils mixed together and collected on the men's clothing. The accumulated mixture aided rotting and added to the stench of dozens of unwashed bodies. One could take a knife and scrape the grimy material off one's clothing in long, curving shavings of brown, clay-like matter. "I guess," recalled a Comanche, "we must have stunk pretty bad."

Winters were certainly mild compared to those of more northern latitudes, but they could be terribly depressing. Mists hung over the forests and lowlands. The mountains seemed always obscured by low-hanging clouds. The wet cold of early morning chilled the men to the very bone. One man, a Muscogee Creek, recalled that during January 1968—the month of the Tet Offensive—"I never once saw the sun." The sun, in Creek tradition, is extremely important and should be greeted every morning by saying a prayer or singing a song of thanksgiving, smoking a pipe, or perhaps offering a pinch of tobacco. Even if this religious tradition went unobserved in Vietnam, not seeing the great and holy fire in the sky would be very depressing for Creeks, Cherokees, and numerous other Indian people.

If the weather and pests were not oppressive enough, the daily cycle of patrolling; gulping down C-rations; digging foxholes; cleaning weapons and equipment; setting up outposts, listening posts, and ambushes; and standing four- to six-hour watches at night wore the men to the point of complete physical exhaustion. It was probably for this reason that the military gave out numerous injections of gamma globulin—a serum containing antibodies—and B-12 vitamins. Presumably these shots increased the body's ability to combat both disease and fatigue. "Every time I turned around," said a veteran, "they hit me with a GG shot. Hurt like hell."

Most of the soldiers in the field sustained themselves on C-rations— boxed, canned meals with various condiments such as crackers, cocoa, jelly, canned fruit, chocolate bars, and coffee. A C-ration boxed meal also contained toilet paper, matches, and cigarettes. The meals themselves were very high in fats and proteins—useful in sustaining high energy levels. Later in the war, the military introduced freeze-dried, long-range rations that could be reconstituted with water. These were much lighter to carry than the cans in the C-ration meals and, according to several men, tasted much better. Packages from home, when they finally got to the field, provided welcome supplements to the soldiers' diets. The two most important condiments sent from home, according to several veterans, were Kool-Aid and Tabasco or Louisiana hot sauces. The former was used to take the chemical or other taste out of the drinking water; the latter to add taste to the C-ration meals. Without these additions, the meals in Vietnam, usually eaten in haste, were, according to one man, "the worstest." The food was cooked on a C-ration stove usually made from an empty can, or it was simply eaten cold. The preferred cooking fuel was C-4 plastic explosive rolled into a ball. The C-4 burned hotter and quicker than the heat tabs that came with the rations. Hot meals were occasionally sent to the field for combat units by helicopter, but these special treats were brought out only for holidays. Beer and soda also were sometimes sent to the field; each man was rationed two cans of either a day. Most were sent special supplementary packs (SPs) of candy, tobacco products, and writing materials. Everyone lost weight in the field. Many became gaunt to the point that their families were shocked. As one man said, "My mother cried when I got home. She said I looked like a skeleton."

Most of the men in the field tried to live as comfortably as possible. If they stayed in a particular area for a period of time, they constructed shelters, or hooches, for themselves out of ponchos, branches, and various bits of cord or bootlaces. As youthful males they formed strong but somewhat tenuous bonds with each other. According to one man:

> You got to be really tight, but you knew that he might be gone the next day. Nobody wanted to get too close at first. When somebody would come into the platoon, you kind of kept away. Some guys didn't want to know a new guy's name. You were just a "cherry" at first, then you'd pick up a nickname and then you'd get really tight with some dudes. You'd get high together, you know, talk about home. The white dudes didn't believe some of the things I did back home. You could count on people.

The outward camaraderie, although in many cases very real, was subject to an acquired harshness in thought and in deed. The reality of the bush often brought out a callous attitude toward suffering and death—a kind of "sorry he's dead but I'm glad it wasn't me" outlook that made them think of things that they would not have dreamed of before coming to Vietnam. One man told a story that seemed to capture this hardened perception of life in the field:

> I remember one day we were sitting on a hill eating. My buddy got a beef-with-spiced-sauce meal from the C-rats. I had ham and limas,

you know, "ham and motherfuckers." The beef-in-spice-sauce you can cook up real good with sugar and Tabasco. The ham-shit, you know, is the worst. Anyway, I just thought to myself for a second that I could just pick up my rifle and waste him and get his meal. That's how bad it got out there. Even that kind of thought crossing your mind—thinking about shooting somebody for C-rations. Blows your mind. It's sick.

Alcohol and marijuana were used to take the edge off living in the bush. And nearly every man admitted that they had used either or both substances at one time or another while in Vietnam. The fatigue, the tension, the bad food, and the terrible weather seemed better to many under the influence of these drugs. Hard drugs, like morphine and heroin, were certainly known, but the Native American veterans for the most part said they avoided them. Morphine, of course, was readily available in the field for the wounded. Heroin would have been much harder to obtain in the field. For most of the men, alcohol was the favored method of numbing themselves to the hardships they endured. But even then there was a certain amount of fear attached to drinking. A soldier could buy black-market liquor just about anywhere, but there was always the nagging doubt in some of their minds that the Vietnamese had put ground glass in the bottles sold to American G.I.'s. Alcohol might relieve the tension for a short period of time, but it did not offer a complete escape from the stress of simply coping with the environment and experience in Vietnam.

COMBAT

Like their non-Indian peers, American Indian troops in Vietnam averaged nineteen years of age. Weary, footsore, plagued by pests, ill-fed, and fearful, these young men hardened into professional soldiers. Despite the adverse conditions of the bush, they developed stamina and remarkable resilience. They knew the capabilities of their weapons and how to use them. But the harsh reality of living in the field was matched and surpassed by that of actual combat. As one man kept repeating, "War's hell, but combat's a motherfucker."

Although Native American veterans took part in more than a few major battles in Vietnam, by and large they were involved in short, violent firefights, ambushes, and defensive stands against line probes and sapper attacks. Most of them described these kinds of encounters as sudden and confusing in the extreme. They could erupt all at once and end in a moment. Often, the veterans were unable to see the enemy, yet they certainly saw the resulting casualties. The sounds of a firefight were a cacophony of whirs, whines, whistles, pops, ricochets, buzzes, cracks, and crashes. The noise level was tremendous and could rise in intensity, then fall into a lull with only a few rifle pops going off. Likely as not, the noise level would rise again to a crescendo of rattling machine-gun and automatic-rifle fire. Grenades went off with a loud "whump," as one man described it. Artillery barrages and airstrikes had noises of their very own. One could actually hear an artillery round coming in, producing a sound like a series of hisses or buzzes, as if the projectile were skipping through the air. If it was a high explosive round, the explosion would literally shake the ground and send shrapnel and debris flying everywhere. A white phosphorus round exploded in a brilliant, white fountain. Both helicopters and fixed-wing aircraft fired rockets and machine guns, and/or cannons. One man likened the sound of the cannon fired by an attacking F-4 Phantom II jet aircraft to that of a chainsaw. Some aircraft dropped napalm, which erupted in a great mass of spreading fire and almost pitch-black smoke. Several saw "Spooky"—C-47 cargo and transport aircraft of World War II vintage, armed with mini-guns, or electrically powered Gatling guns—pouring fire into enemy positions. One man said, "Spooky's guns sounded like little motorcycles." Another, who saw one of the airplanes operating at night, said that the tracers from the mini-guns looked solid like a red line rather than spaced out between five regular bullets. B-52 raids literally shook the earth and produced a distinct rumbling sound. North Vietnamese and Viet Cong rockets and mortars made distinct sounds and sights as well. A Choctaw veteran vividly remembered a rocket attack at night as a series of booming "red geysers."

For the most part, American troops took the tactical offensive if and when they found any major NVA or VC concentrations. Typically, reconnaissance patrols spotted and fixed enemy positions and infantry units attempted to move into blocking positions. One or two units would attack the enemy position in order to drive the enemy soldiers onto the blocking force, which may or may not have been supported with tanks, mortars, or other heavy weaponry. Helicopters were also used, primarily by air-mobile units, to insert ground troops into favorable attacking positions. Artillery, tanks, attack helicopters (gunships), ground support aircraft, and, on occasion, naval gunnery were all used to soften up the enemy troops or to help drive them toward American blocking forces. According to a number of individuals, the trouble was finding the enemy unit in the first place and then holding it in position long enough for American forces to overwhelm it with superior firepower and numbers. If the NVA and VC had one great military asset, however, it was their ability to disperse and literally disappear from the field of battle.

There was no doubt whatsoever in the minds of the veterans that American ground forces held fire superiority. Consequently, enemy units typically engaged the Americans only when they held an obvious advantage. There was an old saying in Vietnam that while the Americans held the day, "Charlie owned the night." To combat "Charlie" (short for "Victor Charlie," the voice alphabet code for *VC*) after sundown, American units set out small ambushes in the effort to interdict enemy movements. The rest of a particular outfit dug fighting holes in a 360-degree defensive perimeter. Three- or four-man listening posts were sent out in front of these perimeters in places where the enemy was likely to advance. Ideally, a listening post would be able to warn the main body of suspected enemy movements and attacks. Enemy attacks most often occurred in the early morning hours and were preceded by machine-gun fire or a mortar bombardment to throw the perimeter into confusion. NVA and VC soldiers would attack at points along the perimeter line, attempting to overrun one or two American positions and infiltrate a group of attackers inside the defensive perimeter. Only two Native American combat veterans in the RCS sample ever took part in beating back what could be called human-wave assaults, like the ones the Chinese regularly launched against American night positions during the Korean War.

On occasion, the North Vietnamese Army launched major attacks on larger combat bases and cities. At these times it fought primarily as a conventional combat force and followed well-thought-out plans of action. Surprisingly, during the Tet Offensive the NVA even utilized tanks. The NVA-VC forces used deception, economy of force, surprise, concentration of force, and a flexible defense to press their attacks. Their failure to defeat American forces in major battles can be attributed primarily to American firepower and to the individual courage and tenacity of the troops.

The perennial problem of finding and fixing enemy positions was a complicated and well-nigh impossible task. The NVA and VC evidently were trained to operate in cells of very small groups of soldiers and live off the land. The ability to disperse, hide, and take refuge among villagers or in sanctuaries in Cambodia and Laos made the enemy forces practically invisible during the day. Accurate intelligence on enemy troop movements and concentrations was extremely difficult to obtain. In addition, the NVA and VC took a great deal of time and effort in building elaborate complexes of bunkers and tunnels in strategic areas. As one man put it, they could literally "be there one minute and gone the next."

As a consequence of the enemy's ability to blend in with the surroundings, either by hiding in tunnel complexes and venturing out only at night or by mingling with villagers friendly to the communist cause, American combat troops took part in seemingly endless rounds of patrols, sweeps, and reconnaissance missions. Artillerymen lobbed tons of high explosives into free-fire zones to harass and interdict NVA and VC troop movements and supply missions. When called upon to do so, aircraft, both helicopter and fixed-wing, struck designated targets with rockets, bombs, and machine-gun and cannon fire. In all cases, the grunts had to go in and reconnoiter the devastation, or, in the parlance of the time and place, "count the meat." One Native American veteran recalled a painful memory from one such mission:

> We went into a ville [village] one day after an air strike. The first body I saw in Nam was a little kid. He was burnt up—napalm—and his arms were kind of curled up. He was on his back, but his arms were curled but sticking up in the air stiff. Made me sick. It turned me around. See, in our way we're not supposed to kill women and children in battle. The old people say it's bad medicine and killing women and children doesn't prove that you're brave. It's just the opposite.

Combat of the sort experienced in Vietnam caused most of the Native American veterans to be confused and doubt the war they were fighting. The forced callousness developed by living in a combat zone was often interspersed with extreme feelings of remorse and the realization that what they were doing to the Vietnamese roughly paralleled what had been done historically to their own people. One veteran saw striking similarities in the condition of the Vietnamese peasants and his own tribe "back in the world"—the United States:

> We went into their country and killed them and took land that wasn't ours. Just like what the whites did to us. I helped load up ville

after ville and pack it off to the resettlement area. Just like when they moved us to the rez [reservation]. We shouldn't have done that. Browns against browns. That screwed me up, you know.

Still another veteran was forced to take a hard look at the racial aspects of the war. During a search-and-destroy mission, this particular man was approached by one of the Vietnamese farmers whose home had just been burned to the ground. The old farmer looked at the Native American soldier, compared their skin and hair color, and said, as if confused, "You . . . me, same-same." Robin LaDue reported a similar kind of exchange between another Indian veteran and an NVA soldier. In her informant's words:

I was told I was destined to be a warrior as my father and grandfather were before me. Then when I was eighteen I enlisted in the Army and I went to Vietnam. I did not get drafted, I went voluntarily. Then I was in the war and I killed and I got to be very good at killing. One day, this VC prisoner we had pointed to my skin and hair and eyes and said "Same, same" meaning he and I were alike. I hated him for saying this but one day, out on patrol, I realized he was right, that I had been a red man killing yellow men for the white man. I put my gun down and I couldn't kill anymore. There was no honor in what I had done. I had shamed myself and the gifts of courage and strength that had been given me.[10]

The actual act of killing another human being—NVA, VC or not—troubled every single one of the Native American combat veterans. Quite often, these veterans would not directly admit to taking a life. They frequently would put up a smoke screen. As one said, "I really don't know. I just fired in a direction. You know, PDF [principal direction of fire]." Sometimes they really did not know if they had killed an enemy soldier. Said one man:

Things get confused in a firefight. Rounds going off, smoke, trying to get to cover, somebody yelling in your ear. Sometimes you don't know if you were the one who busted a cap on a dude. You know, a lot of the bodies had lots of bullet holes.

A soldier's field of vision was often limited in Vietnam. One simply could not see well through the smoke of burning huts, or around one's comrades, or through the trees, high grass, and jungle foliage. In addition, soldiers had to devote part of their attention to simply operating their individual weapons. The more complicated the weapon, the more attention required to fire it. Moreover, several of the men admitted to not even aiming their rifles during a firefight. One man commented, "Man, I just kept down and raised my rifle up and pulled off bursts. If I hit something it'd be a big surprise."

Among those who knew and admitted they had killed enemy soldiers in combat, feelings about their acts were decidedly mixed. One said:

> I killed a VC in an ambush. When we went out to check out the place, I looked at him real good. I know I was the one that got him, 'cause he dropped when I pulled off the round. I just stood there and shook—my hands, my guts. Damn, it was strange.

Another recalled killing an NVA soldier in a spider hole:

> I kept firing—emptied the whole magazine in the hole. Then we drug the guy out. He fell apart. No shit, his arm came off, his intestines fell out. I started barfing till I couldn't throw up anything else.

Others stated that after a period of time they were unaffected by the act of killing and the sight of dead bodies. According to one soldier:

> You kind of got used to it. Some of the guys screwed around with the VC bodies. You know, took pictures, put them into stupid positions, put cigarettes in their mouths. Everybody had a piece of gook equipment. I remember a dude from another company taking a NVA pack off a gook that was dead for awhile—he was stiff. Man, that was bad. You see that all the time and it doesn't bother you anymore.

If there was a common complaint voiced by Native American veterans, it was that their immediate commanders in the field habitually singled them out for numerous dangerous duties simply because they were American Indians. One man became a "tunnel rat" because his commanding officer thought that Indians had been born with remarkably keen eyesight. He was certainly not the smallest man in his platoon, even though most tunnel rats were small of stature elsewhere, nor was he eager to search the forbidding darkness of NVA and VC underground complexes. After he had been in the tunnels, however, he began to trust himself more and more with the job, in spite of the danger.

He quickly became a consummate professional in exploring the dark, dank underground world of the enemy. Indeed, he seemed to have developed his own system of exploration in the tunnels:

> I carried a knife and a .45. The blade was better than the pistol, because if I was going to run into somebody up close I could use the knife . . . I carried a flash, but I'd rather feel my way through. Some little guy might be there waiting for me to turn on a light so's he could blow me away.

The men often talked about how they were assigned the duty of walking point on patrols far more frequently than their non-Indian peers. Troops in Vietnam considered walking point exceptionally dangerous because the point man acted as a scout and walked ahead of a unit's main body. Generally, the danger in walking point had to do with the topography or the foliage in an area of operations. If a unit was moving through tall elephant grass, for example, the point man could literally walk into a concealed enemy position. He would also be in the position most likely to trip mines and booby traps. In ambush situations, the point man would often be allowed to pass by in order for the ambushers to attack a unit's middle in the hope of taking out the command structure or the unit's machine guns. The point man could then be cut off from support and be killed at leisure. In many units the point position was given to a "cherry," or new man, because, simply put, it was thought that his life was not as important as a veteran's. Some of the men scoffed at this idea and said that in their units point duty was assigned to a veteran who presumably knew what he was doing. Most American Indian infantrymen stated flatly that they were ordered to walk point time and again because of white stereotypes. A Menominee from Wisconsin related that his platoon commander thought that since Indians "grew up in the woods" they should know how to track and generally "feel" when something in the immediate area was disturbed or out of place. Apparently, his platoon commander thought that Native Americans were endowed either by heredity or circumstances of birth with the ability to read their environments. The fact that this particular individual spent a good deal of his youth in an urban environment made not one bit of difference in the opinion of the platoon leader. The racism involved in this kind of stereotype is of the same type as that expressed by people who argue that the mascot Indians of professional football and baseball teams, like the Washington Redskins and the Atlanta Braves, are positive images. Presumably, the "Red-skins" and "Braves" are courageous, tenacious foes who play to win. Commanders like the one mentioned above very likely thought he was paying tribute to his Menominee point man's abilities and courage, when he was really putting the man in grave danger. But these kinds of racial stereotypes placed many of the Native American veterans in great peril. A Navajo man, as did numerous others, concurred about the false labeling. In his particular case, he said he walked point all the time because he was:

> stereotyped by the cowboys and Indian movies. Nicknamed "Chief" right away. Non-Indians claimed Indians could see through trees and hear the unhearable. Bullshit, they even believed Indians could walk on water.

The ability to track and know an environment well enough to say that something in it is out of place cannot, of course, be passed along on a strand of DNA. One can only speculate that Native Americans walked point because Indian lives were expendable or because these platoon commanders really believed that putting an Indian, simply because he was an Indian, on point was a tactically sound maneuver. The idea would be laughable had it not been so dangerous for the men who had to do it.

In several instances, disproportionately many given their numbers, Native American veterans indicated the situation was such in Vietnam that their commanders committed them exclusively to scouting activities, not just to walking point. Usually, this came through their volunteering (or "being volunteered") for service in Long Range Reconnaissance Patrol (LRRP, pronounced "lurp") platoons formed within each U.S. Army infantry battalion deployed in Southeast Asia. This was especially hazardous duty involving the sending of very small teams (usually six men) into remote locales thought—and in many cases known—to be occupied by significant numbers of enemy soldiers. The LRRP team would explore its assigned area and report back what it found by radio. In the event it was discovered by NVA or VC troops during its scouting mission, the team would frequently be wiped out. In some cases a team might only be saved from annihilation by a timely and very courageous helicopter evacuation.[11] One Indian veteran, a Creek-Cherokee, explained his motivations for joining his particular battalion's LRRP outfit:

They kept running me on point during the day, and putting me out on listening posts at night. The company I was with, Fourth Division, you know, it was all draftees who didn't have a clue what to do if we got hit. So, I knew I was going to die the minute we made serious contact [with enemy forces]. I'd be out there all by myself, and there'd be nobody to back me up. So I volunteered to run LRRP missions. At least then I knew the people around me knew what they were doing. Besides, in the LRRPs our objective was to avoid contact, not seek it out. It was scary business, but all things considered I figured my best shot at living through Vietnam was to be a LRRP. Crazy, ain't it?

A Lakota veteran testified to the LRRP's overall mission of stealth and the hazards it involved. He and his team were once dropped from helicopter by ropes into thick jungle. They regrouped and departed on a mission that took them ever deeper into the undergrowth—"I've never seen it so thick." On the other hand, the density of the undergrowth and foliage probably saved their lives:

We were spread out when a whole NVA regiment started coming down this little trail. I just froze and kept as still as I could, hoping that I was under cover. I was hoping that nobody else got caught, because the gooks knew that where you found one of us, you'd find more. They would have taken us and put us in tiger cages and let us rot. We waited it out until the whole regiment passed. I've never been so scared in my life.

Of course some LRRP teams were caught and had to fight their way out against terrible odds. Billy Walkabout, a Cherokee from Oklahoma, received a Distinguished Service Cross, the second highest United States decoration for gallantry in combat, for his actions during one such incident in November 1968. Walkabout's citation for the DSC not only attests to his personal bravery, but also to what could befall a LRRP unit operating against an enemy who had more personnel and a complete knowledge of the terrain on his side:

[After] a long range reconnaissance patrol southwest of Hue . . . [Sergeant Walkabout's team] radioed for immediate helicopter extraction.

When the extraction helicopters arrived and the lead man began moving toward the pick-up zone, he was seriously wounded by hostile automatic weapons fire. Sergeant Walkabout quickly rose to his feet and delivered steady suppressive fire on the attackers while other team members pulled the wounded man back to their ranks.

Sergeant Walkabout then administered first aid to the soldier in preparation for medical evacuation. As the man was being loaded onto the evacuation helicopter, enemy elements again attacked the team.

Maneuvering under heavy fire, Sergeant Walkabout positioned himself where the enemy were concentrating their assault and placed continuous rifle fire on the adversary. A command detonated mine ripped through the friendly team, instantly killing three men and wounding all the others.

Although stunned and wounded by the blast, Sergeant Walkabout rushed from man to man administering first aid, bandaging one soldier's severe chest wound and reviving another soldier by heart massage.

He then coordinated gunship and tactical air strikes on the enemy's positions. When evacuation helicopters arrived again, he worked singlehandedly under fire to board his disabled comrades.

Only when the casualties had been evacuated and friendly reinforcements had arrived, did he allow himself to be extracted.[12]

After 1968, the various LRRP units were consolidated as the Seventy-fifth Ranger Group. Those Indian soldiers who had actively sought out such an occupational profile with this unit all too frequently landed in the even more esoteric reconnaissance or hunter-killer units formed with the Special Operations Group created by the Military Assistance Command, Vietnam (MAC-V-SOG). This secret unit—it is still highly classified and euphemistically referred to as the "Studies and Observations Group"—consistently undertook suicidally high-risk operations with casualty rates sometimes exceeding 1,000 percent per year due to soldiers and their replacements being wounded, sometimes on multiple occasions, or killed.[13] So prevalent was American Indian participation in these operations that it has been enshrined in the public consciousness in the character of Billy in the motion picture *Predator*, starring Arnold Schwarzenegger.

The U.S. Marine Corps had its equivalent to the LRRPs in its Force Recon battalions. "There were plenty of 'skins' [slang for Indians] in

Force Recon," said a Winnebago veteran of the First Battalion. "I knew a Navajo and a Pawnee and knew of two Siouxs and either a Menominee or an Oneida from Wisconsin. There were a couple of Chippewas, too, I heard." Normally, Force Recon personnel received training beyond that of Marine riflemen in regular infantry regiments. All were jump-qualified (parachutists), and some had demolitions training with the Navy SEALs (still another specialized counterinsurgency, covert-operations unit), and had attended special jungle warfare, amphibious operations, and intelligence schools. Like all other Marines, they were also basic infantrymen. As one veteran said with a great deal of pride and a certain amount of arrogance, "We were the elite of the elite."

Force Recon platoons usually scouted possible enemy sanctuaries. Stealth was their most important tactical asset, for their primary mission was to find and fix enemy positions so that they could be attacked. The duty led to numerous hair-raising brushes with NVA and VC patrols, during which the Marines were supposed to "lay chilly" and avoid contact. "I've had hard-core VC walk within three feet of me," said a former Recon Marine. "You could smell their breath."

Despite their dangerous assignment, and perhaps as a consequence of their bravado, Force Recon Marines stirred some resentment and not a little envy among other Marines. One Apache Marine Corps veteran testified that he witnessed more than one recon team get "its butt kicked." But his statement also attested to the risks Marine recon teams took in gathering information on enemy movements.

Akin to reconnaissance teams and the Army's hunter-killer operations were Marine Corps killer teams. Basically, these teams were comprised of Marines in a regular infantry battalion who were sent in small groups into free-fire zones dressed in the black pajamas of the Vietnamese peasant. They wore the Vietnamese conical hats and essentially attempted to pass relatively unnoticed in enemy territory. They were expected not only to gather information but also to conduct small-scale raids on known enemy sympathizers and disrupt enemy troop movements. It was no doubt a counterguerilla operation designed to harass and hit the enemy when most vulnerable. The teams were exposed to several dangers, not the least of which were being sighted and attacked by American or South Vietnamese artillery and air strikes. But more dangerous perhaps was being alone and operating, like the Army's LRRPs, deep in enemy territory and possibly encountering a larger and stronger NVA or VC force. A killer team might even have been more vulnerable, because when dressed like the Vietnamese the men were unlikely to carry a radio. Without a radio, of course, they could not call for helicopter extraction. Not only that, but they were expected to make contact with the enemy and/or kill enemy sympathizers. They also attempted to take prisoners. Still, there were enough men who took on the duty and lived to tell about it. According to one veteran:

> Killer teams were the way we got back at the gooks. We did the same things they did. I once slit a man's throat. I've seen prisoners choked and shot. I'm not proud of it, but it was the same thing that they'd do to us.

Several of the men stated that the composition of killer teams was frequently based on race. In order to penetrate enemy territory, members of the killer team were supposed to "look" Vietnamese. The selection of individuals for the teams narrowed, according to several veterans, to Native Americans, dark-skinned Latinos, Asian Americans, Pacific Islanders and lighter-skinned blacks. Some of the Americans were too large to fit into Vietnamese clothing and would have been more than conspicuous in the Vietnamese countryside. Indians apparently were the right size and shade.

Most of the Native American Marine Corps veterans neither served with Force Recon units nor participated in killer team operations. As one man stated, "We didn't need anybody to find gooks, they always found us." It was the same for most of the Army veterans. They served in regular infantry or other units, and although they walked point more than was usual, they basically lived and fought as grunts. But the terror and excitement of a firefight was more than enough trauma, even without stalking an elusive enemy, when the odds were decidedly in the enemy's favor. Most of the men remember incidents specific to their personal views of battle. In combat, an individual rarely sees the battle as a whole and often, especially in Vietnam where the numbers of enemy dead counted more heavily in military terms than territory gained, does not remember how or at what point in time an engagement was won or lost. Seemingly minor incidents in combat, from the standpoint of those in command, become imprinted on the minds of those directly participating in them. The personal view of combat might not be sufficient to explain a given battle, but it definitely provides insight into how battle affects combatants both physically and psychologically. And since battles turn on how well troops are physically and emotionally prepared for combat, the personal view of battle is an important aspect of military history and the understanding of combat in general.

The assertion of terror and of horror in combat was all too common in the testimony of Native American Vietnam veterans. Although each veteran had a combat experience uniquely his own, there was a certain amount of sameness to the stories about the battles between American troops and the NVA and VC in which they fought. A common theme was the suddenness with which a battle could erupt. "All at once everybody opened up" [began firing their weapons] was a common statement. Equally common was "the gooks just disappeared," or "they got out of there fast," or "they made their bird in a hurry." There were certainly prolonged battles, such as the defense of Khe Sanh, the battle for Hue, the attack on Hamburger Hill, and the great thrust and counter-thrust operation in the Ia Drang valley in 1965. But for the most part the men were ambushed or attacked in set positions; or they assaulted bunkers, manned blocking positions, chased fleeing figures through the brush, and endured sniper fire; or they were bombarded with mortars, rockets, and artillery. They also saw limbs blown off and bodies torn apart by mines and booby traps.

Two incidents reported by Native American veterans more than serve the purpose of capturing the terror and the horror of the "common" engagement during the Vietnam War. The first, related by a former Marine, is testimony to the terror of being attacked and knowing beforehand that one was almost certain to become a casualty. The Marine's company was in a defensive position inside a Vietnamese village when the attack occurred:

We were pinned down. I was behind a wall—plaster or something like that. Anyway, the gooks had a machine gun and it seemed like they were shooting directly at me. I watched the bullets take away my damn wall piece by piece. I'd pull off a round, then get back down and watch that wall get lower and lower. It was being shot away. I tried to get smaller and smaller and the wall kept getting smaller and smaller. I knew pretty soon that the wall would get smaller than I would. I got out of that fight flat on my back in a medevac chopper.

The second incident was a gruesome reminder of the horror of what could happen in a night attack. Again, the person who related the story was a Marine who served in the northernmost tactical zone of South

Vietnam known as I Corps. The incident occurred while the informant's company was in a night defense perimeter:

> They came around two o'clock in the morning. One of our holes got overrun and the gooners just got inside the perimeter for a little while. We killed most of them and the rest blazed out of there. . . . After an attack like that we all just stayed up, you know, the rest of the night. In the morning, my platoon commander took a head count and found one guy missing. We had one KIA [killed in action] and two WIA [wounded in action]. We saddled up to go outside the perimeter to look for bodies, drag-trails, and the missing guy—he was one of the guys who was in the hole that got overrun. The other guy in the hole was dead. We found him in an old bomb crater not very far from the perimeter. They'd shot him in the back of the head, like an execution. Man, that was fucking horrible. They drug him out in the bush and blew his head off. I didn't know the dude very good but it really tore me apart inside. I can't forget him lying in that crater on his knees, pushed over like that, stiff. Pitiful. We rolled him on a poncho and carried him back.

CASUALTIES

As can be seen from these two statements, the terror and the horror these two Native Americans witnessed stem directly from their knowledge of what the weapons used in Vietnam were capable of doing to the human body. On both sides, the infantrymen carried arms that were essentially of the same types as those utilized by their fathers during World War II—semiautomatic and fully automatic rifles, machine guns, mortars, bazookas, flame throwers, grenades, and antipersonnel mines. Artillerymen fired light to heavy field guns and howitzers. As in World War II, ground forces in Vietnam could call upon air strikes, employ tanks, and, between 1968 and 1972, use naval gunfire to bombard enemy positions.

There were, however, two main differences between the weaponry of World War II and Vietnam. The first was the use of—indeed, the dependence on—the helicopter. During World War II, the helicopter was experimental and unknown in terms of its usefulness in warfare. In Vietnam, the helicopter became a tactical necessity. It could perform resupply duty, deliver ordnance on the enemy with pinpoint accuracy, insert and extract troops as the tactical need arose, and, of course, evacuate casualties. The second difference was the higher level of sophistication of weaponry in Vietnam. The term *sophistication* in military parlance usually means getting "a bigger bang for the buck," or technologically improving a piece of weaponry to make it more deadly to greater numbers of enemy soldiers in the same time frame as its predecessors on the battlefield. Improving the rate of fire or the accuracy of a weapon without making it too cumbersome or complex automatically makes it more sophisticated; so does increasing the range of a firearm or extending the killing radius of an explosive device. The M-48 Patton tank used in Vietnam was more sophisticated than the Sherman tank of World War II vintage because it had greater speed, thicker armor, and a faster and more accurate gun. The fact that it was more complicated, but not too complicated to operate simply, added to its level of sophistication.[14]

Casualties in combat most always occur in what are known as killing or beaten zones. These areas are usually fairly narrow and determined by the effective range of the weapons employed during a battle. Thus, the killing or beaten zone during the era of muscle-powered weaponry was very narrow, perhaps even a mere sword's length wide. Bows, crossbows, and firearms extended killing zones significantly over those of lances and swords; but still they remained relatively limited until the profusion of rifled musketry and cannon in the mid-nineteenth century. Even the Brown Bess muskets of the formidable British fighting squares of the eighteenth century were not very effective (i.e., possessing the ability to cause casualties) beyond 100 yards. In the 1840s a French army officer, Captain Claude-Etienne Minié, perfected a conical bullet that could be dropped down the barrel of a rifle easily, yet when fired its hollow base would expand and fit tightly in the weapon's spiral grooves. The new projectile spun as it left the barrel, increasing the rifle's range and accuracy at least threefold.[15] In other words, although the principle of rifling was well known, a rifle could not be loaded as fast as a smoothbore musket until the perfection of the minié ball. After its creation, a musket could be loaded just as fast as ever and kill at greater distances. Further inventions increased the rifle's effective range and widened a given army's killing zone very considerably.

Another factor that can be used in the calculation of an army's killing zone is that of time. Increasing a weapon's rate or rapidity of fire simply means that more projectiles can be fired into a given killing zone, thus creating an even greater potential for inflicting wounds and death on an enemy force. The Americans R. J. Gatling, Hiram Maxim, John M. Browning, and I. N. Lewis all contributed to the final perfection of the machine gun, a weapon that did not necessarily extend the limits of an infantry unit's killing zone but certainly created more casualties within its boundaries. Artillery pieces were given similar increases in accuracy and rate of fire. Airplanes and intercontinental ballistic missiles essentially have extended killing zones to include the entire earth's surface. Weapons sophistication, then, means simply widening and making the killing zone more deadly.

In Vietnam, infantry killing zones normally were short due in large part to the foliage and the nature of enemy attacks. The NVA and VC attacked from ambush and made quick assaults. As much as possible the Americans did the same. Consequently, the Vietnam War led to the rise of the relatively short-range, but fast-firing and quickly reloaded, assault rifle. Infantry tactical doctrine rested on the idea of filling a short killing zone with large numbers of projectiles. And, compared to World War II, there were many more types of weapons that could literally spray a given area with flying, fast-moving bits of metal—claymore mines, fleshette rounds, the M-26 hand grenade, the M-60 machine gun, and the M-16 rifle. The NVA and VC had some equivalents to these weapons and their principal assault rifle, the AK-47, was probably better than the Americans'.

As expected, raising the level of weapons sophistication has produced frightening changes on the battlefield. Of course, battlefields were already frightening places well before there were great technological innovations like the minié ball and the machine gun. On the other hand, modern technology has made weaponry and warfare far more insidious. Militaries (and modern police forces) use the descriptive terminology *stopping power* to measure small-arms capabilities in combat. *Stopping power* carries a slightly different connotation than does the term *lethality* in connection with firearms. Lethality is, of course, the ability to kill; stopping power is the ability of a firearm, or any other weapon, for that matter, to force the unfortunate victim to cease any and all activity. A rifle transfers chemical energy by the means of a projectile from one point to another. The energy from a speeding bullet is wasted unless it strikes something or someone. Then the energy is directly transferred to the victim's body, causing an immediate reaction of the nervous system. The victim collapses as though stunned, rather than being violently thrown off his or her feet. The desired effect of a hit is to immediately incapacitate an enemy. The victim's death is a secondary consequence. In fact, an enemy's instantaneous death might very well be an unwanted side effect of a firearm's stopping power.

This other, perhaps even more grisly, side to modern ballistics is a weapon's ability to maim, but not necessarily kill, a targeted human being. The intent of severely injuring enemy soldiers on the battlefield is to tie up more and more personnel in medical support units. The cost of treating the wounded in both human resources and economic terms is far greater than the cost of simply burying the dead. The ultimate goal of maiming enemy soldiers in combat, then, is to make the cost of medical care overwhelming. More people in medical units, in absolute terms, means fewer people carrying arms on the battlefield.

The emotional cost in battlefield deaths, however, forces modern militaries to provide treatment and care for the wounded in spite of the heavy burdens on financial and human resources that they impose. If soldiers are not well taken care of when wounded, other soldiers might, with good cause, mutiny. Not only that, but how can military elites recruit and retain soldiers in the armed forces if potential recruits know that being wounded in combat automatically means long-term, painful infirmity or lingering death?

The weaponry of the Vietnam era produced terrible wounds and frightful deaths. The majority of American battle deaths (51 percent) in Vietnam were produced by small-arms fire (assault rifles, light machine guns, and, rarely, pistol shots). This did not mean that those hit with small-arms fire were instantly killed on the battlefield. Some, even some with head wounds, died while in transit from the battlefield to the aid station or while in the hospital itself. Fragmentation weapons (mortars, grenades, rocket-propelled grenades, rockets, artillery pieces, and mines) produced 65 percent of the nonfatal wounds.[16] Both bullet and fragmentation wounds were particularly terrifying in terms of their malevolent ability to maim rather than instantly kill.

"I took an AK [short for AK-47, the standard Communist Block assault rifle] round in the thigh," said a Yaqui veteran. "It didn't even hit bone, but it screwed up the muscle and nerves so bad that I can't hardly walk around now." Another man had been hit with metal fragments and hot debris blown outward by a Bouncing Betty mine. A Bouncing Betty was a particularly terrifying weapon. When detonated, either by trip wire or direct contact with the firing mechanism, it shot from a buried canister to a height of about three feet before exploding. The man's arm, leg, chest, and back were pocked with small scars and tiny tattoo-like blue marks:

The powder and shit got under my skin. . . . they operated on me three times trying to get all the shrapnel out. During one operation they dug out a piece of bone from one of the other guys who got hit the same time I did. One doc told me that I'll have pieces of shrapnel and stuff working out of my skin for the rest of my life. I'm probably carrying around a few ounces of scrap metal that will be there from now on.

One veteran was shot in his right shin. "The bullet went in and splintered the bone. They operated six times trying to get me to walk right again," he said.

The types of wounds they described attest to the physiological destructiveness of modern weaponry. Rifles like the AK-47 and the American M-16 had high rates of fire and shot relatively lightweight steel or copper-alloy jacketed projectiles at supersonic velocities, producing what are known as cavitation wounds. Generally, high-velocity, steel-jacketed bullets made small, neat entrance wounds and left behind large, gaping holes when exiting a victim's body. The destructiveness, however, was not all that simple.

These kinds of projectiles do a number of things when they hit a human target. First, the jacketing prevents a bullet from immediately flattening out or breaking apart, like hunting bullets do, upon striking living tissue. On the other hand, their lightness and high velocity make them unstable on impact. Thus, if a bullet of this type strikes a glancing blow to bone, it usually ricochets and wobbles or tumbles inside the body before exiting. Sometimes the bullet will strike a dense bone and actually travel along the bone's path through softer tissue. If it is struck head on, the bullet simply splinters bone. In addition, a supersonic bullet essentially expends its energy into the victim's flesh, driving fluids away from its trajectory and causing a breakdown of the surrounding tissues; hence "cavitation" wounds.[17]

These bullets apparently could be as strangely erratic as they were exceedingly dangerous. A Choctaw Army veteran was struck in the head during an exceptionally violent engagement with Viet Cong troops. He kept firing through the firefight, pausing only to wipe away what he thought was sweat from his forehead. At one point, he looked at his hand and discovered blood. He actually did not realize that he had been seriously wounded. The bullet had evidently struck a glancing blow to his head and left in its wake a cracked skull and a large gash. Lightness, supersonic speed, and inherent instability caused the bullet to ricochet easily off the man's cranium rather than penetrate solid bone. Of course, the bullet probably struck at a lucky angle; otherwise it surely would have entered the man's brain. The extreme excitement of the firefight—the adrenaline rush—made him almost impervious to pain. A Marine veteran also testified to the erratic characteristics of modern rifle bullets:

> We got hit pretty hard outside of Cam Lo. We got pinned down inside a tree line. This black guy off to my right kept standing up and firing bursts from his rifle at the gooks. Then he stood up and bang! He drops like somebody kicked his legs out from under him. Well, I don't see him for a minute or two. I thought he was wasted. Next minute I see him staring off, holding his helmet. He took a round right between the steel pot and the helmet liner. The round just followed the shape of the helmet around to the back and dropped out. Weirdest thing I ever saw.

What ultimately made these wounds so terrifying was that they were incredibly difficult to treat. John Keegan, the internationally respected British military historian, once categorically stated that the rifled musket of the American Civil War era inflicted "the worst small-arms wound ever known in warfare."[18] His statement is no doubt accurate. The Civil War minié ball was a .56 to .58 caliber (nearly three times the diameter of a modern .223 caliber M-16 round) bullet weighing nearly two ounces that traveled at subsonic speed. It was not jacketed and therefore it flattened and/or broke up on impact. If a minié ball struck a human being in the head or chest, the victim was very likely to be killed instantly. If a hit was scored on a human being's extremities, the minié ball literally blew away large chunks of the victim's flesh and bone. Most of the casualties of the Civil War were caused by rifled muskets.[19]

The wounds of the Civil War era were appalling to be sure; but they were also relatively easy to treat from a medical standpoint. The reason that the numbers of amputations during the Civil War were so incredibly high was that it was simply the best method of dealing with minié ball wounds in the limbs. Civil War surgeons were forced to admit that there was literally nothing left of a limb to save after it had been struck by such a destructive projectile. The same logic applied to wounds created by explosive cannon shells. The cannon projectiles of the period were powder-filled iron balls that, when exploded, flung out large, irregular chunks of metal. Victims could be torn apart and instantly killed or wounded in the extremities with nearly the same effect as that produced by a minié ball.

As we have seen, the Vietnam-era weapons produced wounds far more maliciously subtle. Bullet wounds in Vietnam shredded tissue and splintered bone. Debriding a wound of this type required great diligence and long hours over the operating table. Attempts to reconstruct or repair damaged muscles, nerves, and bones often involved several intensive surgical procedures. And even then the damaged tissue would never be completely restored.

Fragmentation or shrapnel wounds were equally, or perhaps more, difficult to treat. A quick look at the history of the hand grenade perhaps explains the relative difficulty in dealing with fragmentation wounds during the Vietnam War. A hundred and fifty years ago or so, the grenade was a powder-filled, hand-thrown, antipersonnel bomb not unlike those fired from smoothbore cannons. It exploded in flame, irregular fragments, and flying debris. Most Americans are probably familiar with the pineapple grenade of World War II vintage. This grenade's outer casing was segmented into metal squares not much more than half an inch wide. The pineapple worked on the same principle as the very first hand grenade, but with an important difference: segmentation meant that the metal casing would explode in a definite pattern of more regularly shaped chunks of metal. The American grenades of the Vietnam era were even more insidious. This grenade had a very thin outer casing. Inside, along with the explosive charge, however, was a scored metal coil that would explode into hundreds of tiny fragments. The obvious function of the weapon was to make medical treatment exceedingly difficult. Smaller fragments meant that surgeons would have had to spend more time on a single patient searching for pieces of wire coil not much more than one-eighth of an inch long. Just one such fragment entering the lower abdomen, for example, could make an almost imperceptible hole in the bowel, which, if not found, would cause peritonitis and prolonged, painful death. Smaller fragments could also nick rather than completely sever arteries. If an artery is completely cut in two, the ends will automatically draw back and close off, naturally slowing down the flow of blood. A nicked artery, on the other hand, simply continues to spurt blood with every beat of the victim's heart. If the surgeon cannot stop the bleeding immediately, the victim will quickly go into shock as a result of the rapid decrease in blood pressure and perhaps die of exsanguination.

It is certainly a tribute to American medical personnel—helicopter crews, medics, corpsmen, nurses, and surgeons—that no more soldiers died of wounds in Vietnam than actually did so. On average the wounded in Vietnam were evacuated from the battlefield to a hospital in fifteen minutes.[20] Making it to a hospital virtually assured a wounded soldier's life. The death rate of those wounded who got to medical care units was only 2.6 percent. During World War II, 4.5 percent of the wounded died of their wounds in hospitals.[21] A final tribute to American medical personnel is the fact that 83 percent of the wounded were able to return to light or full duty. While this might not have been a pleasant prospect for the wounded man who had to return to his unit in the bush, it nevertheless meant that he had not only survived but that he had fully recovered.

TO STAND IN BATTLE

Given their terrifying prospects on the field of battle, what gave these modern Native American warriors the "will to combat?" The motivation to stay on a battlefield is different than simply answering an appeal to warriordom and nationalism. Actually hearing shots being fired and watching bodies fall is quite different than listening to nationalistic rhetoric and seeing the flag wave. Many of the Native American warriors had truly been trained to kill instantly, almost instinctively, and without remorse. Not only that, but in a modern killing zone an individual realizes that he has accepted the possibility of death or painful wounds. He could not do otherwise in Vietnam, where the agents of wounds and death came in many forms: tied to tree trunks in the form of booby traps, under the surface of rice paddy water or on the ground in the form of mines, or in the hands of a long-time warrior who came with mortars, rifles, grenades, and shoulder-fired rocket launchers in the middle of the night. What gives human beings the seemingly suicidal capacity to stand in battle and face these terrible realities? John Keegan's *The Face of Battle* is an attempt to get to the heart of this "will to combat." In his analysis of three battles—Agincourt in 1415, Waterloo in 1815, and the Somme in 1916—Keegan concludes that leadership, professionalism, peer pressure, nationalism, coercion, excitement, the will to survive, religion, and even chemical dependency all play a part in a person's ability to do combat and not simply run away from war's obvious horrors.[22]

Certainly all of these factors influenced Native Americans to stand and fight in Vietnam, despite their objections to the war itself. They responded to positive, demonstrative leadership and would have done just about anything to prevent their comrades in arms from thinking them cowardly or unreliable. "You took care of each other," said one man. "Officers were good," according to another, "when they took care of the troops." For an officer, taking care of the troops usually meant not sending them on suicidally dangerous missions, making sure that they were well-supplied, calling in artillery or air strikes when necessary to avoid taking too many casualties, and not asking his men to do anything that he was unwilling or unable to do himself.

Some veterans felt compelled to fight not only for those who were in the bush with them but because the military itself coerced them into combat. They felt that if they did not stand in battle they would surely be court-martialed and imprisoned:

> In the Nam they had you going and coming. Where the hell could you desert to? I figured I was in hell anyway—might as well do my year than get thrown in prison. Once you got out they'd just send you to the bush again anyway to do your time.

Simple survival, nearly every Native American agreed, was a predominant factor underlying their willingness to fight. "This 'why didn't you refuse to kill?' is bullshit. When somebody's shooting at you, you'd better shoot back," one veteran said. Every Native American veteran asserted that getting back home was of primary importance. "Everybody wanted just a small wound. Just enough to get you back home. But nobody wouldn't fight if they thought they were going to get killed," said another veteran. Most Native Americans became seasoned professionals who knew what to do in almost any given combat situation. They trusted themselves and often believed that they held their own fate in their hands. They learned the lay of the land and maintained their weapons in working order. They became thoroughly professional because, as one man put it, "we wanted to get out of the Nam alive."

If tradition can be defined as a set of religiously held beliefs, then one of the most important factors underlying the American Indians' ability to sustain themselves in combat was their adherence to ancient, ancestral values. The two words *warrior tradition* became symbolic of their identities and bolstered their resolve in combat. "I always prayed for help and for courage," said a Kiowa veteran, "like the old war songs say." A Navajo carried sacred corn pollen "to keep me safe and to give me strength and courage."

Many alluded to a heritage of family pride in the achievements of relatives in combat—any combat—and seemingly would have done anything not to besmirch ancestral honor. A Cherokee listed ancestors and relatives who had fought with determination against the whites, during the Civil War, in the trenches in France in World War I, and in World War II. In Vietnam, he said, "I tried to live up to the ways of my ancestors and be a warrior." Another said that he became a member of the 173rd Airborne Brigade because "I wanted to uphold the warrior ways of my family." Surely family honor is just as compelling in combat as American nationalism, if not more so.

Many, like the Navajo veteran mentioned above, carried medicine with them into combat. An Ojibwa veteran said:

> My grandfather gave me some sacred tobacco. When you smoke it the prayers in it go straight to the Creator. The smoke disappears into all things and raises the spirit. That's what my people say. I knew that I'd come back alive.

Others carried small arrowheads and fetishes carved in the shape of animal spirits. "My uncles gave me a prayer plume to carry with me," remarked one individual. "I held it when I prayed and it helped me see that I was going to make it through."

Several of the men had these kinds of spiritual experiences while in Vietnam. A Kiowa said that he was:

> looking into a small stream and saw an old Kiowa man. I couldn't make out who it was but he was dressed in the old way. He wore one eagle feather. He said, "Take heart, be strong, this is what you must do." After that I didn't have any fears.

One veteran was praying and an eagle appeared before him. "The eagle told me that he would be my eyes in battle. After that I knew everything that was going on. That's what helped me survive." Another had a strikingly similar experience:

> I could ask the ground when I was on patrol to take care of me, or ask the tree, "Show me where is my enemy," or ask the animals to watch over me, be my guide, and a lot of times it worked. They warned me when my enemy was around. At night I would ask the crickets and little four-legged creatures, insects, "Be my eyes for tonight" and it worked.

Still another told of having his life saved in a most timely fashion:

> We were on a night movement. I was going to take a step when a bird or bat or something flew in my face. I heard, "Don't step there, grandchild, the danger is very near." I stopped right there and signaled for somebody to come up. The squad halted and spread out and we caught a bunch of gooks in the bush. They laid an ambush and I just about tripped a booby trap. I know that it was my grandmother's voice. She had passed away a few years before but I know she warned me.

The veterans seemed to view the Vietnam War, perhaps all warfare, just as many of their ancestors had viewed it. An ethos perhaps stronger than all other factors appears to have sustained them in Vietnam. According to one veteran:

> The old warriors knew hardships and pain. But they knew that they were the ones everyone else looked to for courage and wisdom. In my language, the word for warrior means something like "defender of the people." That's what I believe. I became a warrior in Vietnam; now I protect my people.

To most of them the war was a rite of passage that transformed them from boys to men. They had seen human nature in its lowest and most malicious form. The horror they witnessed and the terror they endured made them understand war as a disruptive, yet almost natural, force. In that sense, it was more than simply a painful human experience; it had spiritual significance as well. The war brought out both the best and the worst in them and became an everyday ritual of survival.

HEARTS

Tain nah zeddle bey nah Vietnam toyah.
They had strong hearts in Vietnam.

—HONOR SONG COMPOSED BY KIOWA
ELDER JACK ANQUOE IN 1983

They came home individually, trickling back to their homes one by one. Some were immediately honored in their communities for taking part in the fighting in Vietnam. Some were ritually cleansed of the war's emotional effects. Some families ceremonially thanked those who had prayed for their loved one's safe return. Many—too many, perhaps—simply stored their uniforms in old trunks, attempted to take up life where they left off before their military service, and tried to forget the bloodletting and pain. It was a foregone conclusion that they would be unable to store the war away in a remote part of their minds. It had been too traumatic, too exciting, too terrifying and too intense an experience to ever block out or forget. There was certainly no dishonor in the way they fought, for they fought with tenacity, courage, and great skill. They had endured the filth, fatigue, fear, and fighting. Of the Native Americans it can truly be said: they indeed had strong hearts in Vietnam.

But a great irony was in store for them. They had carried on an ancient tradition of arms and had performed well in combat, yet the U.S. military, by rotating them individually, not collectively, in and out of Vietnam, did that tradition a severe disservice. They returned separately, usually at night, slipping silently back home, just as their warrior ancestors had done only in defeat. While the war itself had been a shared experience—like a war party of old—the actual homecoming was not.

They returned severally to an American society undergoing a crisis precipitated by several factors, not the least of which was that it had never really been placed on a wartime footing. The Johnson administration had actively tried to avoid rallying the public to war. Johnson's fear of doing so stemmed from his concern that a full-scale war would shift the public's interest away from the domestic reforms of his Great Society. Public interest shifted anyway, primarily because the government's war effort was deceptive, piecemeal, and, arguably, intended to draw out rather than end the fighting.[1] Richard M. Nixon took office as president in a period of almost monumental public frustration with the Vietnam War. Nixon's efforts to gain "peace with honor" through increasing the bombing, extending the war openly into Cambodia, and negotiating at the Paris Peace Talks simply seemed to prolong an already overlong war. In the end, Nixon too relied on secrecy and deception to continue the war effort in the midst of ever-growing opposition to the conflict.[2]

In many ways the secrecy and deception of the Johnson and Nixon administrations in making war was made in the attempt to cope with the forces of change then taking place in American society itself. The civil rights movement had precipitated Johnson's Great Society and his War on Poverty in the first place. These policies were efforts to create a more just American society in terms of socioeconomic opportunity for minority groups. But the historic oppression of racial minorities in America had led to a demand for significant and far-reaching change: more than simply voting, sitting in an available seat on a bus, or going to an all-white school. It led to a demand to put an end to a greater phenomenon, that of domestic colonialism. By the 1950s it became fully recognized that blacks, Latinos, and Native Americans were living in communities controlled by outsiders. Few people who lived in the ghettoes and barrios and on the reservations owned the businesses that siphoned off their hard-earned wages. Those who ran the businesses invested their profits elsewhere. The result was acute poverty, lack of control, and the inability to gain access to the American political system. For Native Americans, the situation was even worse. They were subjected not only to an economic system that systematically extracted what wealth they did have, but also to a bureaucracy that seemingly controlled their very lives in social, political, cultural, and economic terms.[3] In the 1960s American Indians began to demand that they have the right to take control of their own destinies and end the cyclical pattern of domestic colonialism. They demanded self-determination—Red Power—in maintaining their own cultural viability and retaining their special relationship with the spirit world. But the federal government, it seemed, was determined to retain its control over Indian affairs. Native American Vietnam veterans returned to a war at home.

A SENSE OF BETRAYAL

Each year that has passed since the end of World War II and the implementation of the policies of termination and relocation has led to a greater sense of betrayal among Native Americans. Older Indian veterans—those of World War II—were given the accolades befitting their courage and tenacity in war and were placed in the position of representing their people. As a group they were forced into trying to reconcile the irreconcilable. They had given their all to a government that was, for all intents and purposes, continuing a policy of abusive domestic colonialism. Some of them opted to deny the magnitude of the extent to which their people had been betrayed and become "responsible leaders" who worked within the increasingly oppressive colonial system. Others retreated into their own societies and cultures, maintaining their ceremonies and keeping a wary eye on the federal government.[4]

Many Indian Vietnam veterans returned to a Native America at last coming to grips with an intolerable situation. Native Americans were openly questioning termination, relocation, the appalling poverty of the reservations, and their "responsible leaders." Native Americans took up a crusade to restore treaty rights, curb bureaucratic intrusions into their lives, change an educational system under which Indians were taught self-hatred, preserve a sense of tribal identity, and force their leaders to become more responsive to tribal wishes, rather than to a distant federal government.

During the early 1960s, Native Americans generally viewed the civil rights movement as inappropriate or perhaps not even applicable to their own situation. According to Vine Deloria, Jr.:

> The ideology of civil rights, however, was anathema to the majority of Indians. In the past they had experienced so many betrayals through

policies which purported to give them legal and social "equality" that they suspected anyone who spoke of either equality or helping them to get into "the mainstream." The policy of terminating federal services to Indians, which had dominated the previous decade, was based upon giving Indians civil rights under the theory that by abolishing treaty rights, Indians would receive full citizenship . . . when black leaders spoke of the Indian reservations as rural ghettos, a chill went up the spines of Indians, comparable to that in the old days when the bugle rang across the hills. While some of the tribes had been moved from their ancestral homes, the majority of the tribes still lived in the lands of their origin. Far from considering their reservations as ghettos, they were determined to save the remnants of their homelands and, if possible, prevent any further intrusion of whites into them. . . . The tribes were concerned about their separate existence as dependent nations for whom the United States had a responsibility.[5]

As time wore on, however, a number of young Native Americans began to look upon some of the tactics of the civil rights movement as being useful. For a long time, resentment between whites and Indians had been festering in the state of Washington over fishing rights. The state had been infringing on tribal treaty fishing rights for years in the effort to keep the rivers running full of salmon for sport, rather than Indian, fishing. Sport fishing, in the end, supported Washington's tourist trade. While not quite that simple—the controversy involved all kinds of legal subtleties—the tribes of Washington nevertheless found themselves threatened economically, culturally, politically, and spiritually. In 1964, a small organization of Native Americans known as the National Indian Youth Council helped organize a series of "fish-ins" on Washington rivers to publicize the controversy and test state versus treaty rights. The state reacted harshly, beating and jailing Indians and destroying Indian property.[6]

Over the next ten years Native American protests increased in militancy. The whites responded with increased violence. In 1968, Canada restricted Indian movement back and forth across the border with the United States. By treaty, the Mohawks had been guaranteed free access to their relatives across the international borders. In response to the restrictions, a group of Mohawks blockaded the Cornwall Bridge in upstate New York. The police took them into custody and charged them with resisting arrest. The charges were dismissed. During that same year a group of Native Americans in Minneapolis began patrolling their section of the city and keeping a close watch for reported police discrimination and brutality toward Indians. Their patrols cut the Indian arrest rate significantly. This group would form the nucleus of the American Indian Movement, or AIM. In November 1969, more than three hundred Indians occupied Alcatraz Island in San Francisco Bay. After the San Francisco Indian Center burned down earlier in the year, Indians occupied and claimed the abandoned federal property on the presumed stipulation put in an Indian treaty that said abandoned federal lands would revert to Indian ownership. Richard Oakes, the Mohawk leader of the occupation, made plans for the occupation of several additional sites in California. Actually, the treaty basis for these takeovers was rather dubious. A Sioux treaty of 1868 did indeed contain a provision stating that abandoned American forts would revert to Indian ownership, but only a few of the activists were Sioux and none were duly elected tribal officials who could take administrative control of the property in the name of the tribe. Still, the takeovers continued, if for no other reason than to publicize the revival of Indian activism and notify whites that Indians were going to assert tribal rights wherever and whenever possible.[7]

The early 1970s saw a number of confrontations between Indians and whites based on Oakes' interpretation of tribal treaty rights. In 1970 the Pit River Reservation in California erupted in violence over fishing rights and land claims.[8] When state and federal law enforcement officers moved in, the scenes of violence were roughly reminiscent of Vietnam. Another violent confrontation occurred over the murder of Raymond Yellow Thunder in Gordon, Nebraska. Finally in 1972, Indian activists organized a massive march on Washington, D.C., known as the Trail of Broken Treaties. The caravan was to form on the West Coast and wind its way across the nation picking up followers as it went. It was to arrive in Washington during the final week of the presidential campaign.

Indians poured into the city. The bulk of them assembled at the Bureau of Indian Affairs building to await word regarding where they were to be housed during their stay in the capital. Eventually they were told that they were to be housed in the Department of the Interior auditorium. As they were leaving the BIA, guards began to push a number of people out the door. The young protesters turned on the guards and seized the building. The occupation of the BIA lasted for nearly a week before the Indians agreed to leave. In return, the federal government agreed not to prosecute the protesters. Extensive damage was done to the offices, but much of it was apparently done after the occupation, perhaps in an effort to discredit protest leaders, as well as the entire Native American movement itself.[9]

It was into this atmosphere of tension and turbulence that the Indian Vietnam veterans returned. Many immediately felt that instead of fighting for the government in a far-off country, they should have taken up arms against it in this land. They deeply felt the incongruity of their situation and experience. As one veteran related to Robin LaDue:

> I am a treaty fisherman, an American Indian and a Vietnam combat veteran. I've got three strikes against me before I ever start. I saw things in Vietnam I can't forget, people dying because of me. Then I came home to the reservation and I see my people die and I can't stop it. It's like a war zone all over again. Sometimes I feel like my whole life has been a war.[10]

Others foreswore their obligations as American soldiers to take up the causes of Native American activism. As Sidney Mills stated on October 13, 1968:

> I am Yakima and Cherokee Indian, and a man. For two years and four months, I've been a soldier in the United States Army. I served in combat in Vietnam—until critically wounded . . . I hereby renounce further obligation in service or duty to the United States Army . . . I have served the United States in a less compelling struggle in Vietnam and will not be restricted from doing less for my people within the United States . . . My decision is influenced by the fact that we have already buried Indian fishermen returned dead from Vietnam, while Indian fishermen live here without protection and under steady attack from the power processes of this Nation and the States of Washington and Oregon.

Mills went on to relate the story of Richard Sohappy:

> Sergeant Sohappy is back in Vietnam on his third tour of duty there. He was arrested three times in June for illegal net fishing, while home on recuperative furlough recovering from his fourth series of

combat wounds and while attempting to secure income for his large family. For his stand in Vietnam, this Nation awarded him a Silver Star and Bronze Star, among others. For fighting for his family and people, this Nation permitted a professional barber acting as Justice of the Peace to interpret his Treaty, to ignore his rights, and to impose punishment and record under criminal conviction.[11]

Said a Creek-Cherokee veteran:

I went into the army and to Vietnam because I'd seen the same John Wayne movies as everyone else and thought I was doing an honorable thing, that war was the "Indian way." And, of course, the government was saying at the time that we had this treaty—the SEATO treaty—to uphold. So I went . . . But when I got to Vietnam, I found that my job was to run missions into what everybody called "Indian country." That's what they called enemy territory . . . I woke up one morning fairly early in my tour and realized that instead of being a warrior like Crazy Horse, I was a scout used by the army to track him down. I was on the wrong side of everything I wanted to believe I was about . . . then I found out the SEATO treaty never even required the United States to do what it was doing in Southeast Asia. It was all a total lie. Besides, by then I'd figured out that even if it did, it didn't matter. Why was I fighting to uphold a U.S. treaty commitment halfway around the world when the United States was violating its treaty commitments to my own people and about 300 other Indian nations? . . . I was fighting the wrong people, pure and simple, and I've never gotten over it.

These veterans, along with numerous others, were experiencing what sociologists have termed "cognitive dissonance," and of the most extreme sort. This is when a person's values and philosophical beliefs turn out to be dramatically at odds with the operant realities he or she encounters. The Native Americans experienced guilt from surviving the war, compounded by guilt over having entered the U.S. military service in a time of deep political turmoil among their own people. Among many Native American Vietnam era veterans like the ones quoted above, this psychological disjuncture manifested itself primarily in aggressive political activism. And it seemed to coalesce at the most important Native American protest of the period: Wounded Knee II.

The background of the occupation and siege of Wounded Knee, South Dakota, is fairly well known.[12] Numerous authors have attempted to record the history leading up to the takeover and subsequent seventy-one-day occupation of the tiny village on the Pine Ridge Reservation. No one, it seems, has gone into the extent of veteran participation in the historic event or the military aspects of the siege from the inside; of those we can pick up only bits and pieces of information. As in all battles, there were personal as well as general views of the conflict. What we can determine is that Indian Vietnam veterans played an important part in the occupation and the defense of the village. Not only that, but the defensive arrangements made within Wounded Knee—makeshift as they were—actually held a most formidable opposing military force at bay for over two months and probably helped save many lives.

The occupation and siege of Wounded Knee resulted from a widespread disenchantment on the Pine Ridge Reservation with Bureau of Indian Affairs policies and the Oglala Lakota tribal president, Richard Wilson. Within a few months after taking office in early 1972, Wilson had been specifically accused of mismanagement of funds, fraud, and several other offenses ranging from refusing to publish the minutes of council meetings to denying certain Oglalas the rights of free assembly, due process, and protection from unreasonable searches and seizures.[13] The BIA was also accused of culpability in Wilson's mismanagement of tribal funds. Traditional Lakota elders were seen as Wilson's primary opponents because they had insisted for several years that the real foundation of the relationship between the Lakotas and the federal government was based on the Treaty of 1868 and that Wilson's government had simply become a BIA puppet authority. Wilson organized an auxiliary tribal police, known as the Goon Squad, to keep the traditional opposition in check. The Goon Squad broke up traditional assemblies, harassed individuals, and illegally searched traditional homes and vehicles.[14]

Oglala traditionals responded by forming the Oglala Sioux Civil Rights Organization and made an attempt to impeach Wilson. The impeachment process ultimately failed because Goon Squads impeded Oglalas from making their views heard. The group, in turn, called upon the American Indian Movement for protection and to counter the power of the auxiliary tribal police.[15] Wilson immediately cast his tribal foes and AIM not only as habitual malcontents but also as agitators against the ideal of Oglala tribal sovereignty. On November 10, 1972, he and the Oglala tribal council barred members of the American Indian Movement from using tribal property on the basis that the group threatened "the sovereign dignity of the Oglala Sioux Tribe."[16]

When AIM and the members of the Oglala Sioux Civil Rights Organization occupied Wounded Knee on February 27, 1973, one of their avowed purposes was to produce a crisis in the Oglala tribal government. In effect, they were protesting the existence of Wilson's centralized form of constitutional government on the basis that the 1868 Sioux treaty had been made between two sovereigns. Wilson's government was based on an "imposed" constitution that had been instituted in 1935 under the supervision of the U.S. Department of the Interior and was therefore not the same sovereign Lakota-Dakota entity that participated in the 1868 treaty negotiations. It followed then that if the Sioux Nation was sovereign, the people had the right to establish the type of government they wanted. Wilson was not, according to this line of reasoning, a legitimate tribal authority. He therefore could not have authority over the lives of the Oglala people. The Wounded Knee protesters entered Wounded Knee to declare their separation from the Oglala constitution of 1935 and stated during the siege that they were establishing a sovereign Sioux Nation under the treaty of 1868.[17]

Wilson and various federal agencies moved quickly to surround the protesters in the village in an effort to contain what Wilson concluded was an insurrection led by outside agitators. The Federal Bureau of Investigation brought in helicopters, armored personnel carriers, and enough military assault rifles to equip Wilson's tribal police. The BIA police and U.S. marshals joined in the operation. Both sides dug in for a prolonged siege.

The defenders of Wounded Knee were armed primarily with .22s, hunting rifles of 30.06 caliber, and a few smallbore shotguns.[18] Among the collection of arms carried by the Wounded Knee defenders was an AK-47 of Czech origin. Although the *Arizona Republic,* as did other conservative newspapers, made a great deal of the existence of this particular weapon, asserting that it was of Chinese Communist manufacture and therefore AIM was a Communist front organization, the AK-47 came into very little, if any, use at Wounded Knee, 7.63 mm ammunition being very expensive and hard to obtain in the United States.[19]

The warriors inside Wounded Knee established a perimeter around the village in two concentric lines. They built bunkers and dug fighting holes and trenches in rough imitation of those built by American forces in Vietnam. Apparently, the trenches and fighting holes were laid out in such a manner that these fortifications allowed defenders to overlap and support the fire of the other positions around the perimeter. The Wounded Knee defenders, of course, had no access to a military supply dump and had to create fortifications out of materials already available in the village. Bunkers were constructed with plywood and old wood boards. Sandbags were created from pillowcases and garbage bags.[20] Visitor Angela Davis, a California college professor and leader in the Black Power movement, said that Wounded Knee looked "just like a Vietnam battlefield out there."[21]

By contrast, the FBI agents, federal marshals, BIA police, and Richard Wilson's auxiliary police were armed with assault rifles, tear gas, flack jackets, searchlights, flares, and Starlight scopes through which they could see movement inside the Wounded Knee defenses at night. Their bunkers were made from real sandbags and railroad ties. They were well-fed and well-clothed, and every other night they slept in motel rooms.[22] They could also concentrate a heavy amount of firepower on the village defenses. Several witnesses reported that during an average firefight at Wounded Knee, literally thousands of rounds were exchanged. A reporter for *Akwesasne Notes*, a Native American newspaper, tape-recorded the sounds of what he estimated to have been more than 7,500 bullets being fired into the village perimeter. When food was airlifted into the perimeter the resulting exchange of gunfire amounted to around 4,000 rounds of ammunition. It was during this particular battle that one of the Wounded Knee defenders, Frank Clearwater, was mortally wounded. During a single engagement that lasted two days and claimed the life of another Wounded Knee defender and Vietnam veteran, Lawrence "Buddy" Lamont, the two sides were said to have exchanged nearly 40,000 rounds.[23] Since the military assault rifles carried by the FBI agents and the U.S. marshals have much higher rates of fire than .22s, 30.06s, and .410 shotguns, and since the federal officers had a much better resupply system, it can be asserted with a great deal of certainty that the great majority of those 40,000 bullets were fired into the Wounded Knee defenses, rather than outward toward the federal positions. That only two of Wounded Knee's defenders were killed and a handful wounded can be credited to those who organized and set up the village's defenses. The Wounded Knee fortifications withstood several intensive federal fusillades without crumbling. According to Roger Iron Cloud, a Vietnam and Wounded Knee veteran, "We took more bullets in seventy-one days than I took in two years in Vietnam."[24] Significantly, most of the men who dug the trenches, patrolled the perimeter, built the bunkers, and stood long watches in the fighting holes learned their military skills in the jungles and rice paddies of Vietnam.

Native American Vietnam veterans had indeed channeled their feelings of betrayal into aggressive political activism and attempted to reconstruct the actuality of indigenous traditional warrior societies. A number of AIM leaders, including John Trudell (Santee Dakota), Carter Camp (Ponca), Stanley Holder (Wichita), Bill Means (Oglala Lakota), and John Arbuckle (Omaha), were combat veterans. Another Oglala Vietnam veteran, Stanley Wilson, headed security forces at Wounded Knee.[25] A former president of the Oglala Lakota Nation, Enos Poorbear, a World War II combat veteran himself, related the following about his son, who was wounded while defending Wounded Knee:

> It ain't right. My boy was a paratrooper in Vietnam and he got a purple heart fighting for his country. Now federal marshals have shot him. I tell you, it ain't right. In 1890, the Bluecoats shot down our people here and they gave 18 of the soldiers the Congressional Medal of Honor for shooting mostly children and women, some of them pregnant—if them soldiers got medals, then my boy ought to get a Medal of Honor, too, for getting shot here.[26]

Akwesasne Notes summed up the connection between Vietnam veterans and Wounded Knee:

> The young men defending Wounded Knee are militarily skilled and trained. Almost all are Vietnam veterans, and most of those were in the Special Forces—the Green Berets. In Southeast Asia, they learned about guerilla warfare, courtesy of the U.S. Government, and now they are using what they learned for their own people.[27]

POLITICAL ADJUSTMENT

As has been fully documented by authors Ward Churchill, Jim Vander Wall, Peter Matthiessen, and others, the political problems and outright armed confrontations between Indians and federal officials did not end with the evacuation of Wounded Knee. For several years following the occupation and siege of Wounded Knee, federal agents conducted covert, Cointelpro-type operations to discredit and eventually to put behind bars the entire leadership of the American Indian Movement.[28]

Obviously the federal government, as well as the then leadership of the Oglala Lakota Nation, thought that AIM was a serious threat. And it may well have been thought of as such because much of AIM's membership had been trained in military arms and tactics in the school of the Vietnam War.

As sociologist and Vietnam veteran Wilbur J. Scott has pointed out, there is a political, as well as a psychological, dimension to Vietnam veteran readjustment. As part of a broader hypothesis, Scott points out that veteran readjustment, or adjustment, takes place on numerous levels:

> Veterans of all wars must readapt to civilian life once their military service has ended. This calls for several tricky adjustments. They must recover from their wounds, recognize that the strategies of survival in the combat zone are inappropriate in the civilian sphere, incorporate their war experiences into their civilian selves, and reestablish their familial and occupational careers. Veterans carry out some of these adjustments privately within a network of friends and family. Others are carried out in public arenas that process the experiences of veterans and the costs of going to war.[29]

In short, involvement in political issues—even, or perhaps especially, aggressive political participation—specific to their group (Native American, Vietnam veteran, or Native American Vietnam veteran) may be part and parcel of the readjustment process. Native American Vietnam veterans certainly found a number of political issues and causes to be involved in upon their return from the war. In the RCS study, slightly more than 30 percent of the veterans surveyed became associated with national Native American organizations—the American Indian Movement, National Indian Youth Council, and the National Congress of American Indians—that have been and are deeply involved in the political relationships between the federal government and Native American tribes. On the tribal level, approximately 11 percent have sought and gained tribal office and over 60 percent regularly vote in tribal elections. This level of voting participation is only slightly higher than what they demonstrate outside their own tribes (52 percent) in local, state, and federal elections. Indian Vietnam veterans have also joined numerous Indian veterans' groups—Native American Veterans' Association (NAVA), Vietnam Era Veterans' Inter-Tribal Association, and several all-Indian American Legion and Veterans of Foreign Wars posts, to name a few—that have been active in publicly promoting veterans' issues specific to Native Americans. By 1989, the Vietnam Era Veterans' Inter-tribal Association could count more than one thousand members scattered throughout the United States in a number of chapters. The veterans have also joined other national veterans' groups like the Disabled American Veterans, Order of the Purple Heart, Vietnam Veterans of America, and others which specifically deal with veterans' concerns. While some of these organizations certainly attract members for social reasons, they nevertheless actively take political stands. Native American veterans of the Vietnam War have also testified before Congress on veterans' and Indian veterans' issues and have participated in getting PTSD placed in the American Psychiatric Association's *Diagnostic and Statistical Manual* (DSM-III), building the Vietnam Memorial, and publicizing the Agent Orange controversy. There were also Indian veterans who testified in the "Winter Soldier" investigations for the Vietnam Veterans Against the War in the 1970s; these were a series of staged confessions of war crimes.

If this level of political participation says anything, it bespeaks a healthy interest in political institutions and something of Indian veteran attitudes toward the federal government in particular. Their frustration with, and wariness of, the federal government is particularly pronounced. More than 80 percent of those who answered the RCS survey stated flatly that the federal government had not pursued just policies toward their people. Many of them also indicated that they felt the federal government was failing to own up to its responsibilities toward all Vietnam veterans. Fully 79 percent of them said that they felt the federal government had not treated Vietnam veterans as a whole fairly. Or, as one man said: "Man, the government don't give a damn about any of us. We fight its wars and don't get shit." Still another stated: "I'm a Indian and a Vietnam vet; that's two strikes against you when you need something from the feds." They feel that government attitudes toward them reflect those of the dominant society. The RCS survey revealed that a healthy majority of those who answered the questionnaire (66 percent) felt that non-Indians did not have positive attitudes toward Vietnam veterans in general. Not only that, but 67 percent said they felt that non-Indians still held basically negative attitudes toward Indians.

Their reasons for feeling this way were not only rooted in the climate of racism that has traditionally surrounded their home communities, but also in the way they were treated personally by whites upon their return from the war. "When I was growing up," said a Dakota, "the local cowboys used to call us everything from blankethead to prairie nigger." During the Wounded Knee siege, AIM leader Russell Means stated accurately that "the South Dakota mentality toward Indians made the Ku Klux Klan look like Girl Scouts."[30] When the veterans returned from Vietnam, their greeting from the whites was hardly what they expected. It seemed as if American society, of which they were only a peripheral part to begin with, had sent them to war and then rejected them for actually serving. Several stated that they were called "baby-killers" and "war-mongers." One man described his arrival back in the "world" with a great deal of bitterness:

> We fought a white man's war, you know, and the first thing that happens when I get back is that some white kid, a girl, at the L.A. airport spits on me.

White American society angered another Native American veteran in a different way: "The white dudes stayed in school, you know, and we fought the war. They don't know nothing about anything except what they get out of a book. But they get the jobs." The idea that they have had two strikes against them in the dominant society—being American Indians and Vietnam veterans—is seemingly supported by the fact that their unemployment rate is very high. The RCS study revealed that of the 170 Indian Vietnam veterans surveyed, 45.7 percent were unemployed by the end of 1986. They attributed their unemployment rate to racism and a general negative attitude toward Vietnam veterans, and not to a lack of job qualifications. They certainly had a point: nearly 89 percent of them qualified as skilled laborers and/or white-collar workers. In addition, they have apparently taken advantage of the Vietnam veterans' G.I. Bill in regard to education. By 1990, 94 percent of the RCS informants had high school educational equivalencies and 62 percent had attended college or technical schools above the high school level.

Since most of them think that the federal government, as well as the dominant society, has not done enough on their behalf, they have largely directed their political energies toward tribal government. A number of them remain critical of their own tribal governments for not doing enough for veterans, or for being unrepresentative of traditional tribal values. Over and over different individuals pointed out that their tribal governments were more concerned with economic development than with preserving tribal culture. On the other hand, several of them argued that the tribes would be exceedingly hard-pressed to preserve culture without some form of economic development. "What can I do?" asked an Apache Vietnam veteran. "I ain't got a job here [on his reservation]; but to get one I got to move away from my family and my culture. We need to get economic development." A number of them (43 percent in the RCS survey) have said that their own tribal governments are not paying enough attention to veteran-specific problems. Again, since very often veterans' concerns center on employment, several tribal leaders have indicated that some form of economic development would undoubtedly help alleviate their veterans' considerable financial difficulties, and thus better their overall readjustment.

SOCIAL AND CULTURAL ADJUSTMENTS

Despite their general frustration with the perceived negative attitudes toward them on the part of the federal, state, and tribal bureaucracies and the dominant society, Native American Vietnam veterans feel that other Indians look upon them in a more positive light. Vietnam veterans were readily accepted in the Red Power movement immediately upon their return home, in spite of their prior service in the armed forces. In fact, there seemed to have been a genuine feeling among many Indian activists that Vietnam veterans felt a special sense of betrayal that motivated them to do battle with federal authority. Several Indian veterans were put into positions of leadership in the movement itself because they had already demonstrated their courage and perseverance in a dangerous situation. In a sense, they were honored in the movement of the late 1960s and early 1970s in a very traditional manner. Who better to lead in combat than those who have known, yet survived, its terrible consequences?

Of course, not all Native American veterans of the Vietnam War joined in the political movements or protests of the period. Political activity was not, it seems, enough to heal their wounded souls. They had been engaged in a genuine, human-created disaster and felt not only survivor's guilt but a strong sense of betrayal. They seemed to feel that their experiences were absolutely meaningless within the context of the larger American society. In this sense they shared a common ground with numerous non-Indian veterans of the war. The VA study *Legacies of Vietnam* mentioned this feeling of betrayal:

Many combat veterans continue to dwell on the belief that they were sent to fight a war they were not intended to win . . . They often emphasize public antipathy to the war and feel that their sacrifice was not appreciated . . . More important, perhaps, is the fact that American society has created an environment in which men who were exposed to combat continue to define the experience in a negative way.[31]

There can be no doubt whatsoever that, upon their immediate return from Vietnam, many Native American veterans of the war looked upon their combat experiences as being wholly negative and the ultimate cause of their emotional suffering. And their emotional scars were deep. Said one Native American veteran:

> I saw faces, you know, looking at me. Their hands up like they were telling secrets. I had a rage . . . Sometimes I thought that the top of my head would just blow off.

Another said:

> I couldn't get the war out of my head. So, I stuck my head in a bottle. I hated everybody except when I was drunk. It took me five years, five years, man, to get straight, and now I've been sober for quite a while.

Other vets still are drinking.
One veteran engaged in daredevil activities to relieve the pressure:

> I rode bulls, I drove stock cars, I piled up my own cars and a couple of motorcycles. I drank all the time . . . Goddamn war put me in a world of shit. I think now that I had some sort of death wish.

Another veteran told of how one particular incident brought him to the point of suicide:

> Once one of my nephews came up to me one day, stuck this toy M-14 at me . . . and all I remember seeing . . . he was creeping up on me, I was sitting there and he came up and all I remember seeing was a shadow and that barrel . . . and I reached down and I grabbed him and almost killed my nephew. I was going to smash him and I missed him with the rifle butt. It was just a natural reaction, just like that . . . and my sister, if she hadn't come in and yelled at me, I think I might

have hurt him. She told me, "damn, you're crazy, that war made you crazy." I thought I must be crazy . . . I went out and bought me a pistol, and I was so angry, the damn war fucked me up so I took the pistol and stuck it in my mouth, I was going to kill myself. Nobody gives a shit about me, nobody cares about me, my family . . . my family is calling me crazy, and people don't respect me. I have nothing to come home to.[32]

Flashbacks plagued one man:

You can be sitting there, talking, then all of a sudden, like a TV comes on in your head and you re-vision it. You know, like watching a movie, a Sam Peckinpah movie. You see all this blood and gore and you can't get it out of your mind. You don't want to die over here because you're back over here but you feel like you're going to die. It makes you sweat. It makes you taste again. It makes you feel everything you felt the first time. You smell cordite, you smell gunpowder. You smell blood. You smell intestines. It's everything you see. You can see and smell it again. I have flashbacks. I have times of depression. Other than my wife, or a few select friends, I'm beginning to make, there are very few people in this world I trust. And when you can't trust people in the world, you're in big trouble.[33]

Rage, drinking, drug abuse, feelings of depression, nightmares, and flashbacks were the most common problems that Native American combat veterans seemed to experience when they came home. As shown in Table 6, the RCS survey of 170 Indian Vietnam veterans found that 138 (or 81.1 percent) said that they experienced mild to severe problems with alcohol consumption; 54 with other substances; 136 with depression; 130 with sleep intrusions; 108 with flashbacks; and 121 with extreme feelings of rage. This very high rate of problems associated with the readjustment process following their combat experiences, however, is offset to a certain extent by the fact that some of them claim to have worked through, resolved, or have adjusted somewhat to their situations. The second group of numbers in Table 6 represents those who have stated that they have resolved in some fashion problems with alcohol, drugs, depression, sleep intrusions, flashbacks, and rage. The third group of numbers is important. It shows that of those veterans who have seemingly worked through these problems, a large percentage of them have also participated in traditional tribal ceremonies designed

TABLE 6. Problems Associated with PTSD in American Indian Vietnam Veterans: Frequency, Resolution of Problems, and Participation in Tribal Ceremonies

Type of Problem, Mild to Severe	Frequency		Persons who claimed to have resolved or worked through problem		Persons who claimed to have resolved or worked through problem *and* have taken part in ceremonies	
	No.	Percentage	No.	Percentage	No.	Percentage
Alcohol	138	81.1	56	40.5	23	41.0
Drugs	54	31.7	18	33.3	15	83.3
Depression	136	80.0	34	25.0	24	70.5
Sleep Intrusions	130	76.4	35	26.9	23	65.7
Flashbacks	108	63.5	28	25.9	22	78.5
Anger-Rage	121	71.1	26	21.4	22	84.6

to either honor a combat survivor and/or heal a returning warrior of his battlefield trauma. In other words, a high correlation apparently exists between the resolution of their problems and the participation in tribal rituals connected with warfare and/or ceremonies of healing. The return to their older traditions may very well have aided their readjustment— just as they were and are intended to do.

A good deal of testimony from the veterans themselves lends support to this hypothesis. A Kiowa veteran related the following:

My people honored me as a warrior. We had a feast and my parents and grandparents thanked everyone who prayed for my safe return. We had a Special and I remembered as we circled the drum I got a feeling of pride. I felt good inside because that's the way the Kiowa people tell you that you've done well.

One Cherokee veteran living in Oklahoma City went—at the insistence of his wife—to see a Cherokee doctor more than one hundred miles away. The Cherokee medicine man purified him in a Going to the Water ceremony and gave him some "fixed" tobacco to aid him in the future. "Fixed" tobacco is that which has been made sacred—"the prayers are already in it." Another man, a Menominee veteran in Wisconsin told of how he presented an eagle feather to another veteran at an intertribal pow-wow. The recipient, a Sioux from South Dakota, was paid one of the highest honors a Menominee could bestow on another person. Only a very few people in Menominee society can publicly present eagle feathers to others. Those who can do so are proven warriors, medicine people, elders, and some tribal officials. "I felt honored by giving that feather away," the veteran stated. "That's the Indian way."

Some Indian veterans took part in ceremonies both before they went to Southeast Asia and after they returned home. These ceremonies ranged from the relatively simple to the highly elaborate. The Cherokee veteran mentioned above said that an elderly uncle awoke him before dawn to watch the sunrise and smoke a pipe of tobacco on the last day of leave before being sent overseas. His uncle said a few prayers and gave the informant some protective medicine. A Navajo veteran was given a Blessing Way ceremony prior to his overseas tour. This ceremony, which lasts for several days, is a highly formalized narrative of the Navajo creation legend. It is also a curing ritual, complete with sand paintings and songs, intended to make sure an individual is in harmony with his or her surroundings and people. It was utilized in the case of this particular veteran as protective medicine.

Upon his return home he was given a Squaw Dance or Enemy Way ceremony. This four-to-seven-day ritual involves the recital of the story of the Hero Twins who killed the monsters of the world in order to make a safe place for human beings. As the story goes:

> The Twins were successful in their attempts to kill all the Monsters. However, in the process of destroying the Monsters, the twins abused their special powers and weapons and disrupted the harmony in nature by killing some people. As a consequence the Twins became ill and misfortunes set in upon them. Another Holy Being recognized that the Twins had put themselves out of harmony with nature by killing, and thus need a special ceremony to restore them to harmony. Thus was born the first "Enemy Way."[34]

According to the Navajo veteran:

> When I got back I had a lot of trouble. My mother even called in one of our medicine men. It cost them but my folks had an Enemy Way done for me. It's a pretty big thing . . . It snapped me out of it.

Another Navajo veteran had an Enemy Way done for him even though he thought that he had adjusted to civilian life fairly well and was skeptical of the ceremony's ultimate benefits and wary of its monetary cost:

> As far as my relatives and my home community are concerned, they accepted me. I didn't volunteer to go over to Vietnam—I was drafted. I was forced to go. I went in, I served, I came back. My relatives and immediate family accepted me. They noticed I was experiencing a lot of social problems. I wasn't the same. I didn't really think I'd changed that much. That's when they started talking about the Enemy Way ceremony. The Enemy Way ceremony is a seven-day ceremony. It's a ceremony which allows you to adjust back into society. I didn't completely believe in the ceremony, but I went through it. It did purify me. It's real, it's not something that is just symbolic. I found that it's real.

He went on to describe the Enemy Way as a community effort to bring the returning warrior back to a state of harmony:

> For an Enemy Way ceremony to happen, it takes the whole community. There is a lot of money involved, gift giving, it's a seven day ceremony, there is a lot of preparation. The last three days of the ceremony is when it is most busy. There are several medicine men involved, it takes a lot of work, there's a lot of fasting, a certain type of food that you have to eat. There's a lot of herb gathering. It's a tedious ceremony. It's very tiresome. There is a lot of songs involved and prayers. I personally feel it's a really good outlet. It's something that the Navajo people still have. They have retained it. Many of their culture and tradition come through that ceremony. I felt that it's a good thing that we still have it. Every summer we still have it. There are still a number of veterans going through it. There are some veterans who are going through it twice. There is a number of veterans that really gained from that ceremony. It's recognized by many of the doctors in our home community, white and Indian doctors, and I just hope we perpetuate the ceremony in some way.[35]

In effect, the ritual removes the stigma of death and the disharmony caused by war. Other Native American veterans were honored with special dances, peyote ceremonies, and prayer meetings. All of the individuals who took part in these ceremonies had the strong support of their extended family groups. In fact, few, if any, of these ceremonials could have been arranged without the intercession of certain family members. In regard to their ability to help in the healing process and give the individual veteran a sense of well-being and self-esteem, we again have the testimony of the veterans themselves and the observations made by witnesses. Beatrice Chevalier, writing in 1982 for *Inter-Com*, a national Native American newsletter, described one veteran's feelings after experiencing a Wisconsin pow-wow during which a special warrior song was sung for returning Vietnam veterans:

> Now, he feels good about himself, he knows where he stands within himself. The very thing that makes him proud and sets his ego soaring is the Indian veteran songs. This makes him special for awhile, but the memories of war are a constant invasion of his well being.[36]

The pow-wow songs held a great deal of meaning for another veteran:

> The songs had some special meaning for me. I felt tears in my eyes several times . . . thinking of my cousins [two of the man's cousins were killed in Vietnam], and I just wish they were here to participate. So these pow-wows really do mean a lot to me. I feel like I'm here representing my tribe, the Indians around the country, and also veterans in general, the blacks, the whites, Americans . . . all those veterans who have served. I think that we are also honoring them. So it gives me special pride to go step out there, hold a feather . . . it really gives me pride."

Another stated:

> The Indian ceremony of getting back to my roots . . . listening to the old songs . . . and the feeling of tranquility that it does send in me . . . [helped me] because basically, I like to be at peace with myself . . . I now have peace of mind.

He went on to say that the pow-wows:

> make me feel not as white people look at me, like I'm a killer, like I'm dirt . . . The Indians don't treat me like I'm dirt . . . it embarrasses me when they honor me because I'm just like anyone . . . I'm not treated like a killer . . . The ceremonies do it—the songs—the old songs.

One veteran said that the ceremonies "saved my life," a statement commonly heard from others. Those who have been able to participate in these tribal ceremonies apparently have found some degree of psychological and spiritual solace in their performance. Perhaps of equal psychological value is the fact that many of these men received a certain amount of social prestige as a result of their wartime service. Although the idea of gaining status in a Native American tribe by entering the armed forces and "fighting a white man's war" seems incongruous, it is nevertheless understandable. Indeed, the healing of war trauma seems to be as much a social and cultural process as it is individual and psychological.

The social value of these and other tribal ceremonies cannot be overestimated. Nearly every Indian society in America possesses rituals of renewal and restoration, and, although they are often ignored as products of mysticism, they serve specific functions. Ceremonies like the Sun Dance, the Green Corn Dance, the Blessing Way of the Navajos, and the Stomp Dances of the Creeks, Seminoles, and Cherokees reaffirm group cohesion, reassert the individual participant's value in the community, and attest to the tribal obligation to the Creator. Whether or not the individual fought in an unpopular war matters little, because the purpose of the ceremony is to restore the tribal bond.

The veterans, simply by taking part in these time-honored ceremonies, essentially have demonstrated a commitment to their maintenance. Thus, they share with their relatives an effort to preserve cultural continuity. Without these rituals, taboos, songs, and many other aspects of culture too numerous to mention, the tribal identity could not be maintained. In short, the tribe's special place in the world depends on the continued existence of these rites. The individual who keeps tradition is indeed a respected person, for he or she has made a contribution to the social cohesion of the group. Moreover, a person who honors tradition has created a special relationship with the tribal elders who conduct and sponsor these rituals. Several tribes in the United States—the Kiowas, the Comanches, the Cheyennes, and others—have syncretized service in the American armed forces with several of their own warrior traditions and societies. For these tribes, certain functions can only be performed by veterans. At many northern-style pow-wows, for example, if a dancer drops an eagle feather, it can only be retrieved by a veteran who performs a dance accompanied by the singing of an appropriate honor song. At some tribal gatherings, veterans are still asked to count coup or tell a war story before any ceremonies can begin.

As psychologist John P. Wilson has pointed out, many Vietnam veterans experience an emotional phenomenon known as "age acceleration."[37] According to Joel Osler Brende and Erwin Randolph Parson, Vietnam veterans have a:

> perception of their own ages as paradoxically both excessively young and excessively old. On the one hand, they still feel like the teenagers they were when they first went to Vietnam. On the other hand, they feel as if they were prematurely aged by the experiences they endured.[38]

In combat, a person is exposed to the deaths of others who are of a similar age. These very young, inexperienced men were, in effect, forced to undergo the kinds of emotions that most nonveterans only experience toward the end of their lives. Seeing members of one's peer group die forces an individual to think about—perhaps dwell on—one's own mortality. The combat veteran, then, is old before his time. And, since American society as a whole seems to abhor even the idea of aging, age acceleration is dealt with as a very negative aspect of the combat experience.

But in Native American tribal societies, growing old has a very different meaning. Elders function as links to the traditions, customs, and rituals that give identity to the tribe. As children dislocated by 1950s federal Indian policies, Native American Vietnam veterans formed very close bonds with the most senior members of their communities. The RCS survey found that Indian Vietnam veterans had a deep respect for their traditions and for those who understood the value of traditional ways. Not only that, but maturity and experience are normally equated with wisdom in tribal societies. Thus the Vietnam veterans' combat experiences gave them a degree of knowledge about a subject few others are even conversant with; and because they are so knowledgeable, they obtain a certain degree of wisdom and respect. It could be argued that this was certainly the case at Wounded Knee, when the Indian activists there followed veterans like Stanley Holder, Buddy Lamont, and others in digging the bunkers and trenches that held off the besieging federal officers. In short, their age acceleration has been treated in a positive light. A Winnebago elder at a pow-wow in Wisconsin stated it best. Just before the performance of a veterans' honor song, he said: "We honor our veterans for their bravery and because by seeing death on the battlefield they truly know the greatness of life."

In addition to being honored and perhaps purged of the taint of war, several Native American Vietnam veterans have been aided by what can only be called a social absorption of combat-related trauma. A return to the ways in which traditional Cherokee communities in Oklahoma function helps to illustrate this salient point. As related in chapter 4, young Cherokee males are often forced out of their communities for a time by the lure of economic opportunity and the absence of social rewards at home. When they finally return—perhaps after military service—they are resocialized and the community elders listen to the newly returned younger men's adventures and relate those adventures "to the ancient matrix of Cherokee knowledge conveyed through myth and Indian medicine."[39] As a Cherokee veteran said of his return from Vietnam:

After I got home, my uncles sat me down and had me tell them what it was all about. One of them had been in the service in World War II and knew what war was like. We talked about what went on over there, about the killing and the waste, and one of my uncles said that was why God's laws are against war. They never really talked about those kind of things with me before.

This particular Cherokee was ritually cleansed and welcomed back in the community without reservation. Most important was that his experiences in Vietnam were eventually shared on an intellectual level by the community and tended to confirm the Cherokee belief that war was the ultimate in evil. On a personal level, the veteran himself was never told that his actions in war were either disruptive or improper in the Cherokee sense of order. His entrance into the service and his participation in the war were not viewed as political statements. Entering the military is just one thing that young men have to do. The Cherokee's personal bravery and service were cheered, but the war itself, simply because it was a war, was considered a particularly vile human activity. Since it was a vile experience and he was a relative, he had to be relieved of the terrible spell the war had placed upon him. Otherwise, the entire community could become tainted. Distributing the burden of his trauma thus became a community project.

There is every reason to believe that a number of other tribes saw their returning veterans in exactly the same light. A Hopi veteran said that the male members of his mother's side of the family took over the responsibility of listening to his experiences in Vietnam and preparing a purification ceremony for him. A Cheyenne said that he had to tell and retell his stories about combat in Vietnam to his relatives until "everybody knew what I did over there."

It has become increasingly clear that, despite their combat experiences, general dissatisfaction with federal and state Indian policies, and the dominant society's attitudes toward them, several of the Indian Vietnam veterans have developed a more positive view of their duty in Southeast Asia. According to one, "I wouldn't trade that time for anything. Being in the war taught me how to survive." A few others, including those who had seen very heavy combat, felt their wartime experiences had given them knowledge and abilities over and above those of their nonveteran peers. In short, several of them have become reasonably satisfied that their sacrifices in Vietnam had indeed had some meaning—an attitude that appears to have eluded most of the other veterans. One Cheyenne veteran summed it up in a revealing statement: "I'm proud of our warrior status."

It should not be concluded that all American Indian veterans of the Vietnam War automatically have been given status and ceremonies and, therefore, are all well-adjusted war survivors. Many Indian veterans now live in cities far away from their tribal communities. Others have been simply forgotten even among their own people. Some have not received the benefits of ceremonial adjustment because their rituals of warfare have been lost or stripped away by government policies.

As has been demonstrated, both ceremonialism and recognition have aided a number of Indian veterans in making the transition from war to peace and have helped them work through the many problems associated with war-induced trauma. In a broader context, it is possible that ceremonialism might be of benefit to non-Indian veterans. Non-Indians have several cultural features, including ceremonies, associated with warfare, although sometimes they are not viewed as such.

For example, Franklin D. Roosevelt's famous speech requesting Congress to declare war on Japan in 1941 was more ceremonial than political. The United States was already in a shooting war in the North Atlantic in 1941; the beleaguered American troops in the Pacific were certainly not awaiting a formal declaration of hostilities to fire on the attacking Japanese. Roosevelt's speech and the subsequent declaration of war were the rituals by which American society as a whole crossed the line between war and peace. In a like manner, the formal surrenders and the homecoming parades ceremoniously brought World War II to an end. It must be remembered that one of the chief complaints of returning Vietnam veterans was that there were no ceremonies, either at the beginning or the end, to move American society into war and back to peace again.[40] The American ceremonies that closed World War II not only celebrated the return of the warriors but also linked those veterans with a historic past and the possibility of a glorious future. Elderly veterans of past American conflicts marched in the parades next to those just back home from the Pacific and Europe. Politicians quoted great American leaders during war—George Washington, Abraham Lincoln, Woodrow Wilson. Bands played patriotic music and schoolchildren, symbolizing America's bright future, waved small American flags.

Another important part of veteran adjustment after a war such as Vietnam concerns the status a community gives its returning warriors. The recognition given to Indian Vietnam veterans in some Indian communities did not seem to involve political questions, at least those questions regarding the how and why of the war itself. Many Indians, in fact, thought the war neither justified nor honorable. But these political issues were not as important as the issues of social and cultural continuity. Some Indian veterans were viewed in their home communities as having gained wisdom out of living through a truly horrible experience. Others were seen as heroes, even though the war itself was not viewed as a particularly heroic venture. The importance of tribal continuity, of healing a troubled kinsman, and of absorbing war-related trauma within the society in order to gain harmony within the group outweighs almost any other political consideration.[41] In effect, a community's attempt to heal veteran trauma promotes community cohesion and sense of purpose. Thus, the war had some positive effects and gave a degree of meaning to the veterans' sacrifices in combat. *Legacies of Vietnam*, the Veterans Administration's study of Southeast Asia war veterans, mentions a phenomenon much like this one in connection with non-Indian veterans from small towns. The study notes that a minority of them felt the war was an "affirmative" experience. While it does not attempt to uncover the reasons behind the positive outlooks of small-town non-Indian veterans, *Legacies* does offer some theories:

> The small town Vietnam veterans may have left and returned to a community where service to one's country was considered worthy of respect, even during an unpopular war. Returning combat veterans may more frequently have been regarded as heroes in small towns. And, veterans' doubts about their role may have been mitigated by the attitudes of the community and the welcome they received. Perhaps there is something about small city life that protects combat veterans from dwelling on the traumatic aspects of their combat experiences and encourages them to see military service as a part of life rather than as an inexplicable intrusion into the normal course of things.[42]

In essence, it appears that some non-Indian communities absorb war-related trauma on a societal level in a somewhat similar manner to how many Native American tribes deal with the phenomenon. There was certainly an effort on the part of the federal government to promote parades and other rituals during the Gulf War in order to avoid the social and cultural mistakes made during the war in Vietnam. President George Bush said as much in several speeches explaining to the American public how Operation Desert Storm would be carried out. On the other hand, the white American middle-class veteran seems to remain rather skeptical of the notion of spiritual healing. And since American Christian traditions have tended to lessen the importance of ceremonies that promote group cohesion in favor of salvation on an individual basis, the idea of communal spiritual healing might very well be nonexistent among many non-Indian groups.

CONTINUED HEALING

It must be emphasized that healing war-related trauma is not done at a certain point in time with a single ceremony. One of the strengths of Native American healing is that Indian medicine fully understands the fact that trauma is a recurring illness. As Native American psychologists Don Johnson and Robin LaDue conclude:

> It must be clearly understood, acknowledged and accepted that many of the healing ceremonies are not cures, but simply a part of the healing process provided through the entire community. The trauma is a point on the circle of life that must be passed through over and over again . . . The medicine person takes the circle and the community's support to the injured person through the appropriate ceremony . . . It is recognized that each time one returns to the trauma point on the medicine circle there will be some deflection of the path. Here we depend upon the effects of past healing and repetition of appropriate ceremonial healing.[43]

Thus it is recognized that Native American veterans will have to continue to participate in community ceremonies so that they will be able to adjust to their war experiences. Not only that, but with the continuance of these ceremonies comes the greater chance that more veterans will be able to participate in them. "All I have to do is have patience," said one Native American traditional healer with typical Indian humor, "and I'll get more patients." Ultimately, complete healing will come as a person grows older and becomes wiser. For Native American veterans of the Vietnam War, a more complete understanding of the older traditions of warriorhood has undoubtedly helped along the process of their readjustment. They are fast becoming elders themselves and perhaps better able to subordinate their egos to the continuity of their societies and cultures—exactly as the warriors did in the past. As one veteran said:

I had to have a purpose in life . . . the old warrior instinct came back and I had to preserve the people, preserve my family . . . You protect them first, you do all you can. Your life is to be given for them.

The Native American Vietnam veterans are finally returning from the war and are on the path that leads them back to a better understanding of who they are. For some the cycle has not yet been completed. Many others, however, have completed the circle and truly understand, as did their warrior ancestors, that all life is sacred.

NOTES

1. FORGOTTEN WARRIORS

1. The quotations used in this text, unless otherwise noted, are taken from my field notes and tape recordings of interviews with veterans and tribal elders, letters written to me, or from statements written on the 170 questionnaires returned from the survey done for the American Indian Working Group, Readjustment Counseling Service, Veterans Administration. To protect the privacy of the individuals quoted I have refrained from using their names.

2. Tom Holm, "Indian Veterans of the Vietnam War: Restoring Harmony Through Tribal Ceremony," *Four Winds* 3 (Autumn 1982): 34–37.

3. "Vietnam Era Veterans' Inter-Tribal Association: Chronological History of the Organization," *First National Vietnam Era Veterans' Convention Agenda and Program*, Shawnee, Oklahoma, November 5–7, 1987.

4. See especially Robert K. Thomas, "The Redbird Smith Movement," in William N. Fenton and John Gulick, eds., *Symposium on Cherokee and Iroquois Culture*, pp. 159–166.

5. There is an extensive literature on war-related stress and Vietnam veteran adjustment. See especially David E. Bonior, Steven M. Champlin, and Timothy S. Kelly, *The Vietnam Veteran: A History of Neglect*; Joel Osler Brende and Erwin Randolph Parson, *Vietnam Veterans: The Road to Recovery*; J. J. Card, *Lives after Vietnam*; Gloria

Emerson, *Winners and Losers: Battles, Retreats, Gains, Losses and Ru-*
ins from the Vietnam War; Charles R. Figley, ed., *Stress Disorders*
among Vietnam Veterans: Theory, Research and Treatment; Charles R.
Figley, ed., *Trauma and Its Wake: The Study and Treatment of Post-*
Traumatic Stress Disorder; Charles R. Figley and Seymour Leventman,
eds., *Strangers at Home: Vietnam Veterans since the War*; John Helmer,
Bringing the War Home: The American Soldier in Vietnam and After;
W. E. Kelly, ed., *Post-Traumatic Stress Disorder in the War Veteran Pa-*
tient; R. A. Kulka et al., *Trauma and the Vietnam War Generation: Re-*
port of the Findings from the National Veterans Readjustment Study;
Robert Jay Lifton, *Home from the War: Vietnam Veterans, neither Vic-*
tims nor Executioners; Wilbur J. Scott, *The Politics of Readjustment:*
Vietnam Veterans since the War; John P. Wilson, Z. Harel, and B. Kahanal, eds., *Human Adaptation to Extreme Stress: From the Holocaust*
to Vietnam; John P. Wilson, *Trauma, Transportation and Healing*. For
more titles see John A. Fairbank, et al., "A Selected Bibliography on
Post Traumatic Stress Disorders in Vietnam Veterans," *Professional*
Psychology 12 (1981): 578–586.

6. There is indeed a long history of government indifference toward
those who have fought in America's wars. See especially Richard
Severo and Lewis Milford, *The Wages of War: When America's Soldiers*
Came Home—From Valley Forge to Vietnam.

7. There are several anthologies in print that clearly outline the dichotomy in American thought regarding the Vietnam War and those
who fought it. See especially Peter Braestrup, ed., *Vietnam as History:*
Ten Years after the Paris Peace Accords, and Walter Capps, ed., *The*
Vietnam Reader.

8. See Capps' introduction in Capps, *The Vietnam Reader*, pp.
1–12, and Robert Jay Lifton's "Home from the War: The Psychology of
Survival" in the same volume, pp. 54–67.

9. John P. Wilson, "Conflict, Stress and Growth: Effects of War on
the Psychological Development of American Vietnam Veterans," in
Figley and Leventman, *Strangers at Home*, pp. 123–165.

10. These general ideas have been gleaned from the extensive literature on the subject. See especially Emerson, *Winners and Losers*; and
Lifton, *Home from the War*.

11. William Broyles, Jr., "Why Men Love War," in Capps, *The Viet-*
nam Reader, pp. 68–81.

12. See Bernard Spilka, Lisa Friedman, and David Rosenberg, "Death

and Vietnam: Some Combat Veteran Experience and Perspectives," pp. 129–143; and Chaim F. Shatan, "Stress Disorders among Vietnam Veterans: The Emotional Content of Combat Continues," pp. 43–52, both in Figley, *Stress Disorders among Vietnam Veterans*.

13. See especially Mardi J. Horowitz and George F. Solomon, "Delayed Stress Response Syndromes in Vietnam Veterans," in Figley, *Stress Disorders among Vietnam Veterans*, pp. 268–280; Marc Pilisuk, "The Legacy of the Vietnam Veteran," *Journal of Social Issues* 31 (1975): 3–12; and Arthur Egendorf et al., *Legacies of Vietnam: Comparative Adjustment of Veterans and Their Peers*.

14. Egendorf et al., *Legacies of Vietnam*, p. 52.

15. Lawrence M. Baskir and William A. Strauss, *Chance and Circumstance: The Draft, the War, and the Vietnam Generation*, pp. 8–9.

16. Lisa Hsiao, "Project 100,000: The Great Society's Answer to Military Manpower Needs in Vietnam," *Vietnam Generation* 1 (Spring 1989): 14–37.

17. Severo and Milford, *Wages of War*, pp. 109, 111, 125–126, 218–219, 235–237.

18. Cynthia H. Enloe, *Ethnic Soldiers: State Security in Divided Societies*, pp. 190–192.

19. Alex Haley, "Epilogue," in Malcolm X with Alex Haley, *The Autobiography of Malcolm X*, p. 389.

20. Rhoda Lois Blumberg, *Civil Rights: The 1960s Freedom Struggle*, p. 121.

21. Alan L. Sorkin, "The Economic Basis of Indian Life," *Annals of the American Academy of Political and Social Sciences* 436 (1978): 1–12.

22. *Talking Leaf* 2 (1973): 3. This is no doubt a rough estimate of Indian Vietnam veterans probably arrived at by adding up figures drawn from tribal government sources. See also U.S. Department of Defense and Veterans Administration, "Table of the Estimated Number of American Indian Veterans by States of Residence"; U.S. Bureau of the Census, *1980 Census of the Population, Vol. 1, Characteristics of the Population*, Chapter C, "General Social and Economic Characteristics."

23. *Eighth Annual National Vietnam Era Veterans Convention and Pow-Wow*, Program.

24. See especially "Bibliography of Sources Dealing with Minority Issues," in *Vietnam Generation* 1 (Spring 1989): 151–159.

25. See Robert F. Berkhofer, Jr., *The White Man's Indian*, and Brian W. Dippie, *The Vanishing American: White Attitudes and U.S. Indian Policy*.

26. Vine Deloria, Jr., *Custer Died for Your Sins*, p. 12.

27. *Eighth Annual Vietnam Era Veterans National Convention and Pow-Wow*, Program.

28. "Report of a Working Group on Women Vietnam Veterans and the Operation Outreach Vietnam Vet Center Program," Readjustment Counseling Service, Washington, D.C., December 15, 1982. Author's files.

29. "Preliminary Report/Outline of Activities of the Working Group on Black Viet Nam Veterans," Readjustment Counseling Service (Operation Outreach), Washington, D.C., n.d. Author's files.

30. *Needs of the Hispanic Vietnam Era Veteran: Report of the Hispanic Working Group*, Readjustment Counseling Service, Washington, D.C., September 21, 1983. Author's files.

31. Ibid., p. 6.

32. "The 'Worth of the Warrior' Project," Initial Report on Recommendations and Current Activities of the National Working Group on American Indian Vietnam Era Veterans, Readjustment Counseling Service, Washington, D.C., February 17, 1984. Author's files.

33. *Report of the Working Group on American Indian Vietnam Era Veterans*, Readjustment Counseling Service, Washington, D.C., p. 4.

34. Ibid., p. 6.

35. Steven Silver, "Lessons from Child of Water," pp. 12–24; Donald Johnson, "Stress, Depression, Substance Abuse and Racism," pp. 35–38; Donald Johnson and Robin LaDue, "A Cultural and Community Process," pp. 39–42; and Harold Barse, "American Indian Veterans and Families," pp. 43–49, all in *Report of the Working Group on American Indian Vietnam Era Veterans*.

36. Veterans Administration Advisory Committee on Native American Veterans, *Native American Veterans: Third and Final Report*, p. viii.

37. Veterans Administration Advisory Committee on Native American Veterans, *Native American Veterans*, pp. 1–15, and appendix D, pp. 1–2.

38. The appendices in both reports (1988 and 1989) contained letters to the committee from various federal agencies, maps, statutes, and a report on delivering health care to Indian veterans from the Albuquerque, New Mexico, VA Medical Center. Missing, of course, were Robin LaDue's "The Assessment of Post-Traumatic Stress Disorder

among Minority Vietnam Veterans," a paper presented at the Minority Assessment Conference, Tucson, Arizona, 1983; Robin LaDue, *Coyote Returns: The Warrior, Part 5*; my "Culture, Ceremonialism and Stress: American Indian Veterans of the Vietnam War," *Armed Forces and Society* 12 (Winter 1986): 237–251; and my "The National Survey of Vietnam Era American Indian Veterans: A Preliminary Reconnaissance," *Wicazo Sa Review* 1 (Spring 1985): 36–37.

39. U.S. Senate, *Congressional Record*, June 16, 1988, pp. 8012–8017.

40. Veterans Administration Advisory Committee on Native American Veterans, *Native American Veterans*, appendix D, pp. 1–4.

41. U.S. Senate, *Report of the Committee on Veterans' Affairs to Accompany S. 2011, "Veterans' Benefits and Programs Improvement Act of 1988"*, pp. 128–129.

42. *Lakota Times*, November 17, 1993.

43. Vine Deloria, Jr., "Higher Education and Self-Determination," *Winds of Change* 6 (Winter 1991): 20.

2. AN OLDER TRADITION: NATIVE AMERICAN WARFARE AND THE WARRIOR'S PLACE IN TRIBAL SOCIETY

1. One of the best recent studies of human aggression, technology and warfare is Robert L. O'Connell, *Of Arms and Men: A History of War, Weapons and Aggression*. See especially his chapter on the origins of human aggression and his ideas about predatory and ritualized violence entitled "Dialogue with the Sphinx," pp. 13–29.

2. Gwynne Dyer, *War*, p. 9.

3. Ibid., p. 11.

4. See Trevor N. Dupuy, *The Evolution of Weapons and Warfare*; and John Keegan, *The Face of Battle*.

5. Dyer, *War*, pp. 14–15.

6. Ibid., p. 18.

7. O'Connell, *Of Arms and Men*, pp. 35–37.

8. See Samuel B. Griffith's introduction to Sun Tzu, *The Art of War*, pp. 1–56; and John Keegan's analysis of Alexander the Great's battle tactics against the Persians in his *The Mask of Command*, pp. 77–87.

9. Noel Perrin, *Giving Up the Gun: Japan's Reversion to the Sword, 1545–1879*.

10. Daniel K. Richter, "War and Culture: The Iroquois Experience,"

William and Mary Quarterly 40 (October 1983): 529–537; and George S. Snyderman, "Behind the Tree of Peace" (Ph.D. diss., University of Pennsylvania, 1948).

11. Harold E. Driver, *Indians of North America*, p. 310.

12. Ibid., pp. 288–290, 311–324.

13. For one of the best discussions of the origins of North American aboriginal warfare, see Clifton B. Kroeber and Bernard L. Fontana, *Massacre on the Gila: An Account of the Last Major Battle between American Indians with Reflections on the Origins of War*, pp. 148–174.

14. Kirkpatrick Sale, *The Conquest of Paradise: Columbus and the Columbian Legacy.*

15. See Gregory Evans Dowd's discussion of Native American warfare in his *A Spirited Resistance: The North American Indian Struggle for Unity, 1745–1815*, pp. 4–9; and Kroeber and Fontana, *Massacre on the Gila*, pp. 165–174.

16. Kroeber and Fontana, *Massacre on the Gila*, p. 169.

17. Richter, in "War and Culture", sees the mourning war as primarily a social and cultural function and differs from the emphasis placed on it as an emotional and psychological function in tribal societies by Marian W. Smith in "American Indian Warfare," New York Academy of Sciences, *Transactions*, pp. 348–365. I lean toward Richter's views.

18. For culture areas in Native North America see Driver, *Indians of North America*; and Robert F. Spencer et al., *The Native Americans* (New York: Harper and Row, 1965).

19. For an excellent discussion of the deficiencies of the culture area approach to aboriginal North America see Harriet J. Kupferer, *Ancient Drums, Other Moccasins: Native North American Cultural Adaptation*, pp. ix–xiii. Kupferer's approach is from a "cultural ecology" perspective and emphasizes how tribes, simply put, made a living in a particular environment. It is a very practical and understandable method of looking at tribal subsistence patterns and adaptations.

20. Driver, *Indians of North America*, p. 143.

21. James Adair, *Adair's History of the American Indians*, ed. Samuel Cole Williams, p. 169.

22. See G. P. Horsefly, *A History of the True People: The Cherokees*; James Mooney, *Myths of the Cherokee*, p. 455; James Mooney, *Sacred Formulas of the Cherokees*, p. 342; Angie Debo, *The Road to Disappearance*, p. 14.

23. Driver, *Indians of North America*, p. 317.

24. Horsefly, *A History of the True People*, p. 77.

25. See Thomas E. Mails, *Dog Soldiers, Bear Men and Buffalo Women*; Colin Taylor, *Warriors of the Plains*; Robert H. Lowie, *Indians of the Plains*, pp. 105–114; and Bernard Mishkin, *Rank and Warfare among the Plains Indians*.

26. Adair, *History of the American Indians*, p. 416.

27. Tom Holm, "Patriots and Pawns: State Use of American Indians in the Military and the Process of Nativization in the United States," in M. Annette Jaimes, ed., *The State of Native America: Genocide, Colonization, and Resistance*, pp. 358–359.

28. Keegan, *Face of Battle*, pp. 58–62.

29. Dyer, *War*, p. 9.

30. Ernest L. Schusky, ed., *Political Organization of Native North Americans*, pp. vii–viii.

31. Keegan, *Mask of Command*, pp. 8–9.

32. Keegan, *Face of Battle*, p. 165.

33. Mooney, *Myths of the Cherokee*, p. 379.

34. John P. Brown, *Old Frontiers*, footnote, p. 26.

35. Spencer and Jennings, *The Native Americans*, pp. 187–193.

36. Reginald Laubin and Gladys Laubin, *Indian Dances of North America: Their Importance to Indian Life*, p. 244; Adair, *History of the American Indians*, pp. 172–177; Kupferer, *Ancient Drums, Other Moccasins*, p. 226; Mooney, *Myths of the Cherokee*, p. 496.

37. Spencer and Jennings, *The Native Americans*, p. 382.

38. Lowie, *Indians of the Plains*, p. 118.

39. See especially Keith Basso, ed., *Western Apache Raiding and Warfare*; Driver, *Indians of North America*, p. 318.

40. Driver, *Indians of North America*, pp. 311, 318.

41. Quoted in Kroeber and Fontana, *Massacre on the Gila*, p. 57.

42. Lowie, *Indians of the Plains*, pp. 117–118.

43. Ernest Wallace and E. Adamson Hoebel, *The Comanches*, p. 247.

44. Wilbur R. Jacobs, *Dispossessing the American Indian: Indians and Whites on the Colonial Frontier*, pp. 119–120; Ralph A. Smith, "The Scalp Hunter in the Borderlands, 1835–1850," *Arizona and the West* 6 (Spring 1964): 5–22.

45. Archibald Loudon, *A Selection of Some of the Most Interesting Narratives of Outrages Committed by the Indians in Their Wars with the White People*, vol. 2, p. 166.

46. Jacobs, *Dispossessing the American Indian*, pp. 77–81; see also

Lenore A. Stiffarm and Phil Lane, Jr., "The Demography of Native North America, A Question of American Indian Survival," in Jaimes, ed., *The State of Native America*, p. 32.

47. Laubin, *Indian Dances*, pp. 152–170.

48. Richter, "War and Culture," pp. 533–535.

49. Dowd, *A Spirited Resistance*, p. 12.

50. Richter, "War and Culture," p. 534.

51. Driver, *Indians of North America*, p. 315.

52. Adair, *History of the American Indians*, p. 161.

53. Mooney, *Myths of the Cherokee*, p. 353.

54. Snyderman, "Behind the Tree of Peace," p. 14.

55. Arthur C. Parker, *Parker on the Iroquois*, ed. Williams N. Fenton, pp. 52–53.

56. Margot Astrov, *The Winged Serpent: An Anthology of American Indian Prose and Poetry*, p. 90.

57. Ibid., p. 120.

58. Ibid., pp. 168–169.

59. See especially Berkhofer, *The White Man's Indian;* and Richard Slotkin, *Regeneration through Violence: The Mythology of the American Frontier, 1600–1860.* In addition, consult Roy Harvey Pearce, *The Savages of America: A Study of the Indian and the Idea of Civilization;* his "Significance of the Captivity Narrative," *American Literature* 19 (March 1947): 1–20; and "The Metaphysics of Indian Hating," *Ethnohistory* 4 (1957): 27–40.

60. Adair, *History of the American Indians*, p. 167.

61. Ibid., p. 416.

62. Driver, *Indians of North America*, pp. 108, 310, 322, 385, 411–412.

63. Adair, *History of the American Indians*, p. 416.

64. Snyderman, *Behind the Tree of Peace*, p. 58.

65. See Adair, *History of the American Indians*, pp. 171–172.

66. Ibid., p. 409.

67. Alice Marriott, *The Ten Grandmothers*, pp. 3–14.

68. For example, Wilbur Jacobs, a historian of high repute, suggests that Native Americans were defeated "not because they were beaten by better warriors or strategists but because they could not fight off the overwhelming number of the enemy and his two-horned devil, disease and liquor. Even today we imitate him. There is no higher calling in the military service than that of the commando ranger who gallantly fights our battles the world over." Jacobs, *Dispossessing the American Indian*, p. 166.

69. Loudon, *Selection of Some of the Most Interesting Narratives of Outrages*, vol. 1, p. 120.

70. Ibid., p. 242.

71. Ibid., p. 242.

72. Ibid., p. 248.

73. Adair, *History of the American Indians*, p. 181.

74. Ibid., p. 189.

75. Ibid., pp. 411–412.

76. Ibid., p. 416.

77. Lowie, *Indians of the Plains*, p. 116.

78. Brown, *Old Frontiers*, p. 151.

3. WARRIORS INTO SOLDIERS: EURO-AMERICAN WARFARE AND THE MILITARIZATION OF NATIVE AMERICANS

1. For excellent elaborations of this theme see Roy Harvey Pearce, *The Savages of America*; and Richard Slotkin, *Regeneration through Violence*.

2. Barbara Ehrenreich, "The Warrior Culture," *Time* (October 15, 1990): 100. Ward Churchill, American Indian scholar and activist at the University of Colorado, wrote a rejoinder to Ehrenreich's essay in which he pointed out numerous flaws in her facts and logic as well as her "determinist and virulently ethnocentric content inherent to terms like 'pretechnological' when they are used to describe non-industrial societies." Churchill's rebuttal was not, as far as I know, published. I have a copy of it in my files.

3. Tom Holm, "Indian Concepts of Authority and the Crisis in Tribal Government," *Social Science Journal* 19 (July 1982): 59–71.

4. This is just one of the major themes explored in Robert L. O'Connell's excellent *Of Arms and Men*.

5. John Keegan, *Face of Battle*, p. 162.

6. Gwynne Dyer, *War*, p. 49.

7. Keegan, *Face of Battle*, p. 109.

8. Dyer, *War*, pp. 47–49.

9. Ibid., p. 50.

10. Keegan, *Face of Battle*, pp. 79–116.

11. Dupuy, *The Evolution of Weapons and Warfare*, pp. 93–105; and Dyer, *War*, p. 61.

12. Dupuy, *The Evolution of Weapons and Warfare*, pp. 112–115.

13. Ibid., pp. 133–154.

14. O'Connell, *Of Arms and Men*, pp. 141–147; and Dyer, *War*, pp. 60–62.

15. See Keegan's analysis of the Battle of Waterloo for an idea of the destructive power of this kind of weaponry in his *Face of Battle*, pp. 117–202.

16. See Dupuy, *The Evolution of Weapons and Warfare*, pp. 320–324, for a discussion of military theory, theorists, and the principles of war.

17. Joe S. Sando, "The Pueblo Revolt," in Alfonso Ortiz, *Handbook of North American Indians, Southwest*, Vol. 11, p. 195.

18. Ibid., p. 196.

19. John Francis Bannon, *The Spanish Borderlands Frontier, 1513–1821*, p. 83.

20. Sando, "The Pueblo Revolt," p. 197.

21. Robert M. Utley and Wilcomb E. Washburn, *Indian Wars*, pp. 77–80.

22. Joseph R. Friedman, ed., *American Military History*, pp. 33–36.

23. Ibid., p. 35.

24. James Smith's narrative in Loudon, *Selection of Some of the Most Interesting Narratives of Outrages*, pp. 125–127, 242–243, certainly supports the idea that the tribal commanders engineered Braddock's defeat.

25. Quoted in Friedman, *American Military History*, p. 35.

26. Loudon, *Selection of Some of the Most Interesting Narratives of Outrages*, p. 243.

27. Ibid., p. 245.

28. Ibid., pp. 245–246.

29. See Fairfax Downey, *Indian Wars of the U.S. Army, 1776–1865*, pp. 100–115; and Utley and Washburn, *Indian Wars*, pp. 130–135.

30. Dee Brown, *Bury My Heart at Wounded Knee: An Indian History of the American West*, pp. 121–146; and S. L. A. Marshall, *Crimsoned Prairie*, pp. 60–72.

31. Keith A. Murray, *The Modocs and Their War*.

32. Marshall, *Crimsoned Prairie*, pp. 134–168.

33. Ibid., pp. 183–226.

34. On frontier-colonial militias and their weaponry, see Friedman, *American Military History*, pp. 29–30, 38–39; Smith narrative in Loudon, *Selection of Some of the Most Interesting Narratives of Outrages*, p. 206.

35. Cynthia H. Enloe, *Ethnic Soldiers*, pp. 15, 21, 25. See also Jack D. Foner, *Blacks and the Military in American History*; George Hender-

sen, *Human Relations in the Military*; Richard O. Hope, *Racial Strife in the U.S. Military*; Morris Janowitz, *The Military in the Political Development of New Nations*; Warren L. Young, *Minorities and the Military*.

36. I use the terminology *settler state* to distinguish those nations that were originally founded by imperial powers but have since become independent of them. They are not controlled politically by groups indigenous to their territorial limits. The United States, Canada, New Zealand, and South Africa are examples of settler states.

37. See Young, *Minorities and the Military*, pp. 5–18. See also David Bolt, *Gurkhas*. The example of the Maoris is especially interesting given that the British had shortly before considered them "true savages" worthy of being on the receiving end of outright extermination. See A. J. Harrop, *England and the Maori Wars*.

38. Keegan, *Face of Battle*, pp. 180–185.

39. Loudon, *Selection of Some of the Most Interesting Narratives of Outrages*, p. 249.

40. For analysis, see Francis Paul Prucha, ed., *Americanizing the American Indian: Writings by the "Friends of the Indian"*; and his *American Indian Policy in Crisis: Christian Reformers and the Indian*.

41. *The Indian's Friend*, January 1918.

42. Tom Holm, "Fighting a White Man's War: The Extent and Legacy of American Indian Participation in World War II," *The Journal of Ethnic Studies* 9 (Summer 1981): 69–81. Alison Bernstein, in her *American Indians and World War II: Toward a New Era in Indian Affairs*, suggests that Indians joined the military to accelerate their assimilation into mainstream American society. Jere Franco, in her "Publicity, Persuasion and Propaganda: Stereotyping the Native American in World War II," *Military History of the Southwest* 22 (Fall 1992): 1–15, takes a more balanced approach.

43. Harold Ickes, "Indians Have a Name for Hitler," *Collier's* 113 (January 15, 1944): 58.

44. Jack was a very good friend who unfortunately passed away a number of years ago. He is sorely missed by those of us who came to him when he was the coordinator of Indian student services at the University of Oklahoma in the 1970s. He was always there with help and a kind word.

45. Charles J. Kappler, ed., *Indian Affairs: Laws and Treaties*, Vol. 2, pp. 1–3; see also Jack M. Sosin, "The Use of Indians in the War of the American Revolution," in Roger L. Nichols, ed., *The American Indian Past and Present*, pp. 96–110.

46. Quoted in Hendersen, *Human Relations in the Military*, p. 48.

47. See William T. Hagan, *American Indians*.

48. See especially Francis Paul Prucha, *American Indian Policy in the Formative Years*.

49. See Angie Debo, *A History of the Indians of the United States*, p. 75; Hagan, *American Indians*, p. 51; Friedman, *American Military History*, p. 112; Utley and Washburn, *Indian Wars*, pp. 113–114.

50. Hagan, *American Indians*, p. 51.

51. Tom Holm, "Stereotypes, State Elites, and the Military Use of American Indian Troops," *Plural Societies* 15 (1984): 265–282; Fairfax Downey and Jacques Noel Jacobson, Jr., *The Red Bluecoats*; Robert W. Frazer, ed., *New Mexico in 1850: A Military View by Colonel George Archibald McCall*, pp. 30, 180; Hagan, *American Indians*, p. 51; Horsefly, *History of the True People*, pp. 58, 72.

52. Quoted in Michael P. Rogin, *Fathers and Children: Andrew Jackson and the Subjugation of the American Indian*, p. 151.

53. See Ted Alexander, "Muskets and Tomahawks," *Civil War* 10 (September–October 1992): 8–12, 51–52; and David Woodbury, "From Tahlequah to Boggy Depot: Stand Watie's Civil War," pp. 38–46, in the same issue. See also Annie Heloise Abel, *The American Indian as Participant in the Civil War*; and Edmund Jefferson Danziger, Jr., *Indians and Bureaucrats: Administering the Reservation Policy during the Civil War*.

54. Horsefly, *History of the True People*, p. 91.

55. Ted Alexander, "The Chippewa Sharpshooters of Company K," *Civil War* 10 (September–October 1992): 24–25.

56. Ibid., p. 26. Also see David A. Woodbury, "An Iroquois at Appomattox," in *Civil War* 10, pp. 19–23.

57. Brown, *Bury My Heart at Wounded Knee*, pp. 37–65.

58. See Lynn R. Bailey, *Long Walk*; and Lawrence Kelly, *Navajo Roundup*.

59. Stan Hoig, *The Sand Creek Massacre*.

60. George Bird Grinnell, *Two Great Scouts and Their Pawnee Battalion*.

61. Downey and Jacobson, *Red Bluecoats*, pp. 171, 193–194.

62. U.S. Congress, *House Journal*, pp. 327, 337, 340, 363, 365, 366, 371.

63. See especially Prucha, *American Indian Policy in Crisis*; Henry E. Fritz, *The Movement for Indian Assimilation, 1860–1890*; Robert W. Mardock, *The Reformers and the American Indian*.

64. U.S. Congress, *Annual Report of the Secretary of War*, p. 14.

65. Ibid., pp. 14–15.

66. Quoted in Jack D. Foner, *The United States Soldier between Two Wars, 1865–1898*, p. 131.

67. Ibid., pp. 129–130.

68. Tom Holm, "A 'Great Confusion' in Indian Affairs." Manuscript, 1990.

69. Daniel F. Littlefield and Lonnie E. Underhill, "The Crazy Snake Uprising of 1909: A Red, Black or White Affair?" *Arizona and the West* 20 (Winter 1978): 307–324; Matthew K. Sniffen, *The Meaning of the Ute "War."*

70. Commissioner of Indian Affairs, *Annual Report*, 1917, pp. 6–7.

71. Walker J. Norcross, "History and Army Service in World Wars I and II," in Broderick H. Johnson, *Navajos and World War II*, p. 104.

72. Duane K. Hale, "Forgotten Heroes: American Indians in World War I," *Four Winds* 3 (1982): 39. Also see *The American Indian in the World War*, Office of Indian Affairs Bulletin 15; Bureau of Indian Affairs, "Special Issue: Indians in the Military," *Indian Record* (November 1970): 4; U.S. Army Forces Command, Public Affairs, *Native Americans and the Military*.

73. Hale, "Forgotten Heroes," pp. 40–41.

74. 41 *U.S. Stats.*, p. 350; 43 *U.S. Stats.*, p. 253. John R. Finger, in his "Conscription, Citizenship, and Civilization: World War I and the Eastern Band of Cherokee," *The North Carolina Historical Review* 63 (July 1986): 283–308, argues effectively that Indian Office administrators were actively seeking to "civilize" or assimilate Indians using military service as a means to an end. The confirmation of citizenship was, in reality, an "afterthought."

75. Tom Holm, "Patriots and Pawns: State Use of American Indians in the Military and the Process of Nativization in the United States," in Jaimes, *The State of Native America*, pp. 345–370.

76. Commissioner of Indian Affairs, *Annual Report*, 1919, p. 16.

4. A LEGACY OF WAR: THE AMERICAN INDIAN VIETNAM GENERATION

1. Tom Holm, "The National Survey of Indian Vietnam Veterans," *Report of the Working Group on American Indian Vietnam Era Veterans*, p. 26.

2. Richard L. Neuberger, "On the Warpath," *Saturday Evening Post* 215 (October 24, 1942): 79.

3. Richard L. Neuberger, "The American Indian Enlists," *Asia and the Americas* 42 (November 1942): 628.

4. John Collier, "The Indian in a Wartime Nation," *Annals of the American Academy of Political and Social Science* 223 (September 1942): 29.

5. Elizabeth S. Sergeant, "The Indian Goes to War," *New Republic* 107 (November 30, 1942): 708.

6. U.S. Department of Interior, *Annual Report, 1944*, p. 235, Report of John Collier, Commissioner of Indian Affairs.

7. See especially *Indians in the War, 1945*, p. 1; Bernstein, *American Indians and World War II*; Tom Holm, "Fighting a White Man's War: The Extent and Legacy of American Indian Participation in World War II," *Journal of Ethnic Studies* 9 (Summer 1981): 69–81; and U.S. Army Forces Command, Public Affairs, *Native Americans and the Military*, p. 7.

8. Collier, "Indian in a Wartime Nation," p. 29.

9. Jere Franco, "Bringing Them in Alive: Selective Service and Native Americans," *Journal of Ethnic Studies* 18 (Fall 1990): 1.

10. Ibid., pp. 18–19.

11. Neuberger, "The American Indian Enlists," p. 629.

12. *Indians in the War*, pp. 9–24.

13. Ibid., p. 12.

14. Franco, "Bringing Them in Alive," p. 19; and Troy Bryant, "Comanches Used Their Language to Help Confuse WWII Enemies," *The Purple Heart Magazine* (March–April 1993): 20–22.

15. See the *New York Times*, July 5, 1942, and September 19, 1945. For a more in-depth look at the Navajo Code Talkers see Doris A. Paul, *The Navajo Code Talkers*; Bruce Watson, "Jaysho, Moasi, Dibeh, Ayeshi, Hasclishnih, Beshlo, Shush, Gini," *Smithsonian* (September 1993): pp. 31–43, 108; Murrey Marder, "Navajo Code Talkers," *Indians in the War*, pp. 25–27; and David Begay, "The Navajo Code Talkers," *Four Winds* (Winter 1981): 62–64, 90–93.

16. Cozy S. Brown, "Code Talker—Pacific Theater," in Broderick H. Johnson, *Navajos and World War II*, p. 54.

17. See especially Franco, "Publicity, Persuasion and Propaganda."

18. *New York Times*, January 8, 1942, February 21, 1943, June 9, 1943, February 14, 1944, January 30, 1945, April 22, 1945; U.S. Department of the Interior, *Annual Report, 1944*, pp. 237–238.

19. Sergeant, "The Indian Goes to War," p. 709; U.S. Department of the Interior, *Annual Report, 1944,* p. 238.

20. *New York Times,* February 21, 1943, June 9, 1943, February 17, 1944.

21. U.S. Department of the Interior, *Annual Report, 1944,* p. 237; and *Indians in the War,* p. 1. For a look at a single reservation during the war see Robert Ritzenthaler, "The Impact of the War on an Indian Community," *American Anthropologist* 45 (April–June 1943): 325–326.

22. Oswald Garrison Villard, "Wardship and the Indian," *Christian Century* 61 (March 29, 1944): 397–398.

23. O. K. Armstrong, "Set the American Indians Free," *Reader's Digest* 47 (August 1945): 47–48.

24. Ibid., pp. 47, 49.

25. Donald L. Fixico, *Termination and Relocation: Federal Indian Policy, 1945–1960.*

26. Richard G. Braungart and Margaret M. Braungart, "Life Course and Generational Politics," *Journal of Political and Military Sociology* 12 (Spring 1984): 1.

27. See especially Clifford Adelman, *Generations: A Collage on Youthcult;* Lewis S. Feuer, *The Conflict of Generations: The Character and Significance of Student Movements;* Robert D. Laing, *The Politics of Experience;* and Seymour M. Lipset, *Rebellion in the University.*

28. U.S. Senate, *Occupation of Wounded Knee.* See also Ward Churchill and Jim Vander Wall, *Agents of Repression: the FBI's Secret Wars against the Black Panther Party and the American Indian Movement;* Roxanne Dunbar Ortiz, *The Great Sioux Nation.*

29. Holm, "Indian Concepts of Authority and the Crisis in Tribal Government," pp. 63–64; Churchill and Vander Wall, *Agents of Repression,* pp. 171–173.

30. Karl Mannheim, "The Problem of Generations," *Essays on the Sociology of Knowledge,* pp. 276–322; Richard G. Braungart, "The Sociology of Generations and Student Politics: A Comparison of the Functionalist and Generational Unit Models," *Journal of Social Issues* 30 (1974): 31–54.

31. Mannheim, "The Problem of Generations," p. 310.

32. See especially Stan Steiner, *The New Indians.*

33. Mannheim, "The Problem of Generations," p. 310.

34. Everett Stonequist, *The Marginal Man: A Study in Personality and Culture Conflict.*

35. Albert L. Wahrhaftig, "More than Mere Work: The Subsistence of

Oklahoma's Cherokee Indians," paper presented at the Southwest Anthropological Association Annual Conference, San Francisco, Calif., 1973, p. 4.

36. Letter to Editor (unsigned), *Navajo Times*, April 9, 1970.

37. Quoted in Ethel Nurge, ed., *The Modern Sioux*, p. 242.

38. Office of Information, Management and Statistics, "Selected Data on Native American Veterans," 1980.

39. Baskir and Strauss, *Chance and Circumstance*, p. 9. The estimate of eligible American Indian males is from Robert K. Thomas, interview with author, May 2, 1989. See also Sam Stanley and Robert K. Thomas, "Current Demographic and Social Trends among North American Indians," *Annals of the American Academy of Political and Social Science* 436 (1978): 111–120; U.S. Bureau of the Census, *1970 Census of the Population* and *1980 Census of the Population*. Also see Francis Paul Prucha's self-published *Demographic Map of American Indians in the United States*, 1985.

40. For an especially insightful look at military training see Dyer, *War*, pp. 102–128.

41. Ibid., pp. 104–105.

42. Keegan, *Face of Battle*, p. 193.

5. "INDIAN COUNTRY"

1. See especially Harry G. Summers, Jr., *On Strategy: A Critical Analysis of the Vietnam War*. For a discussion of the strategy and tactics of the war see Summers' "Lessons: A Soldier's View," and Russell F. Weigley, "Reflections on 'Lessons' from Vietnam," in Braestrup, *Vietnam as History*, pp. 109–124.

2. See Colonel David H. Hackworth and Julie Sherman, *About Face: The Odyssey of an American Warrior*.

3. See Thomas D. Boettcher, *Vietnam: The Valor and the Sorrow*; George C. Herring, *America's Longest War: The United States and Vietnam, 1950–1975*; Stanley Karnow, *Vietnam: A History*; Michael Maclear, *The Ten Thousand Day War, Vietnam: 1945–1975*; and Friedman, *American Military History*, pp. 619–647.

4. Edwin H. Simmons, "Marine Corps Operations in Vietnam, 1965–1966," in *The Marines in Vietnam, 1954–1973*, p. 39.

5. Ray Bonds, ed., *The Vietnam War: The Illustrated History of the Conflict in Southeast Asia*, p. 31.

6. See Douglas Pike, "The Other Side," in Braestrup, *Vietnam as History*, pp. 71–77.

7. Stanley Karnow, "An Interview with General Giap," in Capps, *The Vietnam Reader*, pp. 127–133.

8. Ibid., p. 126.

9. Several articles and oral histories point out the diversity of experience in Vietnam. See especially Mark Baker, ed., *Nam: The Vietnam War in the Words of the Men and Women Who Fought There*; Al Santoli, ed., *Everything We Had: An Oral History of the Vietnam War by Thirty-Three American Soldiers Who Fought It*; Wallace Terry, ed., *Bloods: An Oral History of the Vietnam War by Black Veterans*; Lea Ybarra, "Perceptions of Race and Class among Chicano Vietnam Veterans," *Vietnam Generation* 1 (Spring 1989): 69–93.

10. Quoted in LaDue, *Coyote Returns*, p. 5.

11. For more on the operational realities of these units, see Michael Lee Lanning, *Inside the LRRPs: Rangers in Vietnam*.

12. *Stars and Stripes*, April 19, 1984, p. 3. For more on Walkabout's exploits on that day, see Gary A. Linderer, *The Eyes of the Eagle: F Company LRPs in Vietnam, 1968*, pp. 178–194.

13. On MAC-V-SOG see Shelby L. Stanton, *Green Berets at War: U.S. Army Special Forces in Southeast Asia, 1956–1975*, pp. 218–229.

14. On the evolution of arms, see Dupuy, *The Evolution of Weapons and Warfare*. Also see Sheila Tobias et al., *What Kinds of Guns Are They Buying for Your Butter? A Beginner's Guide to Defense, Weaponry and Military Spending*.

15. O'Connell, *Of Arms and Men*, p. 191.

16. Bonds, ed., *The Vietnam War*, p. 34.

17. Keegan, *Face of Battle*, p. 265.

18. Keegan, *The Mask of Command*, p. 209.

19. O'Connell, *Of Arms and Men*, p. 199.

20. Keegan, *Face of Battle*, p. 270.

21. Bonds, ed., *The Vietnam War*, p. 34.

22. See especially Keegan, *Face of Battle*, pp. 113–116, 177–179, 269–279.

6. STRONG HEARTS

1. See Larry Berman, *Planning a Tragedy: The Americanization of the War in Vietnam*; and his *Lyndon Johnson's War: The Road to Stalemate in Vietnam*.

2. See Boettcher, *Vietnam: The Valor and the Sorrow*, pp. 444–471.

3. Robert K. Thomas, "Colonialism: Classic and Internal," *New University Thought* 4 (Spring 1966): 37–44; his "Powerless Politics," in Norman R. Yetman and C. Hoy Steele, eds., *Majority and Minority: The Dynamics of Racial and Ethnic Relations*; and Rhoda Lois Blumberg, *Civil Rights: The 1960s Freedom Struggle*.

4. There is no comprehensive study of post-World War II Native American leadership. In general, see Bernstein, *American Indians and World War II*; Fixico, *Termination and Relocation*; Steiner, *The New Indians*; Lawrence M. Hauptman, *The Iroquois Struggle for Survival: World War II to Red Power*; and the relevant sections of W. R. Swaggerty, ed., *Scholars and the Indian Experience: Recent Writing in the Social Sciences*.

5. Vine Deloria, Jr., *Behind the Trail of Broken Treaties: An Indian Declaration of Independence*, pp. 23–24.

6. See especially American Friends Service Committee, *Uncommon Controversy: Fishing Rights of the Muckleshoot, Puyallup, and Nisqually Indians*.

7. Deloria, *Behind the Trail of Broken Treaties*, pp. 27–41.

8. *Akwesasne Notes*, September 1970, pp. 28–33.

9. Deloria, *Behind the Trail of Broken Treaties*, pp. 54–57.

10. LaDue, *Coyote Returns*, p. 5.

11. Quoted in Alvin M. Josephy, Jr., ed., *Red Power: The American Indians' Fight for Freedom*, pp. 81–82.

12. See especially Churchill and Vander Wall, *Agents of Repression*, pp. 103–151; and Peter Matthiessen, *In the Spirit of Crazy Horse*, pp. 58–82.

13. U.S. Senate, *Occupation of Wounded Knee*, pp. 251–252.

14. Ibid., pp. 124–125.

15. Ibid., p. 142.

16. Resolution No. 72–55 of the Oglala Sioux Tribal Council to Protect Property, Interests and Sovereign Dignity of the Oglala Sioux Tribe. American Indian Studies Files, University of Arizona, 1972.

17. U.S. Senate, *Occupation of Wounded Knee*, pp. 251–256, 311.

18. *Akwesasne Notes*, Early Spring, April 1973, p. 20.

19. Quoted in Ibid., Early Summer, June 1973, p. 15.

20. Ibid., Early Spring, April 1973, p. 20.

21. Ibid., p. 43.

22. Ibid., Early Summer, June 1973, p. 30.

23. Ibid., pp. 15, 22.

24. Quoted in Churchill and Vander Wall, *Agents of Repression,* p. 151.

25. *Akwesasne Notes,* Early Spring, April 1973, p. 29.

26. Ibid., Early Summer, June 1973, p. 16.

27. Ibid., p. 5.

28. See Matthiessen, *In the Spirit of Crazy Horse;* Churchill and Vander Wall, *Agents of Repression;* and Ward Churchill and James Vander Wall, *The Cointelpro Papers: Documents from the FBI's Secret Wars against Dissent in the United States.*

29. Scott, *The Politics of Readjustment,* pp. xv–xvi.

30. Quoted in *Akwesasne Notes,* Early Summer, June 1973, p. 14.

31. Egendorf et al., *Legacies of Vietnam,* p. 378.

32. Quoted in Regional Learning Resources Service, Video Script on American Indian Vietnam Veterans, St. Louis Veterans Administration Hospital, June 17, 1985, pp. 12, 14. Author's files.

33. Ibid., p. 13.

34. Gloria Davis et al., "The Veterans Administration's Responsibility: Financing Prescribed Ceremonials for Navajo Veterans," Position Paper, Veterans Administration Office, Albuquerque, New Mexico, 1974, p. 5.

35. Quoted in Regional Learning Resources Service, Video Script on American Indian Vietnam Veterans, June 17, 1985, pp. 14–16.

36. Beatrice Chevalier, "American Indians Have Always Fought for Their Land in a Powerful Way," *Inter-Com* 11 (February 1982): 5.

37. See John P. Wilson, "Conflict, Stress, and Growth: Effects of War on Psychological Development among Vietnam Veterans," in Figley and Leventman, *Strangers at Home,* pp. 123–165.

38. Brende and Parson, *Vietnam Veterans: The Road to Recovery,* p. 112.

39. Wahrhaftig, "More Than Mere Work," p. 4.

40. Egendorf et al., *Legacies of Vietnam,* p. 329.

41. See especially Steven Silver, "Lessons from Child of Water," pp. 21–23; and Johnson and LaDue, "A Cultural and Community Process," pp. 41–42.

42. Egendorf et al., *Legacies of Vietnam,* pp. 378–379.

43. Johnson and LaDue, "A Cultural and Community Process," p. 41.

BIBLIOGRAPHY

Abel, Annie Heloise. *The American Indian as Participant in the Civil War*. Cleveland, Ohio: Arthur H. Clark, 1915.

Adair, James. *Adair's History of the American Indians*. Edited by Samuel Cole Williams. New York: Promontory Press, 1930. Reprint. New York: Arno Press, n.d.

Adelman, Clifford. *Generations: A Collage on Youthcult*. New York: Praeger, 1972.

Alexander, Ted. "The Chippewa Sharpshooters of Company K." *Civil War* 10 (September–October 1992): 24–25.

———. "Muskets and Tomahawks." *Civil War* 10 (September–October 1992): 8–12, 51–52.

American Friends Service Committee. *Uncommon Controversy: Fishing Rights of the Muckleshoot, Puyallup, and Nisqually Indians*. Seattle: University of Washington Press, 1970.

Armstrong, O. K. "Set the American Indians Free." *Reader's Digest* 47 (August 1945): 47–49.

Astrov, Margot. *The Winged Serpent: An Anthology of American Indian Prose and Poetry*. Greenwich, Conn.: Fawcett, 1973.

Bailey, Lynn R. *Long Walk*. Los Angeles: Westernlore, 1964.

Baker, Mark, ed. *Nam: The Vietnam War in the Words of the Men and Women Who Fought There*. New York: William Morrow and Company, 1981.

Bannon, John Francis. *The Spanish Borderlands Frontier, 1513–1821.* New York: Holt, Rinehart and Winston, 1970.

Barse, Harold. "American Indian Veterans and Families." In *Report of the Working Group on American Indian Vietnam Era Veterans,* pp. 43–49. Washington, D.C.: Readjustment Counseling Service, Department of Veterans Affairs, 1992.

Baskir, Lawrence M., and William A. Strauss. *Chance and Circumstance: The Draft, the War, and the Vietnam Generation.* New York: Vintage, 1978.

Basso, Keith, ed. *Western Apache Raiding and Warfare.* Tucson: University of Arizona Press, 1971.

Begay, David. "The Navajo Code Talkers." *Four Winds* (Winter 1981): 62–64, 90–93.

Berkhofer, Robert F. *The White Man's Indian.* New York: Alfred A. Knopf, 1978.

Berman, Larry. *Lyndon Johnson's War: The Road to Stalemate in Vietnam.* New York: Norton, 1989.

———. *Planning a Tragedy: The Americanization of the War in Vietnam.* New York: Norton, 1982.

Bernstein, Alison. *American Indians and World War II: Toward a New Era in Indian Affairs.* Norman: University of Oklahoma Press, 1990.

"Bibliography of Sources Dealing with Minority Issues." *Vietnam Generation* 1 (Spring 1989): 151–159.

Blumberg, Rhoda Lois. *Civil Rights: The 1960s Freedom Struggle.* Boston: Twayne Publishers, 1984.

Boettcher, Thomas D. *Vietnam: The Valor and the Sorrow.* Boston: Little, Brown and Company, 1985.

Bolt, David. *Gurkhas.* London: Weidenfeld and Nicolson Publishers, 1967.

Bonds, Ray, ed. *The Vietnam War: The Illustrated History of the Conflict in Southeast Asia.* New York: Crown Publishers, Inc., 1979.

Bonior, David E., Steven M. Champlin, and Timothy S. Kelley. *The Vietnam Veteran: A History of Neglect.* New York: Praeger Publishers, 1984.

Braestrup, Peter, ed. *Vietnam as History: Ten Years after the Paris Peace Accords.* Washington, D.C.: University Press of America, 1984.

Braungart, Richard G. "The Sociology of Generations and Student Politics: A Comparison of the Functionalist and Generational Unit Models." *Journal of Social Issues* 30 (1974): 31–54.

Braungart, Richard G., and Margaret M. Braungart. "Life Course and

Generational Politics." *Journal of Political and Military Sociology* 12 (Spring 1984): 1–8.

Brende, Joel Osler, and Erwin Randolph Parson. *Vietnam Veterans: The Road to Recovery.* New York: Signet, 1986.

Brown, Dee. *Bury My Heart at Wounded Knee: An Indian History of the American West.* New York: Holt, Rinehart and Winston, 1970.

Brown, John P. *Old Frontiers.* Kingsport, Tenn.: Southern Publishers, 1938. Reprint New York: Arno Press, 1971.

Bryant, Troy. "Comanches Used Their Language to Help Confuse WWII Enemies." *The Purple Heart Magazine* (March–April 1993): 20–23.

Bureau of Indian Affairs. "Special Issue: Indians in the Military." *Indian Record* (November 1970).

Capps, Walter, ed. *The Vietnam Reader.* New York: Routledge, 1991.

Card, J. J. *Lives after Vietnam.* Springfield, Ill.: Charles Thomas; Lexington, Mass.: Lexington Books, 1983.

Chevalier, Beatrice. "American Indians Have Always Fought for Their Land in a Powerful Way." *Inter-Com* 11 (February 1982): 4–6.

Churchill, Ward, and James Vander Wall. *Agents of Repression: The FBI's Secret Wars against the Black Panther Party and the American Indian Movement.* Boston: South End Press, 1990.

———. *The Cointelpro Papers: Documents from the FBI's Secret Wars against Dissent in the United States.* Boston: South End Press, 1990.

Collier, John. "The Indian in a Wartime Nation." *Annals of the American Academy of Political and Social Science* 223 (September 1942): 28–29.

Commissioner of Indian Affairs. *Annual Report.* 1917–1919.

Danziger, Edmund Jefferson, Jr. *Indians and Bureaucrats: Administering the Reservation Policy during the Civil War.* Urbana: University of Illinois Press, 1974.

Davis, Gloria, Marie McCrae, and Michael O'Sullivan. "The Veterans Administration's Responsibility: Financing Prescribed Ceremonials for Navajo Veterans." Position paper, Veterans Administration Office, Albuquerque, New Mexico, 1974.

Debo, Angie. *A History of the Indians of the United States.* Norman: University of Oklahoma Press, 1970.

———. *The Road to Disappearance.* Norman: University of Oklahoma Press, 1967.

Deloria, Vine, Jr. *Behind the Trail of Broken Treaties: An Indian Declaration of Independence.* New York: Dell Books, 1974.

———. *Custer Died for Your Sins*. Norman: University of Oklahoma Press, 1989.

———. "Higher Education and Self-Determination." *Winds of Change* 6 (Winter 1991): 18–25.

Dippie, Brian W. *The Vanishing American: White Attitudes and U.S. Indian Policy*. Middletown, Conn.: Wesleyan University Press, 1982.

Dowd, Gregory Evans. *A Spirited Resistance: The North American Indian Struggle for Unity, 1745–1815*. Baltimore, Md.: Johns Hopkins University Press, 1991.

Downey, Fairfax. *Indian Wars of the U.S. Army, 1776–1865*. Derby, Conn.: Monarch Books, 1963.

Downey, Fairfax, and Jacques Noel Jacobson, Jr. *The Red Bluecoats*. Fort Collins, Colo.: Old Army Press, 1973.

Driver, Harold E. *Indians of North America*. Chicago: University of Chicago Press, 1975.

Dupuy, Trevor N. *The Evolution of Weapons and Warfare*. New York: Bobbs-Merrill, 1980.

Dyer, Gwynne. *War*. Homewood, Ill.: Dorsey Press, 1985.

Egendorf, Arthur, Charles Kadushin, Robert S. Laufer, George Rothbart, and Lee Sloan. *Legacies of Vietnam: Comparative Adjustment of Veterans and Their Peers*. Washington, D.C.: Government Printing Office, 1981.

Ehrenreich, Barbara. "The Warrior Culture." *Time* (October 15, 1990): 100.

Eighth Annual National Vietnam Era Veterans Convention and Powwow. Program. Shawnee, Oklahoma, 1989.

Emerson, Gloria. *Winners and Losers: Battles, Retreats, Gains, Losses and Ruins from the Vietnam War*. New York: Harcourt Brace Jovanovich, 1976.

Enloe, Cynthia H. *Ethnic Soldiers: State Security in Divided Societies*. New York: Penguin Books, 1980.

Fairbank, John A., R. A. Kulka, W. E. Schlenger, R. L. Hough, B. K. Jordan, C. R. Marmar, and D. S. Weiss. "A Selected Bibliography on Post Traumatic Stress Disorders in Vietnam Veterans." *Professional Psychology* 12 (1981): 578–586.

Feuer, Lewis S. *The Conflict of Generations: The Character and Significance of Student Movements*. New York: Basic Books, 1969.

Figley, Charles R., ed. *Stress Disorders among Vietnam Veterans: Theory, Research and Treatment*. New York: Brunner/Mazel, 1978.

————, ed. *Trauma and Its Wake: The Study and Treatment of Post Traumatic Stress Disorder.* New York: Brunner/Mazel, 1985.

Figley, Charles R., and Seymour Leventman, eds. *Strangers at Home: Vietnam Veterans since the War.* New York: Praeger, 1980.

Finger, John R. "Conscription, Citizenship, and Civilization: World War I and the Eastern Band of Cherokee." *The North Carolina Historical Review* 63 (July 1986): 283–308.

First National Vietnam Era Veterans' Convention Agenda and Program. Shawnee, Oklahoma, November 5–7, 1987.

Fixico, Donald L. *Termination and Relocation: Federal Indian Policy, 1945–1960.* Albuquerque: University of New Mexico Press, 1986.

Foner, Jack D. *Blacks and the Military in American History.* New York: Praeger, 1974.

————. *The United States Soldier between Two Wars, 1865–1898.* New York: Humanities Press, 1970.

Franco, Jere. "Bringing Them in Alive: Selective Service and Native Americans." *Journal of Ethnic Studies* 18 (Fall 1990): 1–27.

————. "Publicity, Persuasion and Propaganda: Stereotyping the Native American in World War II." *Military History of the Southwest* 22 (Fall 1992): 1–15.

Frazer, Robert W., ed. *New Mexico in 1850: A Military View by Colonel George Archibald McCall.* Norman: University of Oklahoma Press, 1968.

Friedman, Joseph R., ed. *American Military History.* United States Army Historical Series. Washington, D.C.: Center for Military History, 1985.

Fritz, Henry E. *The Movement for Indian Assimilation, 1860–1890.* Philadelphia: University of Pennsylvania Press, 1963.

Grinnell, George Bird. *Two Great Scouts and Their Pawnee Battalion.* Cleveland, Ohio: Arthur H. Clark, 1928.

Hackworth, David H., and Julie Sherman. *About Face: The Odyssey of an American Warrior.* New York: Simon and Schuster, 1989.

Hagan, William T. *American Indians.* Chicago: University of Chicago Press, 1971.

Hale, Duane K. "Forgotten Heroes: American Indians in World War I." *Four Winds* 3 (1982): 38–40.

Harrop, A. J. *England and the Maori Wars.* Australia and New Zealand: Whitcombe and Tombs Publishers, 1937.

Hauptman, Lawrence M. *The Iroquois Struggle for Survival: World*

War II to Red Power. Syracuse, N.Y.: Syracuse University Press, 1986.

Helmer, John. *Bringing the War Home: The American Soldier in Vietnam and After.* New York: The Free Press, 1974.

Hendersen, George. *Human Relations in the Military.* Chicago: Nelson-Hall, 1975.

Herring, George C. *America's Longest War: The United States and Vietnam, 1950–1975.* New York: Alfred A. Knopf, 1986.

Hoig, Stan. *The Sand Creek Massacre.* Norman: University of Oklahoma Press, 1961.

Holm, Tom. "Culture, Ceremonialism and Stress: American Indian Veterans of the Vietnam War." *Armed Forces and Society* 12 (Winter 1986): 237–251.

———. "Fighting a White Man's War: The Extent and Legacy of American Indian Participation in World War II." *Journal of Ethnic Studies* 9 (Summer 1981): 69–81.

———. "Forgotten Warriors: American Indian Servicemen in Vietnam." *Vietnam Generation* 1 (Spring 1989): 56–68.

———. "Indian Concepts of Authority and the Crisis in Tribal Government." *Social Science Journal* 19 (July 1982): 59–71.

———. "Indian Veterans of the Vietnam War: Restoring Harmony through Tribal Ceremony." *Four Winds* 3 (Autumn 1982): 34–37.

———. "Intergenerational Rapprochement among American Indians: A Study of Thirty-Five Indian Veterans of the Vietnam War." *Journal of Military and Political Sociology* 12 (Spring 1984): 161–170.

———. "A 'Great Confusion' in Indian Affairs." Manuscript, 1990.

———. "The National Survey of Indian Vietnam Veterans." In *Report of the Working Group on American Indian Vietnam Era Veterans,* pp. 25–34. Washington, D.C.: Readjustment Counseling Service, Department of Veterans Affairs, 1992.

———. "The National Survey of Vietnam Era American Indian Veterans: A Preliminary Reconnaissance." *Wicazo Sa Review* 1 (Spring 1985): 36–37.

———. "Patriots and Pawns: State Use of American Indians in the Military and the Process of Nativization in the United States." In *The State of Native America: Genocide, Colonization, and Resistance,* edited by M. Annette Jaimes, pp. 345–370. Boston: South End Press, 1992.

———. "Stereotypes, State Elites, and the Military Use of American Indian Troops." *Plural Societies* 15 (1984): 265–282.

———. "Warriors All." In *Report of the Working Group on American Indian Vietnam Era Veterans*, pp. 8–11. Washington, D.C.: Readjustment Counseling Service, Department of Veterans Affairs, 1992.

Hope, Richard O. *Racial Strife in the U.S. Military*. New York: Praeger, 1979.

Horsefly, G. P. *A History of the True People: The Cherokees*. Detroit, Mich.: Rick Smith Oral History Publication, 1979.

Hsiao, Lisa. "Project 100,000: The Great Society's Answer to Military Manpower Needs in Vietnam." *Vietnam Generation* 1 (Spring 1989): 14–37.

Ickes, Harold. "Indians Have a Name for Hitler." *Collier's* 113 (January 15, 1944): 57–58.

The Indian's Friend. Newsletter, January 1918.

Indians in the War, 1945. Chicago: Department of the Interior–Bureau of Indian Affairs, 1945.

Jacobs, Wilbur R. *Dispossessing the American Indian: Indians and Whites on the Colonial Frontier*. New York: Charles Scribner's Sons, 1972.

Jaimes, M. Annette, ed., *The State of Native America: Genocide, Colonization, and Resistance*. Boston: South End Press, 1992.

Janowitz, Morris. *The Military in the Political Development of New Nations*. Chicago: University of Chicago Press, 1964.

Johnson, Broderick H., ed. *Navajos and World War II*. Tsaile, Ariz.: Navajo Community College Press, 1977.

Johnson, Donald. "Stress, Depression, Substance Abuse and Racism." In *Report of the Working Group on American Indian Vietnam Era Veterans*, pp. 35–38. Washington, D.C.: Readjustment Counseling Service, Department of Veterans Affairs, 1992.

Johnson, Donald, and Robin LaDue. "A Cultural and Community Process." In *Report of the Working Group on American Indian Vietnam Era Veterans*, pp. 39–42. Washington, D.C.: Readjustment Counseling Service, Department of Veterans Affairs, 1992.

Josephy, Alvin M., ed. *Red Power: The American Indians' Fight for Freedom*. New York: McGraw-Hill, 1971.

Kappler, Charles J., ed. *Indian Affairs: Laws and Treaties*, Vol. 2. Washington, D.C.: Government Printing Office, 1903.

Karnow, Stanley. *Vietnam: A History*. New York: Viking, 1983.

Keegan, John. *The Face of Battle*. New York: Vintage Books, 1977.

———. *The Mask of Command*. New York: Penguin, 1988.

Kelly, W. E., ed. *Post-Traumatic Stress Disorder in the War Veteran Patient.* New York: Brunner/Mazel, 1985.

Kelly, Lawrence. *Navajo Roundup.* Boulder, Colo.: Pruett Press, 1970.

Kilpatrick, Jack Frederick, and Anna Gritts Kilpatrick. *The Shadow of Sequoyah: Social Documents of the Cherokees, 1862–1964.* Norman: University of Oklahoma Press, 1965.

Kroeber, Clifton B., and Bernard L. Fontana. *Massacre on the Gila: An Account of the Last Major Battle between American Indians with Reflections on the Origins of War.* Tucson: University of Arizona Press, 1986.

Kulka, R. A., W. E. Schlenger, J. A. Fairbank, R. L. Hough, B. K. Jordan, C. R. Marmar, and D. S. Weiss. *Trauma and the Vietnam War Generation: Report of the Findings from the National Veterans Readjustment Study.* New York: Brunner/Mazel, 1990.

Kupferer, Harriet J. *Ancient Drums, Other Moccasins: Native North American Cultural Adaptation.* Englewood Cliffs, N.J.: Prentice-Hall, 1988.

LaDue, Robin. "The Assessment of Post-Traumatic Stress Disorder among Minority Vietnam Veterans." Paper presented at the Minority Assessment Conference, Tucson, Arizona, 1983.

———. *Coyote Returns: The Warrior, Part 5.* Department of Psychiatry and Behavioral Sciences Monograph Series on the Integration of Traditional Indian and Contemporary Western Medicines. Seattle: University of Washington, 1987.

Laing, Robert D. *The Politics of Experience.* New York: Ballantine Books, 1967.

Lakota Times, November 17, 1993.

Lanning, Michael Lee. *Inside the LRRPs: Rangers in Vietnam.* New York: Ivy Books, 1988.

Laubin, Reginald, and Gladys Laubin. *Indian Dances of North America: Their Importance to Indian Life.* Norman: University of Oklahoma Press, 1977.

Lifton, Robert Jay. *Home from the War: Vietnam Veterans, neither Victims nor Executioners.* New York: Touchstone/Simon and Schuster, 1973.

Linderer, Gary A. *The Eyes of the Eagle: F Company LRPs in Vietnam, 1968.* New York: Ivy Books, 1991.

Lipset, Seymour M. *Rebellion in the University.* Boston: Little, Brown and Company, 1972.

Littlefield, Daniel F., and Lonnie E. Underhill. "The Crazy Snake Uprising of 1909: A Red, Black or White Affair?" *Arizona and the West* 20 (Winter 1978): 307–324.

Loudon, Archibald. *A Selection of Some of the Most Interesting Narratives of Outrages Committed by the Indians in Their Wars with the White People*. Vol. 1, 1808; vol. 2, 1811. Reprint Harrisburg Publishing Company, 1888. Reprint New York: Arno Press, 1971.

Lowie, Robert H. *Indians of the Plains*. Garden City, N.Y.: Natural History Press, 1963.

Maclear, Michael. *The Ten Thousand Day War, Vietnam: 1945–1975*. New York: Avon Books, 1983.

Mails, Thomas E. *Dog Soldiers, Bear Men and Buffalo Women*. Englewood Cliffs, N.J.: Prentice-Hall, 1973.

Malcolm X, with Alex Haley. *The Autobiography of Malcolm X*. New York: Grove Press, 1970.

Mannheim, Karl. "The Problem of Generations." *Essays on the Sociology of Knowledge*. London: Routledge and Kegan Paul, 1952.

Mardock, Robert W. *The Reformers and the American Indian*. Columbia: University of Missouri Press, 1971.

Marriott, Alice. *The Ten Grandmothers*. Norman: University of Oklahoma Press, 1971.

Marshall, S. L. A. *Crimsoned Prairie*. New York: Scribner's, 1972.

Matthiessen, Peter. *In the Spirit of Crazy Horse*. New York: Viking, 1991.

Mishkin, Bernard. *Rank and Warfare among the Plains Indians*. Monographs on American Ethnology, vol. 3, New York: J. J. Augustin Publishers, 1940.

Montour, Frank. "Introduction." In *Report of the Working Group on American Indian Vietnam Era Veterans*, pp. 6–7. Washington, D.C.: Readjustment Counseling Service, Department of Veterans Affairs, 1992.

Mooney, James. *Myths of the Cherokee*. Washington, D.C.: Bureau of American Ethnology Report, 1897–1898, Nineteenth Annual Report. Reprint Nashville, Tenn.: Charles and Randy Elder, Booksellers.

———. *Sacred Formulas of the Cherokees*. Washington, D.C.: Bureau of American Ethnology, 1885–1886, Seventh Annual Report. Reprint Nashville, Tenn.: Charles and Randy Elder, Booksellers.

Murray, Keith A. *The Modocs and Their War*. Norman: University of Oklahoma Press, 1959.

Needs of the Hispanic Vietnam Era Veteran: Report of the Hispanic Working Group. Washington, D.C.: Readjustment Counseling Service, Veterans Administration, 1983.

Neuberger, Richard L. "The American Indian Enlists." *Asia and the Americas* 42 (November 1942): 628–630.

———. "On the Warpath." *Saturday Evening Post* 215 (October 24, 1942): 79.

Nichols, Roger L., ed. *The American Indian Past and Present.* Waltham, Mass.: Xerox College Publishers, 1971.

Nurge, Ethel, ed. *The Modern Sioux.* Lincoln: University of Nebraska Press, 1970.

O'Connell, Robert L. *Of Arms and Men: A History of War, Weapons and Aggression.* New York: Oxford University Press, 1989.

Office of Indian Affairs. *The American Indian in the World War.* Bulletin no. 15. Washington, D.C.: Government Printing Office, 1922.

Ortiz, Roxanne Dunbar. *The Great Sioux Nation.* Berkeley: Moon Books, 1977.

Parker, Arthur C. *Parker on the Iroquois.* Edited by William N. Fenton. Syracuse: Syracuse University Press, 1968.

Paul, Doris A. *The Navajo Code Talkers.* Pittsburgh: Dorrance and Company, 1973.

Pearce, Roy Harvey. "The Metaphysics of Indian Hating." *Ethnohistory* 4 (1957): 27–40.

———. *The Savages of America: A Study of the Indian and the Idea of Civilization.* Baltimore: The Johns Hopkins University Press, 1953.

———. "The Significance of the Captivity Narrative." *American Literature* 19 (March 1947): 1–20.

Perrin, Noel. *Giving Up the Gun: Japan's Reversion to the Sword, 1545–1879.* Boulder, Colo.: Shambhala, 1980.

Pilisuk, Marc. "The Legacy of the Vietnam Veteran." *Journal of Social Issues* 31 (1975): 3–12.

Preliminary Report/Outline of Activities of the Working Group on Black Viet Nam Veterans. Washington, D.C.: Readjustment Counseling Service, Veterans Administration, n.d.

Prucha, Francis Paul. *American Indian Policy in Crisis: Christian Reformers and the Indian.* Norman: University of Oklahoma Press, 1976.

———. *American Indian Policy in the Formative Years.* Lincoln: University of Nebraska Press, 1973.

———, ed. *Americanizing the American Indian: Writings by the*

"Friends of the Indian". Lincoln: University of Nebraska Press, 1973.

Red Smoke. Newsletter of the Vietnam Era Veterans Inter-Tribal Association, Oklahoma City, Okla. 1989–1990.

Regional Learning Resources Service, Video Script on American Indian Vietnam Veterans. St. Louis, Mo.: Veterans Administration Hospital, June 17, 1985.

"Report of a Working Group on Women Vietnam Veterans and the Operation Outreach Vietnam Vet Center Program." Washington, D.C.: Readjustment Counseling Service, Veterans Administration, 1982.

Report of the Working Group on American Indian Vietnam Era Veterans. Washington, D.C.: Readjustment Counseling Service, Department of Veterans Affairs, 1992.

Richter, Daniel K. "War and Culture: The Iroquois Experience." *William and Mary Quarterly* 40 (October 1983): 529–537.

Ritzenthaler, Robert. "The Impact of the War on an Indian Community." *American Anthropologist* 45 (April–June 1943): 325–326.

Rogin, Michael P. *Fathers and Children: Andrew Jackson and the Subjugation of the American Indian*. New York: Vintage, 1975.

Sale, Kirkpatrick. *The Conquest of Paradise: Columbus and the Columbian Legacy*. New York: Alfred A. Knopf, 1990.

Sando, Joe. "The Pueblo Revolt." In *Handbook of North American Indians, Southwest*, Vol. 11, edited by Alfonso Ortiz, pp. 195–198. Washington, D.C.: Smithsonian Institution, 1979.

Santoli, Al, ed. *Everything We Had: An Oral History of the Viet Nam War by Thirty-Three American Soldiers Who Fought It*. New York: Random House, 1981.

Schusky, Ernest L., ed. *Political Organization of Native North Americans*. Washington, D.C.: University Press of America, 1981.

Scott, Wilbur J. *The Politics of Readjustment: Vietnam Veterans since the War*. New York: Walter de Gruyter, 1993.

Sergeant, Elizabeth S. "The Indian Goes to War." *New Republic* 107 (November 30, 1942): 708–709.

Severo, Richard, and Lewis Milford. *The Wages of War: When America's Soldiers Came Home—From Valley Forge to Vietnam*. New York: Simon and Schuster, 1989.

Silver, Steven. "Lessons From Child of Water." In *Report of the Working Group on American Indian Vietnam Era Veterans*, pp. 12–24. Washington, D.C.: Readjustment Counseling Service, Department of Veterans Affairs, 1992.

Simmons, Edwin H. "Marine Corps Operations in Vietnam, 1965–1966." *The Marines in Vietnam, 1954–1973*. Washington, D.C.: Headquarters, U.S. Marine Corps, History and Museums Division, 1974.

Slotkin, Richard. *Regeneration through Violence: The Mythology of the American Frontier, 1600–1860*. Middletown, Conn.: Wesleyan University Press, 1973.

Smith, Marian W. "American Indian Warfare." New York Academy of Sciences, *Transactions*, 2d ser., 13 (1951): 348–365.

Smith, Ralph A. "The Scalp Hunter in the Borderlands, 1835–1850." *Arizona and the West* 6 (Spring 1964): 5–22.

Sniffen, Matthew K. *The Meaning of the Ute "War."* Philadelphia: Indian Rights Association, 1915.

Snyderman, George S. "Behind the Tree of Peace." Ph.D. diss., University of Pennsylvania, 1948.

Sorkin, Alan L. "The Economic Basis of Indian Life." *Annals of the American Academy of Political and Social Sciences* 436 (1978): 1–12.

Spencer, Robert F., Jesse D. Jennings, Charles E. Dibble, Elden Johnson, Arden R. King, Theodore Stern, Kenneth M. Stewart, Omer C. Stewart, and William J. Wallace. *The Native Americans*. New York: Harper and Row, 1965.

Stanley, Sam, and Robert K. Thomas. "Current Demographic and Social Trends among North American Indians." *Annals of the American Academy of Political and Social Science* 436 (1978): 111–120.

Stanton, Shelby L. *Green Berets at War: U.S. Army Special Forces in Southeast Asia, 1956–1975*. San Francisco: Presidio Press, 1985.

Steiner, Stan. *The New Indians*. New York: Delta Books, 1968.

Stonequist, Everett. *The Marginal Man: A Study in Personality and Culture Conflict*. New York: Charles Scribner's Sons, 1937.

Summers, Harry G., Jr. *On Strategy: A Critical Analysis of the Vietnam War*. New York: Dell Publishing Company, 1982.

Sun Tzu. *The Art of War*. Translated and edited by Samuel B. Griffith. New York: Oxford University Press, 1971.

Swaggerty, W. R., ed. *Scholars and the Indian Experience: Recent Writing in the Social Sciences*. Bloomington: Indiana University Press, 1984.

Talking Leaf 2 (1973).

Taylor, Colin. *Warriors of the Plains*. New York: Arco, 1975.

Terry, Wallace, ed. *Bloods: An Oral History of the Vietnam War by Black Veterans*. New York: Random House, 1984.

Thomas, Robert K. "Colonialism: Classic and Internal." *New University Thought* 4 (Spring 1966): 37–44.

———. "The Redbird Smith Movement." In *Symposium on Cherokee and Iroquois Culture*, edited by William N. Fenton and John Gulick, 159–166. Bureau of American Ethnology Bulletin 180. Washington, D.C: Smithsonian Institution, 1961.

Tobias, Sheila, Peter Goudinoff, Stefan Leader, and Shelah Leader. *What Kinds of Guns are They Buying for Your Butter? A Beginner's Guide to Defense, Weaponry, and Military Spending.* New York: William Morrow and Company, 1982.

U.S. Army Forces Command, Public Affairs. *Native Americans and the Military: Yesterday and Today.* Fort MacPherson, Ga.: Army Public Affairs, 1984.

U.S. Bureau of the Census. *1970 Census of the Population, Vol. 1, Characteristics of the Population.* Washington, D.C.: Government Printing Office, 1973.

U.S. Bureau of the Census. *1980 Census of the Population, Vol. 1, Characteristics of the Population.* Washington, D.C.: Government Printing Office, 1983.

U.S. Congress. *Congressional Record.* June 16, 1988.

U.S. Congress. House. *Annual Report of the Secretary of War.* House Executive Document, Vol. 1, serial 2829. 52d Cong., 1st sess., 1891.

U.S. Congress. House. *Journal.* 51st Cong., 2d sess., 1890.

U.S. Congress. Senate. *Occupation of Wounded Knee: Hearings before the Subcommittee on Indian Affairs, June 16–17, 1973.* 93d Cong., 1st sess., 1974.

U.S. Congress. Senate. *Report of the Committee on Veterans' Affairs to Accompany S. 2011, "Veterans' Benefits and Programs Improvement Act of 1988".* S.R. 100–429. 100th Cong., 2d sess., 1988.

U.S. Department of the Interior. *Annual Report, 1944.* Washington, D.C.: Government Printing Office, 1945.

United States Statutes at Large. Vols. 41, 43.

Utley, Robert M., and Wilcomb E. Washburn. *Indian Wars.* Boston: Houghton-Mifflin, 1987.

Veterans Administration Advisory Committee on Native American Veterans. *Native American Veterans.* Washington, D.C.: Department of Veterans Affairs, 1988.

———. *Native American Veterans: Third and Final Report.* Washington, D.C.: Department of Veterans Affairs, 1989.

Vietnam Era Veterans Inter-Tribal Association Newsletter. Oklahoma City, Okla., 1983–1988.

Villard, Oswald Garrison. "Wardship and the Indian." *Christian Century* 61 (March 29, 1944): 397–398.

Wahrhaftig, Albert L. "More Than Mere Work: The Subsistence of Oklahoma's Cherokee Indians." Paper presented at the Southwest Anthropological Association Annual Conference, San Francisco, Calif., 1973.

Wallace, Ernest, and E. Adamson Hoebel. *The Comanches.* Norman: University of Oklahoma Press, 1952.

Watson, Bruce. "Jaysho, Moasi, Dibeh, Ayeshi, Hasclishnih, Beshlo, Shush, Gini." *Smithsonian* (September 1993): 31–43.

Wilson, John P. *Trauma, Transportation and Healing.* New York: Brunner/Mazel, 1989.

Wilson, J. P., Z. Harel, and B. Kahanal, eds. *Human Adaptation to Extreme Stress: From the Holocaust to Vietnam.* New York: Plenum, 1988.

Woodbury, David. "From Tahlequah to Boggy Depot: Stand Watie's Civil War." *Civil War* 10 (September–October 1992): 38–46.

———. "An Iroquois at Appomattox." *Civil War* 10 (September–October 1992): 19–23.

"The 'Worth of the Warrior' Project: Initial Report on Recommendations and Current Activities of the National Working Group on American Indian Vietnam Era Veterans." Washington, D.C.: Readjustment Counseling Service, Veterans Administration, 1984.

Ybarra, Lea. "Perceptions of Race and Class among Chicano Vietnam Veterans." *Vietnam Generation* 1 (Spring 1989): 69–93.

Yetman, Norman R., and C. Hoy Steele, eds. *Majority and Minority: The Dynamics of Racial and Ethnic Relations.* Boston: Allyn and Bacon, 1975.

Young, Warren L. *Minorities and the Military.* Westport, Conn.: Greenwood Press, 1982.

INDEX

Onondagas, 52
Operation Desert Storm, 195
Opotheleyahola (Muscogee Creek
leader), 93
Order of the Purple Heart (organization), 181
Osages, 31, 92, 93, 104
Ostrogoths, 70
Otermín, Antonio de, 78–79
Owen, David, 48

Paiutes, 31
Paris Peace Talks, 170
Parker, Ely S., 94
Parson, Erwin Randolph, 191
Pawnee Battalion, 95
Pawnees, 34, 95, 155
Pea Ridge, battle of, 93
Pershing, John J., 99
Persians, 30
Picq, Charles Ardant du, 76
Pike, Albert, 93
Plains culture area, 31, 34, 35, 46,
57, 62, 67, 68
Plateau culture area, 31, 34
Plume, Sidney, 13
Polynesian-Americans, 16
Pomos, 31, 34, 35
Poncas, 104, 179
Pontiac (Ottawa leader), 49
Poorbear, Enos, 179
Popé (Pueblo war captain), 77
Post Oak Jim, 47–48
post-traumatic stress disorder
(PTSD), 2–9, 17, 25, 184–187
Prairie culture area, 31, 34
predation, 27, 29
Proctor, Redfield, 95–97
Project 100,000, 9
Pueblo Revolt (1680), 77–80, 87

Pueblos, 47, 86, 94, 123
Pyle, Ernie, 105

Rascon, Thomas, III, 13
Reader's Digest (magazine), 107
Readjustment Counseling Service, VA (RCS), 2, 12–14, 16–17, 21, 103, 109, 182
Red Cloud (Oglala Lakota leader),
84
Red Power Movement, 171
"relocation," 108–110, 115
Research Triangle Institute, Inc.
(RTI), 17–18
Revolutionary War, 20, 22, 90, 91
ritual aggression, 27
ritual cannibalism, 48–50
Rome, 30, 70, 86
Roosevelt, Franklin D., 66, 106,
194
Russia, 87

Sacred Pipe, 43
St. Clair, Arthur, 92
Sale, Kirkpatrick, 32
Salish, 31
Sand Creek massacre, 94
Sando, Joe S., 78, 79
Saturday Evening Post, The, 103
scalping, 33, 48, 49, 63
Schlieffen, Alfred von, 76
Schusky, Ernest L., 42
Scots (highlanders), 87
Scott, Hugh L., 97
Scott, Wilbur J., 180
Sells, Cato, 99, 101, 104
Seminoles, 84, 93, 94, 95, 191
Senate Committee on Veterans
Affairs, 17
Senecas, 51, 52, 94, 129